Charles Grey, Giovanni Maria degli Angiolelli

A narrative of Italian travels in Persia, in the fifteenth and sixteen centuries

Charles Grey, Giovanni Maria degli Angiolelli

A narrative of Italian travels in Persia, in the fifteenth and sixteen centuries

ISBN/EAN: 9783337207984

Printed in Europe, USA, Canada, Australia, Japan

Cover: Foto ©Andreas Hilbeck / pixelio.de

More available books at **www.hansebooks.com**

A NARRATIVE

OF

ITALIAN TRAVELS

IN

PERSIA,

IN THE

FIFTEENTH AND SIXTEENTH CENTURIES.

Translated and Edited

BY

CHARLES GREY, Esq.

LONDON:
PRINTED FOR THE HAKLUYT SOCIETY.

M.DCCC.LXXIII.

CONTENTS.

	PAGE
TRAVELS IN PERSIA, BY CATERINO ZENO - -	1
DISCOURSE OF MESSER GIOVAN BATTISTA RAMUSIO ON THE WRITINGS OF GIOVAN MARIA ANGIOLELLO, ETC. -	67
THE TRAVELS OF A MERCHANT IN PERSIA - -	139
NARRATIVE OF THE MOST NOBLE VINCENTIO D'ALESSANDRI	209

A NARRATIVE

OF

ITALIAN TRAVELS IN PERSIA.

The close of the fifteenth century is an epoch in the history of the East, and especially of Persia, of which but little is known. The blast of Timour's invasion had swept over that historic land and left it desolate. These four Accounts of Travels by Europeans are, therefore, especially interesting in a geographical and historical point of view, and will, with the books of Barbaro and Contarini, which are in Ramusio's collection, complete the series of Italian voyages about that period. In order clearly to understand the facts brought forward, it will be necessary to glance at the motives of policy which started the embassies, and the historical changes which influenced their results.

In Eastern Europe the Byzantine empire had, after a long and gradual decline, at length crumbled into ruins beneath the power of the Ottomans, which threatened to be as great a scourge to Europe as that of Timur (or Tamerlane) had been to Asia, while the stability and vitality of their empire offered a great contrast to the ephemeral character of Timur's dominion. Singly, the powers of Christendom could in vain hope to withstand their terrible foe; and Venice, the Great Republic, then rich and flourishing, with a far-sighted policy, endeavoured to induce all the Christian princes to make common cause against the Ottoman Turks.

Hungary and Poland were engaged in continuous warfare with the Musulmans; but the petty jealousies, which no danger, however imminent, could lull, caused the other powers to look coldly on the proposed alliance. Venice, in her need, then cast her eyes to the East, where she found a new dynasty firmly established in the ancient kingdom of Persia, the inveterate foe of the house of Othman. That country, after the death of Timour, had been nominally subject to his descendants, though two rival Toorkoman tribes had established principalities in Azerbigan and Diarbekr. These were the Kara Koinlu, and Ak-koinlu, or the Black and White Sheep, between whom a deadly feud existed; the former were the first to rise to power, under their chief, Kara Mahomed; while his son, the famous Kara Yusuf, threw off the yoke of the descendants of Timour in 1410. Secunder, the son of Kara Yusuf, waged war with Shah Rokh; and, after his death, his brother Jehan Shah, in 1437, not only overran Irak, Fars, and Kerman, but in 1457 besieged and pillaged Herat. The Kara Koinlus kept the throne until 1486.

Kara Koinlu Rulers.

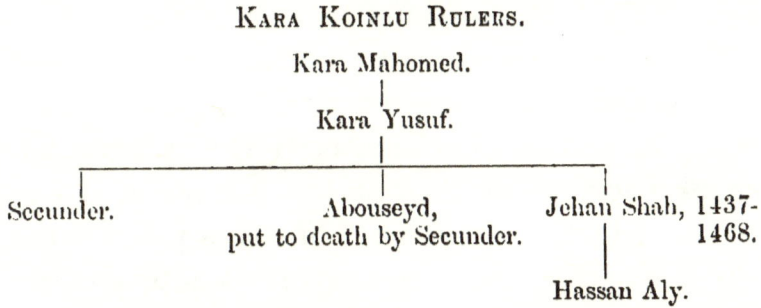

In that year the chief of the rival tribe of the Ak-koinloos, named Uzun Hassan, who had established himself at Diarbekr, succeeded in defeating Jehan Shah in a battle in which the latter fell. The Ak-koinloos were now masters of Persia, and Uzun Hassan carried his victorious arms against Sultan Abouseyd, the reigning prince of the house of Timour, who also fell before him.

Malcolm's account of the reign of Uzun Hassan is very meagre. He was the chief of the Ak-koinlu, or Turks, of the tribe of White Sheep, and established a powerful principality at Diarbekr. He defeated and killed Jehan Shah and his son Hassan Aly, whom he had taken prisoner, with all his family. The dynasty which Uzun Hassan founded is termed Bâyenderee; the family date their rise from the reign of Timour, who made them grants of land in Armenia and Mesopotamia. Hassan, after defeating his rival, engaged in a war with Sultan Abouseyd. He owed his triumph to his skill and activity in a predatory warfare, and at last having taken his enemy prisoner, made himself master of a great part of the dominions of the house of Timour. Malcolm says: "Uzun Hassan, after making himself master of Persia, turned his arms in the direction of Turkey; but his career was arrested by the superior genius of the Turkish emperor, Mahomet II; he suffered a signal defeat, which terminated his schemes of ambition. He died after a reign of eleven years, at the age of seventy. All authors agree in ascribing valour and wisdom to this prince. We are told by an European ambassador, who resided at his court, that he was a tall thin man, of a very open countenance, and that his army amounted to fifty thousand horse, a great proportion of which were of very indifferent quality." He adds that this ambassador was an envoy from Venice, sent by that Republic to solicit the aid of Uzun Hassan against the Ottoman. The personage alluded to by Malcolm must have been M. Josafat Barbaro, the successor of M. Caterino Zeno.

Uzun Hassan had already been in collision with the Turks, having, when ruler of Diarbekr, undertaken to defend Calo Johannes of the noble house of the Comneni, one of the last of the Christian emperors of Trebizond, against Mahomet II. This alliance had been cemented by his marriage with the beautiful princess Despina, daughter of Calo Johannes, in which manner he was connected with some of the princely families of Venice, so that the way for an embassy was easily paved. The Venetians might hope much from the ambitious and turbulent character of the Persian prince; and in this they were not disappointed, as it needed but little persuasion to induce the hitherto almost invincible soldier to take up arms against his hereditary foe. Worn out by a state of anarchy, rival chiefs and tribes struggling for power before the land had fully risen again after the blast of foreign conquest had passed over it, the ancient glory of Persia had paled before the brighter light of its rival; but the old hatred still remained, with the will, if not the power, to oppose the Turkish arms. An embassy to Uzun Hassan being determined on, the difficult task of sending an envoy still remained. The duty would be a hazardous one, as any one proceeding from Venice to Persia would have to run the gauntlet of the Turks. The sister of Queen Despina had married Nicolo Crespo, the Duke of the Archipelago, whose four daughters were in turn wedded to four of the merchant princes of Venice, one of whom was M. Caterino Zeno, a man of courage and talent. He, of all others, appeared the fittest to undertake this honourable but perilous mission, and the patriotism of Zeno induced him to overlook the dangers he would run in traversing hostile and almost unknown regions before reaching his destination. He was rewarded for his courage by arriving safely in the presence of the king, though not without meeting serious obstacles in his journey through Caramania.

Zeno was well received by the monarch; and, being supported in his arguments by his aunt, the Queen Despina, succeeded in inducing Uzun Hassan to take up arms against the Turk.

In 1472 the Persians marched into the Turkish

dominions and ravaged them, but a flying column under Mustafà, the second son of Mahomet II, routed a force of Persians under one of Uzun Hassan's generals. In the following year the Grand Turk invaded Persia with an immense army, but met with a severe check while endeavouring to cross the Euphrates near Malatia, and was forced to retreat. Uzun Hassan, however, following up his success too rashly, was routed by the Turks at Tabcada. M. Caterino Zeno was then sent as ambassador from Uzun Hassan to various Christian princes, among others to Poland and Hungary, to incite them to take up arms against the Ottoman. M. Josafat Barbaro and Ambrogio Contarini were sent from Venice to take his place at the Persian Court; but no arguments could again induce the Persian monarch to meet the Turks in the field.

The account of Zeno's Travels in Ramusio's collection was prepared from Zeno's letters, as the editor was never able to get possession of a copy of Zeno's book. For this reason the geographical details in these Travels are not so explicit as in the others, and Ramusio has in his book put Zeno's narrative after several others, although in date he was the first. It is supplemented by a sketch of Persian history subsequent to M. Caterino's embassy, taken from other sources. MM. Barbaro and Contarini succeeded Zeno. The account of their travels will form a separate work.

The second author in this collection is a M. Giovan Maria Angiolello, who was in the service of the

Turks, and present in their campaign against the Persians. He describes, shortly, the rise of Uzun Hassan, and gives a full description of the Turkish invasion from the Turkish point of view, and the details of the march. Unghermaumet's rebellion against his father Uzun Hassan is also mentioned by him as well as by Zeno. After the death of Uzun Hassan and his son Yakoob, Persia fell into a state of anarchy caused by the civil wars between various members of the dominant Akkoinloo family; from this the country rose at length, through the process of a revolution, almost without a parallel in the history of the world. Not only was there a change in the dynasty and form of government, but the empire was revived in a native Persian family, and an end was put to the long foreign domination. More than all, the very religion of the people was essentially altered: a fact which, by widening the gulf which separated them from their surrounding enemies, consolidated the empire and created a nationality. The family which now rose on the ruins of the Ak-koinlu power traced their descent from Ali, the son-in-law of the Prophet, through Mussa, the Seventh Imaum:—

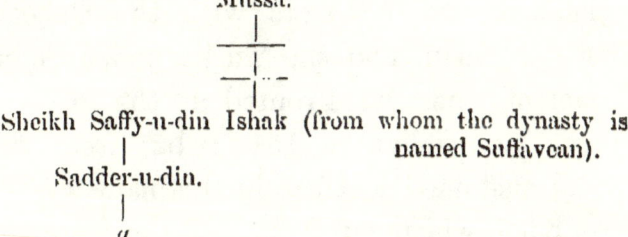

Mussa.
|
—|—
|
Sheikh Saffy-u-din Ishak (from whom the dynasty is
| named Suffavean).
Sadder-u-din.
|

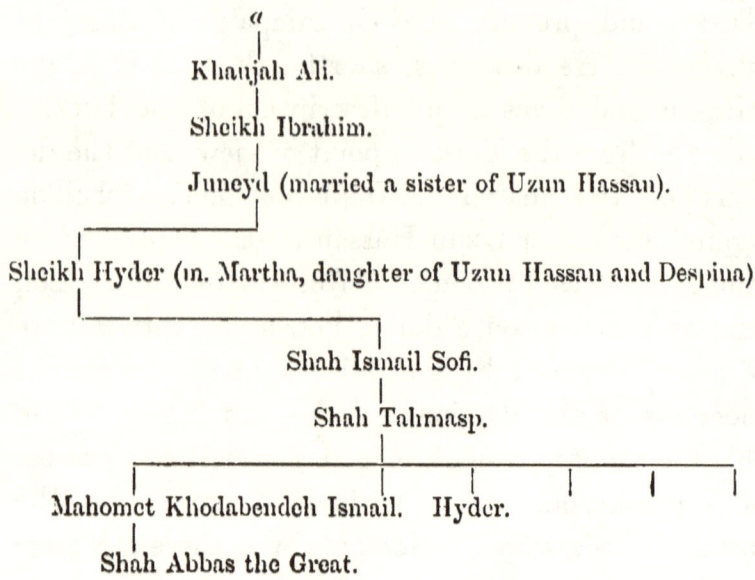

The chiefs of this family were regarded by the Persians as saints, and when Sheikh Hyder, a son-in-law of Uzun Hassan, rose in arms against Rustan, King of Persia, he was joined by great numbers. This insurrection was, however, ineffectual, and it was reserved for Sheikh Hyder's son, afterwards Shah Ismail Sofi, to overthrow the fast decaying power of the Ak-koinlus, which was still further weakened by the struggle for the throne between two brothers named Alwung Beg and Morad Khan. The victorious career of Ismail is treated of by Angiolello, as also his wars with the Uzbegs under Sheibani Khan, and the Turks under Selim I, the former of whom were routed at the great battle of Merv Shah Jehan in 1514; but from the latter Ismail sustained a defeat in the plains of Chalderan, near Khoi, which left Tauris at the mercy of Selim.

Angiolello, leaving Persian history, gives a full and animated account of Selim's expedition against Egypt, which resulted in the conquest by the Turks of that great country and the deaths of the two last Soldans, Khafur el Ghouri and Tomant Bey.

The Third Book of Travels from Ramusio is that of an unnamed author trading from Damascus and Aleppo to Persia, where he remained upwards of eight years, from 1511 to 1520; so that he also was an eye-witness of the glory of Shah Ismail. The style of this latter is more involved; but while his historical facts correspond, his description of the towns and country is more detailed, as is but natural, from his occupation, which was more suited than that of an ambassador for gaining geographical information. He opens his narrative by describing, with a good deal of minuteness, the route from Aleppo to Tauris, finishing with an account of that city and of the historical events that took place during his stay.

There is a long gap between these two latter writers and Vincentio d'Alessandri, an envoy from Venice in 1571 to the Court of Shah Tahmasp, the son and successor of Shah Ismail Sofi, who had died in 1524. This writer is mentioned by Knolles in his General History of the Turks, from whom the following account of the intermediate history is also taken. In the year 1534 Solyman was persuaded by Ibrahim Pasha to make war on Persia, stirred up against the new Shiah religion which had been introduced by Shah Ismail Sofi. The purpose of Ibrahim was also furthered by a Persian named Ulemas, brother-in-law of the King Tahmasp, who had revolted from him,[1] fearing to be called to account for his extortion. After making preparations, Solyman sent Ibrahim and Ulemas with an army into Syria, and in the spring they advanced, without resistance, as far as Tauris. Tahmasp, the Persian monarch, was then absent, engaged in a war with Kezienbassa, Prince of the Corasine Hyrcanians; but, hearing of the taking of his capital, returned in haste for the defence of his empire. Solyman, on reports reaching him of the successes of his generals, crossed the Euphrates at Malatia, and joined them at Tauris. Tahmasp, not daring to join battle with Solyman, retreated to the mountains above Sultania, where the Turkish army, endeavouring to follow him, was greatly distressed, and forced to retreat from the inclemency of the weather. Solyman now retired to Mesopotamia, where he took Bagdad and added the provinces of Babylonia and Mesopotamia to the Turkish empire. In the following year, 1535, Solyman again entered Tauris and ransacked it; but, finding that nothing was to be done against Tahmasp, withdrew to his own dominions greatly harassed on his journey by Persian cavalry, who at last surprised and routed his army near Betilis, under the command of Delimenthes. This last reverse was the occasion of the fall of the great Pasha Ibrahim, the friend and counsellor of Solyman, by whose orders he was murdered. Ulemas was afterwards made

[1] According to Alessandri, Shah Tahmasp would allow no one to be avaricious but himself.

Governor of Bosina. In 1549 the cause of Ercases Imirza, Prince of Shirvan and brother of Shah Tahmasp, was espoused by Solyman against Tahmasp; but, in a tedious war, except the capture of Van by the Turks, nothing of any importance took place, as the Persian monarch, pursuing his usual tactics, acted on the defensive, and retreated to the mountains. Discord being sown between Solyman and Ercases Imirza, the latter fled to Chaldea, where he was treacherously delivered into the hands of Tahmasp, who caused him to be murdered in prison. Bajazet, the son of Solyman, after his rebelion in 1556, fled for safety to the Court of Tahmasp, who received him with favour at first; but his mind becoming embittered against him, he caused his followers to be dispersed and slain, and Bajazet himself to be cast into prison. Solyman used all the means in his power to have Bajazet delivered into his hands, but Tahmasp would not consent; but afterwards, in consideration of a large sum of money, agreed to allow him to be made away with.[1] Bajazet accordingly was strangled, with his four sons. On the accession of Selim II, Tahmasp sent ambassadors to Constantinople to ratify a peace between them, which was concluded in the year 1568. About Vincentio d'Alessandri Knolles says, A.D. 1571 :—

"Whilest these things were in doing, the Venetians, the more to entangle the Turke, thought it good to make proofe, if they might by any means stirre up Tamas, the Persian king, to take up armes against him; who, as hee was a prince

---

[1] Angerius Busbequius legationis Turcicæ epist. 4.

of great power, so did hee exceedingly hate the Turks, as well for the difference between the Persians and them about matters of their vaine superstition, as for the manifold injuries he had oftentimes sustained. There was one Vincent Alexander, one of the secretaries for the State, who, having escaped out of prison at Constantinople, was but a little before come to Venice, a warie wise man, and of great experience, who, for his dexteritie of wit and skilfulnesse in the Turkish language, was thought of all others most fit to take in hand so great a matter. He having received letters and instructions from the Senat, and furnished with all things necessarie, travelling through Germanie, Polonia, and the forrests of Mœsia, in Turkish attire, came to Moncastron, a port towne upon the side of the Euxine or Black Sea, at the mouth of the great river Boristhenes, where he embarked himself for Trapezond, but was by a contrarie wind driven to Sinope, a citie of great trafficke; from whence he travelled, by rough and broken ways, to Cutay, keeping still upon the left hand because he would not fall upon any part of the Turk's armie (which was then marching towards Cyprus through all those countries); neverthelesse, he fell upon a part thereof, from which he with great danger rid himselfe, beinge taken for a Turke, and by blind and troublesome wayes, through rockes and forrests, arrived at length at Erzirum, a strong citie of the Turks, then upon the frontiers of the Turk's dominions toward the Georgians. This journey of Alexander's was not kept so secret, but that it was vented at Constantinople by a spie, who, under the colour of friendship haunting the Venetian embassadour's house at Pera, had got certaine knowledge of the going of Alexander in Persia. Whereupon, certaine courrours were sent out with all speed to beset the three straight passages into Persia, whereby it was supposed he must of necessitie passe, with certaine notes also of the favour of the man, of his stature, and other marks wherby he was best to be knowne. But he in so dangerous a countrie doubting all things, and fearing such a matter, leaving his companie behind him, with incredible celeritie posted from Erzirum to Tauris, and was a great way gone before the Turk's courrours came into those quarters; who, yet hearing of him, followed after as far as they durst, but could not overtake him. Alexander, comming to Tauris, understood that the court lay at Casbin, about twelve days' journey farther up into the country. Comming thither the 14th of August of this year, 1571, he chanced to meet with certaine English marchants, with whom he had beene before acquainted; by whose helpe he not only got to speak with Ayder Tamas, the king's third sonne, but learned of them also the manners and fashions of the Persian court, and how to beare himselfe therein. The Persians, by reason of the intollerable heate, doe most of their business at that time of the yeare by night. Wherefore, Alexander, about midnight brought in to Aider, declared unto him the cause of his comming: and the next night admitted into the speech of his aged father, delivered his letters of credence, and in the name of the Senat, declared unto him, with what perfidious dealing Selymus, the Turkish emperor, was about to take away Cyprus from the Venetians, with what greedinesse and pride he had set upon the Christians, and that discharged of that warre, he would of all likelyhood set upon the Persians; having the selfesame quarrell unto the Persians that he had unto the Venetians, that is, an ardent and insatiable desire of soveraignetie; a sufficient cause for the greedie Turke to repute every king, the richer that he was, the more his enemie. After that, setting foorth to the full the prowesse of the Christians, the wonderfull preparation they had made, both at sea and land, he persuaded the king, with all his power, to invade the Turke, now altogether busied in the warres of Cyprus; and to recover againe such parts of his kingdom as Solyman, the father of Selymus, had taken from him. Warres, he said, were more happily managed abroad than at home; that, sithence he alone (the Christian princes all then at quiet) had withstood the Turk's whole force and power, he needed not now to doubt of his most prosperous successe, the Christian princes now joyning with him. That he was much unmindful of his former losses and wrongs, if he thought he enjoyed an assured peace, which he should find to be nothing els but a deferring of war unto more cruell times; and that the Turke, if he should overrun Cyprus, would forthwith turne his victorious arms upon him. The end of one warre was (as he said) but the beginning of another; and that the Turkish empire could never stay in one state; and that he would observe not the Turke's words, but his deeds; and how that the Othoman emperours, according to the oportunitie of the times, used by turnes sometimes force, sometimes deceit, as best served their purposes. That no princes had at all times, by dissembled peace and uncertaine leagues, more deluded some, untill they had oppressed others. He wished also, that at length this his cunning dealing might appeare unto the world; and that princes would thinke, that being combined together, they might more easily overcome the Turke, than being seperated, defend their owne; that in former times, sometimes will, sometimes occasion, was wanting to them to unite their forces; and that, therefore, they should now combine themselves for their common good against the common enemie; that it conserned no lesse the Persians than the Christians, to have the power of the Turke abated; and that this taking up of armes should be for the good of the Persian king, howsoever things should fall out; if well, he should then recover what he had before lost, with much more that was the Turke's; if otherwise, yet by voluntarie entering into armes, to countenance himselfe, and to give the Turks occasion to think that he feared him not, which was (as he said) the only way to preserve their common safetie, which would be unto all the confederat princes easie enough, if they themselves made it not more difficult than the power of the enemie. The speech of the embassadour was willingly heard; whereunto the king answered, that he would consider thereupon what he had to doe; and, in the meanwhile, a faire house was appointed for the embassadour and his followers, and bountifull allowance appointed for the king's charge. He was also many times sumptuously feasted by the noblemen whom he still requested to be mediatours unto the king, to take that honourable warre in hand. The king had at that time a sonne called Ismael, a man of great spirit, whom he then kept in durance, for that he, with too much insolencie, made roades into the frontiers of the Turke's dominions, to the disturbance of the leagues his father had before made with the late Turkish emperor, Solyman: unto him, Alexander having accesse, was of him courteously heard, who, fretting and languishing for verie griefe of revenge upon the Turkes, wished that either the king, his father, had his mind, or he himselfe the power of a king, and said, That if ever it were his good fortune to obtaine, he would indeed shew what he then in mind thought. But of him more shall be said hereafter. Whilest this matter went more slowly forward in the Persian court than the embassadour would have had it, newes was brought unto the court of the great victorie which the Christians had much about that time obtained of the Turkes at sea; upon which occasion the embassadour solicited the king more earnestly than before, to make himselfe partaker of the victorie of the Christians by entring into confederation with them, and by taking up of armes, rather than to hold uncertain friendship with the Turkes in their miseries, by whom he had been so often wronged. This he said, was the only time for the Persian king to recover his former glorie, the like offer whereof would neither often chance, neither long stay; and that if he suffered so fit an opportunitie to slip away, he should afterwards in vaine wish for the same, when it were so late. This so wholsome counsell was well heard, but prevailed nothing to stir up the aged king, who, then troubled with rebellion in Media, or wearie of the former warres he had had with the Turke, and glad of such peace as he had then with him, answered the embassadour: That, for as much as the Christian princes had made a perpetuall league amongst themselves, he would for two yeares expect the event, and afterward, as occasion served, so to resolve upon peace or warre. This improvident resolution of the king brought afterward unprofitable and too late repentance unto the whole Persian kingdome, when, as within a few yeares after, all the calamities which the Senat had by their embassadour (as true prophets) foretold, redounded unto the great shaking thereof. For the Cyprian warre once ended, and peace concluded with the Venetians, Amurath, the sonne of Selymus, succeeding his father in the Turkish empire, invading the Persian king, tooke from him the great country of Media, now called Silvan, with a great part of Armenia the Great, and the regall citie of Tauris, as shall be here after in due place declared. At which time the Persian, who now refused to take up armes or join in league with the Christian princes, repented that he had not before hearkened unto the wholsome counsell of the Venetians; and, taught by his owne harmes, wished in vaine that the Christian princes would againe take up armes and joyne with him against the Turke."

In the year 1576 troubles arose in the Persian kingdom consequent on the death of Tahmasp, which were taken advantage of by Sultan Murad III. Tahmasp had eleven sons; Mahomed Khodabendeh, who suffered from a weakness in his eyes; Ismael, a turbulent warrior, confined in the fortress of Cahaca, between Tauris and Casbin; Hyder, the third, with a powerful party in the State; and the others, Mahmoud, Solyman, Mustafa, Emanguli, Alichar, Ahmed, Abrahim, and Ismael the younger.

Before his death he appointed Ismael his successor, to the great discontent of Hyder, who, being in the palace, caused himself to be crowned; but Ismael's friends being strong he was imprisoned in his palace and soon after murdered. Ismael, on ascending the throne, caused his eight younger brothers to be murdered, and greatly oppressed the country;[1] he himself, after a year's reign, met with his fate, being murdered by his sister. The Persian chiefs raised Mahomed Khodabendeh to the throne, who, in endeavouring to avenge his brothers' deaths, caused great discord in the kingdom, of which Murad determined to take advantage, inducing the Georgians under Levent Ogli and the people of Shirvan to revolt. After a few years, however, the incapable Mahomet was dethroned by the Persian nobles to make way for his son Abbas. This prince, perhaps the best ruler Persia had had for many centuries, began to reign in 1585, and is known to history as Shah Abbas the Great.

[1] He also sent to put Mahomed Khodabendeh to death, but died himself before the order was executed.

TRAVELS IN PERSIA,

BY

CATERINO ZENO.

RAMUSIO'S PREFACE.[1]

HAVING undertaken to describe a journey made in Persia by M. Caterino Zeno, knight, at the time that our Republic, being at war with the Turk, desired that he should be harassed on the East by the arms of the king Ussun Cassano, who, some years before with great skill in the art of war, had made himself Master of Persia, and a great part of the neighbouring provinces; I have considered it suited to my undertaking, to treat of all the wars, which were waged in Persia, both between the members of the royal family and by the Persians against the Turks. And particularly to narrate the manner in which this Ussun Cassano, a poor nobleman, and the weakest in condition of many brothers[2] (*Giausu*,[3] the eldest, having become King of Persia), not possessing

---

[1] This Preface is by Ramusio; the rest is prepared by the same writer from the official letters of M. Caterino Zeno.

[2] Kara Mahomed, chief of the Kârâ Koinloo.

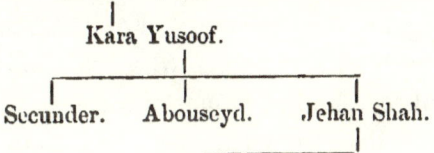

Kârâ Yussoof or Hussun Ali, according to Malcolm.

[3] Jehan Shah. Uzun Hassan was not his brother, as they were the respective chiefs of the rival tribes of Kârâ Koinloo and Ak-Koinloo. The dynasty founded by Uzun Hassan of the Ak-Koinloo tribe is termed Bàyenderee; the influence of the family dates from the reign of Timour, who made them grants of land in Armenia and Mesopotamia.

more than thirty soldiers besides a small castle, afterwards raised himself to such grandeur, that he had the courage to dispute the empire of all Asia with the Ottoman house, which, under Mahomet II,[1] was a terror to the East.

But the arts by which he made himself king, his valour and cunning, I shall narrate as briefly as possible, as I consider these things worthy to be reported to our nation; for, amongst all the kings of the East, who existed since the Government was taken away from the Persians, and transferred to the Greeks, there have been none who equalled the glory of Darius Hystaspes and Ussun Cassano; and if fortune had favoured him in the second battle at Tabeada in the campaign of Tokat, as it did in the first he had with the Turks on the Euphrates, there is no doubt that by these two victories he would have made himself master of all Asia and Egypt. But it is to be regretted that some Eastern kings, great in power and intellect, have not had historians to celebrate their deeds, since among the Sultans of Egypt and among the Kings of Persia, there have been men most excellent in war,[2] and worthy not only of being compared with ancient barbarian kings famous in arms,[3] but even with the great Greek and Roman commanders, in all those things which constitute able generals of armies. For the record of the deeds of such reach us Europeans, who are admirers of the virtues of men abroad and at home, in a condition so mutilated and imperfect, that from the few particulars we

[1] Mahomet II, the first Emperor of the Turks, reigned from 1450-1481.
[2] " Vixēre fortes ante Agamemnona
  Multi."—*Horace*, Book iv, ode 10.
[3] It was by no means the case that at that time the Persian monarchs had no poets or historians to celebrate their deeds, as the Augustan age, so to speak, of Persian literature was just then coming to a close, the two last of the great poets, Jami and Hatifi, flourishing at the Court of Abousaid and his successor Hoossein Meerza, the enlightened descendants of Timour. Hatifi died in 1522; his great poem was written to commemorate the victory of Ismael Shah over the Usbegs at Merv in 1514. The two famous historians, Mirkhond and Khondemir, also flourished at this time.

cannot draw up a complete history. Therefore, let no one marvel if in these my notes I do not describe things as fully in some places as I should have done, if I had had ampler information; since M. Caterino, who, as has been said, went as ambassador to Ussun Cassano, wrote several letters, from which I have drawn the pith of this short history, for the satisfaction of those who, hearing discussions about the Sufi, and of his great pomp, are desirous of being informed of the affairs of the Persian Empire. And I know well that in thus writing to a purport different from what has been written by others, many will be apt to criticise me, as it is difficult to efface early impressions from the mind; but before they do so, I beg they will rather consider my good intentions than impute to me any desire to gain a reputation for being better acquainted with the affairs of the world than other writers. But surely we ought far sooner to credit what is told us of the doings of Ussun Cassano, by one who was connected with him, and who got his information from the Queen Despina, his own aunt, than by those who, in their histories, have only availed themselves of the narrations of some Armenians, who, to take away his reputation, went about spreading the report that he was not born of royal blood, and that while he governed certain places in Armenia, by lavish expenditure, and gaining the favour of the soldiery, he seized an opportunity of casting off the sway of Giausa, and treacherously putting him to death with his son.[1] And they add, to further embellish this lie, that in this Giausa the descendants of Moleoncre, formerly a great sultan of the Parthians, became extinct. These things are all well known not to be true, since how could Ussun Cassano have made himself Lord of Persia, if he had not been of royal blood; particularly, for this reason, that there is no nation which holds noble birth and royal descent in more estimation than the Persians. And to omit the ancient ex-

[1] Jehan Shah, Karâ Yusuf.

ample of Darius Hystaspes,[1] the son of Atossa, the daughter of Cyrus, there is the more recent one of Ismail; for, although he was not born of royal blood on his father's side, nevertheless his mother, called Martha, was daughter of Ussun Cassano, through whom the new king was tolerated, as formerly Darius was, as the son of Atossa. We must not believe that the partizans of the ancient kings[2] (if indeed there was a party, as these authors say) would be so soon swept away; because it is impossible that a new dynasty should appear without causing great commotions and tumults, as we have seen in many kingdoms of Christendom; and, nevertheless, the reign of Ussun Cassano, as regards internal affairs, was not visited by any blast of domestic or civil war, except that raised by his son Unghermaumet; but this was caused by lust of power and not by a faction of a former reign. Therefore, read without chiding these my commentaries, in which, if I had been able to find the "Book of Travels of M. Caterino", who first gave information of the affairs of Persia, and preceded M. Giosafat Barbaro, and M. Ambrogio Contarini as ambassador to Persia from our Republic, I should have touched upon many other particulars, which would have been most acceptable to those who take an interest in such things.

As, in spite of all my research, I have never been able to get into my hands this Book of Travels, if I should find it (and I am sure there is no one so malicious as not to shew it), I will supply what I have now missed. But, as we say, he who does all he can, does much. Since we cannot get further particulars, let us accept these, and praise the industry of the good M. Caterino, and it being evident that, not being able to find more on this subject among his writings, I cannot communicate it.

[1] Darius was the husband, not the son, of Atossa.

[2] There were two rival Toorkman tribes, as has already been noticed, the Kara-Koinloo and the Ak-Koinloo, who were engaged in continual struggles for the supremacy in Persia. Uzun Hassan was a chief of the Ak-Koinloo, or White Sheep.

CATERINO ZENO.

FIRST BOOK.

IN the year of our Lord Jesus Christ one thousand four hundred and fifty, (1450), Giausa,[1] being King of Persia, *Assimbeo*[2] (who, from that time, on account of his deeds, called himself *Ussun Cassano*,[3] which in the Persian tongue signifies "great man"), not contenting himself with being Lord of a small castle, began by little and little to usurp the states, and the jurisdictions of his other brothers less powerful than himself,[4] who, either not being of a warlike disposition or for some other reason, preferred living in ease and not opposing his ambition. Thus he without difficulty raised himself in credit and reputation. Ussun Cassano was a warlike, valiant man, and above all of great liberality, which is a rare virtue, to enable great lords to gain over the affections of the soldiery, provided it is exercised at the proper time and place, and towards the deserving (so that he who makes

---

[1] Jehan Shah.   [2] Hassan Beg, called Alymbeius by Knolles.
[3] He was called Uzun Hassan and Hassan et Taneel by the Arabs, from the fact, as the appellative denotes, of his height, which was far above the standard. Barbaro describes him as a very tall, thin man. Taneel, Arabic, is the translation of Uzun or Oozoon, Turkish, and means "tall", not "great". Oozoon, in Turkish, means essentially long, not great.
[4] *Ak-Koinloo Chiefs:*—

Kârâ Osman put to death by Secunder, chief of the Kârâ Koinloo.
|
Uzun Hassan, first of the Bâyenderee kings.
|
Ughermaumet. Ezeinel. Calul. Yakoob. Martha m. Sheikh Hyder.
|
Alwung Beg (Alumut).   Morad Khan.   Ismael Sofi.

use of it be not esteemed of small judgment or a prodigal). By this means he was soon followed by people of war, so that he brought together five hundred good horsemen, assaulted the great and famous city of *Amitto*;[1] in which fortune was so favourable to him, that he took it with so much reputation that from that time he had the support of all those regions. Hence, he thought he should easily be able to make himself master of the kingdom of Persia, provided his partizans, who now favoured him so readily, continued to do so. Therefore, having made of them a large army, he took the field with the intention, if Giausa[2] opposed him, of trying the fortune of battle. Giausa, who had been half apprehensive

[1] Amida (Diarbekr) was founded, according to Oriental tradition, by Tahmuras of the Paishdadian dynasty, and fortified by the Emperor Constans, who probably surrounded it with the stupendous wall of black stone, from which the city is often called by the Turks Kârâ Amid, or Black Amid. Some of the masonry is evidently Roman, though there are Cufic inscriptions on different parts of the wall. Kinneir says:—
"The houses are built of stone, and have a good appearance, but the streets, although paved, are narrow and filthy. The castle is on the north side of the town; it is also surrounded by a strong wall, and divided into many courts and handsome buildings, where the Pasha and his officers reside. The population of the town is said to amount to thirty-eight thousand souls, of which the greater proportion are Turks, and the remainder Armenians, Kurds, Jacobites, and Catholics. The bazar is well supplied with corn and provisions, and the adjoining country is fruitful and well cultivated. Cotton, silk, copper, and iron are manufactured by the natives, and exported to Bagdad and Constantinople. When viewed from a distance, the city of Diarbekr has a fine appearance. The elevation of the surrounding mountains, the windings of the Tigris and height of the walls and towers with the cupolas of the mosques, give it an air of grandeur far above that of any other city which I have visited in this quarter of the world. In the spring the Tigris rises to a great height at this place, but in the month of December it was so shallow, that the water did not reach much above my horse's knees. It is generally passed on a bridge of twelve arches, situated about half a mile below the town. Diarbekr is sixty miles from Merdin, two hundred and eighty-seven from Orfa, and a hundred and seventy-two and a half from Malatea. Its position is fixed in latitude 37° 55′ 40″ N., and longitude 39° 52′ E., as ascertained from actual observation by Mr. Simon."

[2] Jehan Shah.

of the designs of his brother[1] hearing of the assault and capture of Amitto,[2] did not think it politic to keep himself aloof and so allow Ussun Cassano to increase in power and also to repair the other disadvantages, which usually follow in the course of war. Therefore, having levied an army, he advanced, with almost all the forces of Persia, against Ussun Cassano. At this juncture, some Persian lords, who were friends of both, knowing what desolation would follow in Persia if they came to blows, thrust themselves between the brothers, and would have brought, with much difficulty, matters to a good understanding, if it had not been that Giausa, demanding a tribute of three hundred boy slaves from Ussun Cassano, and the latter not being willing to consent to it, proved the cause of all proposals of reconciliation being broken off. As he said, " Have I command over the sons of my vassals, that I should pay them as a tribute to Giausa; or can I forsooth dispose of them as my own? If Giausa wished to take them by force of arms from the hands of their fathers and mothers, I should never consent to it, even if I were certain of losing my life, as it is equally enjoined on the Prince to defend his people, as on the people to obey; it is not now to be thought of, that I should give them of free will."

This answer so touched to the quick, as it were, the hearts of those people, that there was not one who would not have risked his life for Ussun Cassano. Being held in this favour he artfully drew Giausa[3] to the plains of *Arsenga*,[4] where, having come to an engagement, he defeated and took him, pursuing his son, who sought safety in flight beyond Tauris.

[1] Uzun Hassan was not a brother of Jehan Shah, but of a different tribe.   [2] Diarbekr.
[3] Jehan Shah was killed in the battle and his son Kara Yusuf taken prisoner.
[4] Erzingan, Eriza, a town and district of the same name. The town is situated on the eastern branch of the Euphrates, below Erzeroum. The fine plain slopes gently from north to south, acting as a kind of

The Persian histories say, that Mahomet the Second, the lord of the Turks, who was afraid lest the greatness of Ussun Cassano should harm him in time, undertook to favour and replace Giausa in power. Wherefore, Ussun Cassano, expecting some great commotion on this side, sent Unghermaumet, his son, a valiant young man, as far as Tauris, which was the chief place of a great region; while he himself on the other side went on reducing the whole of Persia to his sway, and conquered as far as the Indian Sea, possessing a mighty empire; which empire was comprised in these limits—on the east, the river Indus and the Tartars;[1] on the west, Gorgora,[2] Trebizond, Caramania, Soria,[3] and Lesser Armenia, on this side of the Euphrates; on the south, the Arabs and the Sea of India; on the north, the *Sea of Baccu*.[4] This his country was for the most part inhabited by Armenian Christians, and by native Persian races, separated by a continuous rampart of mountains, inhabited by Kurds, an independent people, and partly ruled over by the Lord of *Betelis*,[5] who, some years later, seeing the greatness of Ussun Cassano, gave in his submission. And be-

vast drain for the waters of the mountains on the north and two other sides—viz., the Mezoor Dagh and the Kesheesh Dagh, thus conveying them to the Kara Su. Otherwise, it is a perfect level, free from stone or elevation of any kind, but some artificial mounds at the east corner. It is a garrison town, with new barracks just built; the town and villages contain about twelve thousand houses, or, by the usual calculation, sixty thousand inhabitants. The soil is rich, producing abundance of grain, cotton, fruits, and melons.

[1] His dominions hardly extended so far, even after defeating Abou Said, the reigning prince of the House of Timour. as Khorassan, Herat, Cabul, etc., were governed by the successors of that prince.

[2] Georgia.   [3] Syria.   [4] The Caspian Sea.

[5] Bitlis, the Armenian Pangesh, about an equal distance between Diarbekr and Van, the scene of the signal defeat sustained by Solyman the Magnificent in 1535. Kinneir says:—

"The town extends across the greater part of the valley, the houses being built at some distance from each other in the manner of Rutouz. The castle is situated on the top of a high mountain, which bounds the plain to the west. The inhabitants of the town and the neighbouring

cause at that time the Turkish arms were more than ever flourishing and illustrious under Mahomet II, Grand Turk, and made themselves felt gloriously in Asia and in Europe, Ussun Cassano, as generally happens to great Princes who live in jealousy about their states if they see another Prince of enterprise make great progress in war, fearing lest the immense power of the Ottoman house should in time destroy the Persian kingdom, made a close alliance and connection with Caloiane,[1] Emperor of Trabisonda, taking as a wife Despina, his daughter, under the condition that she might live in the Christian faith. This same Emperor had also married another of his daughters to the Lord Nicolo Crespo, Duke of the Archipelago, from whom were born four daughters, who were afterwards most honourably married to as many Venetian gentlemen, of the first nobility, and of one named Fiorenza settled in the Cornaro house, was born Madame Caterina, the Queen of Cyprus, and M. Giorgio, the Procurator; Valenza married to M. Giovanni Loredano dalla Samitara, son of the late M. Aluise, the Procurator, had no issue; of another, called Lucretia, married into the house of Priuli, was born M. Nicolò, the Procurator. Lastly, from Violante, who married M. Caterino Zeno, knight, who was afterwards ambassador in Persia, was

villages amount to about twenty-six thousand—Kurds, Turks, Armenians, and Syrians. The Armenians have four churches and four monasteries, and, upon the whole, enjoy more liberty and are treated with greater respect than in most Mahomedan States. The lands around Betlis are highly cultivated, and produce grain of several kinds—cotton, hemp, rice, olives, honey, truffles, and mushrooms. There is abundance of gravel in the neighbourhood, and the mountains are infested by lions, wolves, and bears. Quarries of red and white marble have also been discovered at a short distance from the town."

[1] Calo Johannes, or Black John, brother of David, last Christian Emperor of Trebizond, was of the noble family of the Comneni, which became extinct with them. Trebizond was taken in 1461 by Mahomet II, Sultan of the Turks. Uzun Hassan had married Despina while still Prince of Diarbekr, before he had gained the throne.

born M. Pietro, who begot M. Caterino, who died last year, whose soul God hath taken to himself, and whose son, M. Nicolò, still lives. This same M. Caterino, knight, in the misgivings which nearly all the powers of the world had of the power of Mahomet, the Grand Turk, was despatched as ambassador from our Republic to Ussun Cassano, in order that if they were not able to raise the Sovereigns of the West to combat the common enemy, who, insatiable in his lust of power, aspired to the empire of the world, they might at least induce those of the East, by the same misgivings to become anxious and mistrustful of their affairs.

Fortune, which often opposes itself to the loftiest desires of men, caused that our Republic, being then at the zenith of its greatness, and most flourishing through many acquisitions, having in recent years waged a glorious war in Lombardy against Philippo Visconte, and having increased her dominion in that province, excited a certain jealousy in the Sovereigns of Europe, who feared lest such power and opulence should in time prove their ruin; and especially lest this Republic, being superior to the Roman in civil government, might in course of years attain the same grandeur; therefore, as if they had conspired together, when she invited each one into a league against Mahomet, they all plainly declined. On this account our ancestors, who, animated by an honourable zeal, were eager for this politic enterprise, were filled with much anxiety, seeing that envy of their greatness would occasion the ruin of Christendom. As, in the event of a Republic, which was powerful at sea and in Greece, and enriched by many large islands,[1] which were in her possession, meeting with any slight defeat, what obstacle would remain to the Turk, to prevent him attacking Italy, as was afterwards shown in the capture of Otranto.[2]

[1] Rhodes, Cyprus, etc.
[2] Otranto was taken by the Turks in 1480, under Achmet Pasha, who

But what gave them greater disgust and anxiety of mind was, that the Turk knowing the importance of keeping this Republic friendly, sought for peace; and the senators saw that after the other Powers had been beaten by his arms, they themselves his allies, would remain an easy prey to the conquerors. Now, while they found themselves in this dilemma, four ambassadors sent by Ussun Cassano, arrived at Venice,—namely, Azimamet, Morat, Nicolo and Chefarsa, venerable men, and of great authority with the king, who, with many proffers from their master, offered to make a league and an honourable alliance against the Turk and against the Soldan, provided the Venetians would not fail with their fleet to attack both powers. These (Venetians) being delighted to have the greatest and most powerful king of the East as their confederate and ally in this war, accepted the offer, and professed to have always been good friends with the king, and assured him that this war would be more agreeable to them than ever so many others they had waged.

And thus, Azimamet remaining at Venice, the other three passed on to the Pope and to the King of Naples to excite, if possible, both of these powers to enter the league. Hence the Senate thought proper to elect an ambassador to reside at the Court of the King Ussun Cassano; as much to be ready to inflame and excite him to take up arms for the common offence and defence as to represent the grandeur and dignity of the Republic. Therefore, M. Francesco Michele was first elected, who refused; then the senators elected M. Giacomo da Mezo, who also would not accept this charge. At last, in the year 1471, M. Caterino Zeno was elected, who cheerfully undertook the journey moved only by zeal

embarked at Vallona in Macedonia, and ravaged a great part of Apulia; but, being called away to join Mahomet in his wars in Asia, the Turkish garrison, after holding the place for a year, surrendered at discretion to Alfonso, Duke of Calabria.—Knolles, *Hist. of the Turks*, p. 433.

for the holy faith. He was the son of M. Dragon Zeno, who died at Damascus, having been many years before as far as Bassera,[1] to Mecca and to Persia; therefore, M. Caterino had some acquaintance with those regions, and from the knowledge that he was nephew of the Queen Despina, wife of Ussun Cassano, considered himself alone fitted to serve his country well and efficiently in this embassy. But, because this journey was unknown, long, and full of dangers, and there was no one to be found to go with M. Caterino, our Government, not wishing to desist from the enterprise, and perceiving this difficulty, provided more pay and better provisions for those attendants who would go with him, by which means they procured some valiant men, accustomed to all kinds of hardships, who, induced by the high salary, and by a desire to see the world, gladly entered his service. By this means M. Caterino was despatched on the 6th June of the same year that he was elected, with a commission to Ussun Cassano, our Government offering to arm one hundred galleys and many other large and small ships, and with them to attack the empire of the Turk from the sea, if he from the East would not fail to press them with all his forces. With these commissions M. Caterino left Venice, arrived at Rhodes in a few months, and thence having entered the country of the Caramanians, with much difficulty reached Persia. I cannot give the particulars of his journey, because, as I mentioned above, I could never, with all my research, get his book that was printed, into my hands.

M. Caterino, having arrived at the Court of Ussun Cassano,[2] was received by him with great rejoicing and honour, as the ambassador of a Republic so illustrious and power-

---

[1] Bussora, or Basra, was founded by Omar in 636; has a population of sixty thousand at the present time. It is situated on the western bank of the Shat-ul-Arab and seventy miles from its mouth, with an immense trade. It was conquered by the Turks in 1668.

[2] At Taunis, or Tabreez. See *Travels of a Merchant*, cap. 7.

ful, his new confederate and ally; then, after having visited the king, he asked to be allowed to visit the Queen Despina. This matter, as it was not the custom to grant it to any of the Persians, was refused, it being the habit among them for the ladies not to allow themselves to be seen by any one, and they consider being seen as bad as if among us a person committed adultery.

Therefore, while they walk about the cities and the fortresses, or ride with their husbands to the war, in the following of the king, they cover their faces with nets woven of horsehair,[1] so thick that they can easily see others, but cannot be seen by them. Nevertheless, M. Caterino, by the special permission of the king, was allowed to visit her in the name of the Republic. Then, being taken into the presence of the queen, and she being informed who he was, he was welcomed and received by her with the greatest favour as a dear nephew and relation, asking him with great instance if all her nephews were alive, and in what condition they were. M. Caterino replied with great pleasure, and gave satisfactory answers to all her questions. Afterwards, when he wished to return to his lodging, she would not hear of it, but kept him in her palace, giving him separate apartments for himself and suite, and presenting him every day (a thing which is considered very honourable from the King of Persia) with the same victuals, which were put before their majesties. And then, having heard more particularly the reason of his coming, she promised him all her influence, and showing herself friendly towards our illustrious Government. And in reality this queen was instrumental, through M. Caterino, in inducing Ussun Cassano to declare war against the Turk. Nor can one deny that through the relationship M. Caterino had with Despina, he attained to such favour and intimacy with Ussun Cassano, that he even went in and out of the private apartments of the king and queen at

[1] This covering, called Peychar, is now only used in Bagdad.

whatever time and hour he pleased, and what is still more extraordinary, even when both their majesties were in bed; which I do not think any other Mahometan or Christian king ever granted, even to their nearest relations. This Despina was the most religious lady in the world, always remained a good Christian, and every day had mass solemnly celebrated in the Greek manner, which she attended with much devotion. Nor did her husband, although he was of a different faith and an enemy of her own, ever say one word to her about it, or persuade her to change her religion; certainly it is curious that the one bore so much with the other, and that there was so much love and affection between them. Nor did M. Caterino fail, after seeing this good Christian, to incite her to persuade her husband to wage a stubborn war with the Turks, bitter enemies of all the Christians and most particularly hostile to her and to her race, as they had slain her father,[1] and taken away his realm. Prevailed on by these arguments, the queen did so much and said so much to her husband, that he who was of himself much inclined to humble the greatness of the Ottoman power, wrote with his own hand orders to the King of Gorgora, Lord of the Georgians, to commence war with the Turks in that quarter. And Despina, while her husband was engaged in this project and was collecting troops, hurriedly dispatched M. Caterino's chaplain, with letters written by her own hand to the most Illustrious Government and all her relations.

But the spring having passed, and there being no news of the preparations which M. Caterino said our Republic was making to attack the Ottoman, the king began to lose hope and to give less credit to him than before. On this account, having in readiness a magnificent army, he thought of leading it against some Tartar chiefs, his enemies. But our Republic, which did not fail to send messages and letters, to

[1] David, last Emperor of Trebizond, was Despina's uncle. Her father had died before.

keep him acquainted with affairs and to confirm him in his knowledge, that the Venetians would never fail in what they had promised, on the 6th of January, twenty months after the departure of M. Caterino, elected M. Giosafat Barbaro ambassador to Persia, and sent with him several gifts to the king, which were six immense siege guns, arquebuses, and field-pieces in great number, powder, and other munitions of war; six bombardiers, one hundred arquebusiers, and other men skilled in artillery. And, on the other hand, they made a captain-general of the sea, and sent him with a great fleet to the coasts of Caramania, where, having arrived, and after waging some minor battles with the enemy, he took some castles which the Turks had occupied, giving them over to the generals of the Caramanian prince.[1] This chief, for having given a passage to M. Caterino, was unexpectedly attacked by the Turk, and deprived of his power;[2] having left several fortresses well garrisoned with men and munitions, he fled to Ussun Cassano, by whom he was graciously received, and given hopes of being reinstated, provided those fortresses, which he said still held for him, remained in his allegiance. But hope, which often disappoints the desires of men, now disappointed the Caramanian; since the captains who had charge of these strong places, corrupted by Turkish gold, although with the dishonoured name of traitors to their sovereign, gave up the fortresses in their possession, to the enemy. Having made this acquisition, Mahomet sent ambassadors from Constantinople to Persia, to excuse himself to Ussun Cassano for what he had done, and to confirm an honourable peace and friendship with him.

But very early on the day they were to have had an audience of the king, M. Caterino entered his room, and spoke to him with such convincing arguments, that, being

---

[1] Peer Ahmed, who was afterwards defeated and killed in 1486 by Bajazet II, for having aided his brother Zizim in his revolt. See Knolles, *Hist. of the Turks*, p. 446.   [2] See Angiolello, cap. 2.

backed up by Despina and by pity for the Caramanian monarch exiled from his home, and who, having come into his presence, supplicated, and entreated him not to abandon him in his adversity, the ambassadors were dismissed without ceremony. And having given immediate orders for war, he put his army in readiness; and he himself having arrived in great haste at the city of Betilis,[1] sent for M. Caterino, and said that he wished him to come with him to his army that he might see with what promptitude he had undertaken the war, partly for his own sake and for the safety of the kingdom of Persia, and partly incited by our Republic, and by the recent injury done to the Caramanian lord, his friend and ally, whom he could not desert, as he had thrown himself altogether into his hands.

These things M. Caterino heard with great delight, and thanked him with many words for the affection he had for our most illustrious Government, and joining one of his captains, called Amarbei Giusultan Nichenizza, went to make a muster of the king's warriors, who, as he writes in a private letter, were one hundred thousand horse, reckoning attendants, who accompanied their masters; some of them and their horses armed after the manner of Italy, and some covered with strong, thick hides, able to save the wearer from any heavy blow. Others were clothed in fine silk with doublets quilted so thickly that they could not be pierced by arrows. Others had gilt cuirasses and coats of mail, with so many weapons of offence and defence, that it was a marvel to behold how well and skilfully they bore themselves in arms.[2] Their servants also were excellently

[1] Bitlis. See p. 8.
[2] Kinneir, speaking of the Persian soldiery, says:—"What is denominated the standing army of the empire consists of the king's bodyguard, which amounts to about ten thousand men, and the Gholaums or royal slaves, in number about three thousand. The former are a kind of militia, which are obliged to have their habitations in the capital or its vicinity, and are liable to be called out at a moment's warn-

mounted, with cuirasses of polished iron and in place of bucklers which our people use, they have round shields, with which they cover themselves, and make use of the keenest scimitars in battle; the masters made a total of

ing: the latter are in constant attendance upon his majesty and more feared and respected than any other troops in his service. But it is the numbers and bravery of the wandering tribes which constitute the military force of the Persian empire. When the sovereign is desirous of assembling an army, the chiefs of the different tribes are commanded to send to the royal camp a number of men proportionate to the power and strength of his tribe: each town and village is also under the necessity of furnishing its quota. The army thus assembled, is consequently entirely irregular, chiefly consisting of cavalry; and, as they seldom receive either clothing or pay, only kept together by the hope of plunder. The present king, as an extreme effort, might probably in this manner be able to collect together a force of a hundred and fifty thousand or perhaps two hundred thousand men. To their cavalry, which is excellent, the rulers of Persia have hitherto, with success, solely entrusted the defence of their dominions. Their arms are a scimitar, a brace of pistols, a carabin, and sometimes a lance, or a bow and arrow—all of which they alternately use, at full speed, with the utmost skill and dexterity. The pistols are either stuck in the girdle or in the holsters of the saddle; the carabin or bow is slung across the shoulder; and the lance, which is light and shafted with bamboo, is wielded in the right hand. There is one great defect inherent in the constitution of their cavalry—a defect which cannot fail of proving highly detrimental to its success in the field, and of repressing the natural impetuosity and courage of the troops. His arms and horse in general belong not to the public, but to the individual; his whole property is often vested in these articles; and, as he receives no compensation in the event of losing them, his whole attention is naturally turned towards their preservation. This single circumstance, as must be obvious, may often be productive of the most disastrous consequences, and has, on more than one occasion, proved fatal to the honour and reputation of the Persian arms. They are not so gaudy in the trappings of their horses as the Turks; their saddles and bridles are more adapted for use than show; and the Arabian bit and stirrup were thrown aside by the orders of Nadir Shah for a plain snaffle and light iron stirrup. The saddle also is much more light than that in use among the Turks or Mamelukes, but somewhat too short in the seat, and inconvenient to a person who has not been accustomed to it. They ride with very short stirrups; but have, notwithstanding, a wonderful command over their horses, and can stop them in an instant in the midst of their career. Their cavalry, like all irregular horse, are incapable of acting in unison or of making any serious impression on

forty thousand men, all brave soldiers, and their servants sixty thousand, and finer cavalry were never seen in any army : the men were tall and very muscular, and very dexterous in wielding their weapons, so that it is reported that a small troop of them would have routed ever so great a squadron of the enemy. The muster being completed, he made forced marches with the whole army towards the country of the enemy, and with him went Pirameto,[1] the Caramanian chief, and all the king's sons who were valiant young men. And M. Caterino, who also wished to be with them, went to bid adieu to the Queen Despina; but the army marched ahead with such speed that he could not re-

a body of troops disciplined in the European fashion : but, as their evolutions and movements are extremely rapid and each individual is aware of the part he ought to act, they are nearly as formidable when broken and dispersed as when united. The Persian armies, as I have said before, receive no regular pay, and are only kept together by the hope of plunder; we therefore find, that it is considered as incumbent on the king to take the field once a year, either against the Russians, Affghans, or Turkomans, his immediate neighbours. They know nothing of the modern science of war, being entirely ignorant of the principles of fortification and of the arts of attack and defence. The field artillery is chiefly composed of zumbarooks or small swivels, mounted on, and fired from, the backs of camels. There are also small field-pieces attached to the army; but the roads on the frontier are but ill adapted for the transportation of cannon, and as the carriages are of a miserable construction, they are either broken by the rocks and precipices, or go to pieces after firing a few rounds. Another great defect in the organisation of the armies of this country is the total want of good officers, and therefore of a proper degree of subordination. Without able and experienced men to direct and command, and a regular system of payment, it is next to impossible that an army can arrive at anything like perfection. There is no separation of the civil from the military authorities. The troops are commanded by the chiefs of their own tribes, who are jealous of each other, and therefore not likely to act in concert or yield that obedience so absolutely necessary in military affairs. In the absence of the King and Prince, the Grand Vizier is the general-in-chief; and, as he is not unfrequently raised to that dignity from offices entirely civil, the army may be commanded by a man who has never witnessed an engagement."

[1] Peer Ahmed. See p. 15.

join it, and therefore was much disgusted. Going on his way with a squadron of five hundred horse he was attacked in Giauas[1] by the people of the country, who caused them much loss; thus, having lost many soldiers, and having suffered several other inconveniences, he turned towards Tocat, and led them at last to the city of Carpeto,[2] where he heard, to his great comfort, that Ussun Cassano was soon to arrive. The Persian army entered Giauas in the month of September, and carried fire and sword through the country far and near, plundering and cutting people to pieces, to the great terror of the inhabitants, so that every one fled before this tempest. And passing Arsenga[3] and Tocat, he burnt the towns and villages everywhere with the same fury, and assaulted and took Carle, which belonged to the Caramanian.

Mustafà, the son of the Turk, who, with Acomat Pasha, was in Lulla, a city of Caramania, being alarmed at this, fled towards Cogno :[4] and removing his mother, sent her to Saibcacarascar,[5] four days' journey in the interior, towards Constantinople. But the Persians coming towards Cogno, the Turk wrote letters to his son that he should retreat, and not rashly seek to come to blows with the enemy, because any little victory would raise their courage, and make them attempt anything. On account of these letters Mustafà, who knew that his father was right, retired to Cuteia,[6] where he found Daut[7] Pasha, Beglerbeg of Natolia, making great assemblies of people of war. The Grand Turk then did not

[1] Gerjannes, a district of Erzingan.
[2] Kharput, in the Valley of Sophene, as it was called by the ancients. See *Travels of a Merchant*.   [3] Erzingan. See p. 7.
[4] Konieh (Iconium). Konieh, a city of Asia Minor, with a population of thirty thousand, employed mostly in the manufacture of carpets; it was a capital of the Seljook Sultans.
[5] Ofium Kara Hissar, a town of fifty thousand inhabitants, two hundred miles from Smyrna, where opium is raised in great quantities.
[6] Kutaieh.   [7] Daood.

think it right to linger lest his men, missing his presence, might lose spirit and allow the enemy boldly to enter the country and to capture the strongholds. On this account, having passed into Asia with his whole court, he expected soon to encounter Ussun Cassano with the Persian army. But having heard from his spies that the disturbances in those provinces arose from a captain of Ussun Cassano's, who, with forty thousand horse, went plundering, burning, and slaughtering, and who just then was marching towards Bursia[1] to burn it (the king having remained behind with the rest of the army), the Turk despatched Mustafà with sixty thousand of the best cavalry of the army, who moved by forced marches towards the enemy, desirous of encountering them and of putting a stop to such devastation. The Persian army being warned of this, commenced a retreat, knowing themselves to be much inferior in number to the enemy; and, as they were loaded with booty and made slow progress, four thousand Turks who pursued at great speed under Armaut,[2] came up with them and at once attacked, when the Persians, beginning to fight bravely, pressed them hard, and routed them in a moment, and cut to pieces two thousand Turks with their leader Armaut. Scarcely was this action over when Mustafà arrived with the rest of his men, who, closing in one squadron, attacked the Persians fiercely; while the latter, on their side, resisted not less courageously. Both parties bore themselves bravely for many hours, and it is thought that anyhow the victory would have been on the side of the Persians, if they had not first fought with those four thousand horse, since Mustafà, who came up with fresh men, found them fatigued with that battle and with the journey, and thus remained the conqueror, although with great loss on his side.[3] The number

---

[1] Boorsa. [2] Amurath.

[3] This, according to Knolles, was a Persian victory, Mustafa being forced to fly.—*History of the Turks*, p. 410. See below, p. 25.

of the slain is not given in the letters from which this history is taken; it is only mentioned that Usufcan,[1] the general of Ussun Cassano, was taken prisoner by the Turks, and that Pirameto,[2] the Caramanian Prince, fled and saved himself with a great part of the army. The whole of the succeeding winter the king and the Turk busied themselves in making fresh preparations for war, that they might in the spring again confront each other.

And Ussun Cassano, in the beginning of the summer, took the field with his army, and having captured some of the spies of the Turk, commanded their hands to be cut off and hung round their necks, and that they should be sent back to the Ottoman in this manner.

At this very time arrived letters for M. Caterino, written by M. Pietro Mocenigo, who was afterwards Doge, then Captain-General of the Sea, and M. Giosafat Barbaro[3] giving him intelligence, both of the presents which our most Illustrious Government was sending to the king, and of the arrival of the fleet on the coast of Caramania. And above all, he heard with great satisfaction of the castles which they had taken and restored to the generals of the Caramanian Prince; these letters filled Ussun Cassano with such joy and hope, that he ordered the news to be spread through the whole army, and commanded as a greater token of affection and honour towards our Republic, that at the sound of the trumpet, and Zamblacare,[4] the Venetian name should be lauded and saluted, and such was the din, that the noise might be heard at several miles' distance.

The Turk also having made greater exertions than before, passed into Asia, and shut himself up in Amasia, a city of Cappadocia, which was the Sangiacato[5] of his son Bajazet,[6]

---

[1] Yusuf Khan.   [2] Peer Ahmed.
[3] M. Josafat Barbaro's account of his travels is in Ramusio's Collection.
[4] Zumburka.   [5] Sanjak.
[6] Afterwards Bajazet II, reigned from 1481-1512.

who together with Mustafà, went with his father to this war, Gieu,[1] his third son, remaining in Constantinople. And since the difficulty of leading armies into Persia consists in supplying provisions, it being the custom of the Persians to desolate the country for fifteen or twenty days' journey on the side on which they expect an invasion; so that, whoever, in attacking Persia, does not go well provided with necessaries, either dies of hunger on the road, has to retire much to his dishonour, or else becomes a prey to the enemy. Mahomet, who had deliberated well about this with his people, after having made a good provision of victuals, divided all his army into five columns.

The first he led in person, in which, with the corps of Janissaries, were thirty thousand soldiers—the flower of the Turkish nation, so to speak.

The second, of another thirty thousand, Bajazet commanded.

Mustafà led the third, also of thirty thousand, including twelve thousand Wallachians, led by Basaraba, their captain, who came to the aid of the Turks in this war.

The fourth was under Asmurat Palæologus, a Turk, Beglerbeg of Roumania, numbering sixty thousand men, among whom were many of his Christian subjects.

The fifth was under Daut, Beglerbeg of Natolia, of forty thousand men. There were besides, the Acangi,[2] volunteer cavalry, with their chief, to the number of thirty thousand. These traversed the country thirty, forty, and fifty miles before the Turkish armies, plundered, burnt, and slaughtered whatever they found before them. They are most valiant in person, and it is their duty to bring provisions to the camp.

With this immense army the Turk started from Amasia,

[1] The unfortunate Djim-Zizim, or Zemes, who, being defeated by Bajazet in his struggle for empire, fled first to Egypt and then to Rhodes. He was sent to Rome to the Pope Innocent VIII, but was poisoned at the instigation of the infamous Alexander Borgia, who had been forced to give him up to Charles VIII of France.   [2] Ikindjis.

and having with him several large pieces of artillery, took the road to Tocat in capital order, and leaving on the left the town of Siuas[1] on the river Lais,[2] which flows from the mountains of Trebizond, entered a low plain between that city and Mount Taurus. On their way they found Nicheset,[3] a very strong Persian castle, which they did not attack, in order not to lose time on the way. Thus marching, they had on the left the city of Coiliutar,[4] situated among mountains, and surrounded with villages; descending the mountain they halted near the city Carascar,[5] famous for its mines.

The inhabitants of this place had all fled to the mountains; therefore, without halting, the army proceeded to the city of Argina,[6] situated in a wide plain. Here they found in a church a philosopher studying with many books around him, and who,[7] not ceasing to read, in spite of all the noise and uproar they made, was cut to pieces by the Acangian[8] horsemen. All the other people had fled beyond the Euphrates. Having left this, the Turks passed the country called Arsenga,[9] which is Lesser Armenia, and approached the Euphrates not far from Malatia,[10] where, on eleven dro-

[1] Siwas, sixty miles from Tokat on the Kizzil Irmak, with manufactures of coarse woollen, etc.
[2] River Iris, the present Kizzil Irmak. [3] Niksar.
[4] Koili Hissar, according to Kiepert's Map on the Schonak or Owadmish Schai, which falls into the Yekyl Irmak. It is a little below Shebban Kara Hissar; it is also called Koyunlu Hissar.
[5] Shebban Kara Hissar, still noted for its alum mines. The castle is built on an isolated mountain about six hundred feet high and three miles in circumference, and is of great natural strength; it has the same contrivance common to most of the old castles for the supply of water during a siege, namely, a staircase excavated in the solid rock. It was probably one of the treasure-cities of Mithridates mentioned by Strabo. The trade in alum has greatly diminished, as it is now exported to Turkish provinces solely.
[6] Probably Egin on the Euphrates, on the route from Erzingan to Malatia. See Angiolello, cap. 6.
[7] Compare the death of Archimedes.
[8] Ikindjis. [9] Erzingan. See p. 7.
[10] Malatia, the ancient Melitene, near the Euphrates or Murad, in lat. N. 30 deg. 26 min., long. E. 38 deg. 27 min.

medaries, there arrived before the sovereign the ambassadors of the Soldan of Cairo to deliver an arrow with a letter on its point, to which an answer was soon given; and they having remounted their dromedaries departed, getting over a deal of ground in one day, the dromedary being so swift as to travel without intermission further than any other animal. And St. John Chrysostom, upon Matthew, explains the difficult passage as to how the Magians could have come from the East to Judæa to worship Christ in such a short space of time, as is mentioned in the Evangelist, by supposing that they came upon dromedaries, which are said to be the fastest animals for a long journey. Leaving this place the Turkish army marched along the banks of the river towards the north-east, going up against the course of the stream, when on the other bank Ussun Cassano presented himself with the whole Persian army in array.

In this place the Euphrates, which is an immense river with very high banks, forms many sandy islands; so that it is easy to ford it from one side to the other.[1]

Ussun Cassano had a magnificent army of Lesdians who are Parthians, of Persians, Georgians, Kurds, and Tartars, and the principal captains who led them were Unghermaumet, Calul, and Ezeinel, his sons, and Pirameto, the Caramanian Prince.[2] But, although his army was so large, he nevertheless saw that of the Turk as immense, and occupying as large a space of ground, a thing which he had not at first believed, from hearsay. He marvelled at it for a time, and then all astonished, said: "Hai cabesen ne dentider,"[3] which in the Persian tongue signifies "Oh, son of a ——, what an ocean"; comparing this immense army to a sea. Then the Turk, who thought that by boldness he might anticipate and check the forces of Ussun Cassano, commanded the Beglerbeg of Roumania, Asmurat Palæologus, to

---

[1] This is only in the dry season, as there are no islands, only sandbanks.
[2] Peer Ahmed.   [3] See Angiolello, cap. 7.

cross the river with his men and gain possession of the other bank, which would be an evident defeat for Ussun Cassano and his whole army; and since Palæologus was young and bold, in order that his rashness might not cause some mistake, he joined to him Mahomet Pasha to direct him in any emergency.

He led out an immense squadron to the sound of kettle-drums and other martial instruments, with banners flying, descended into the bed of the river, and crossed from one sand-bank to another. Then Ussun Cassano, irritated by this bold proceeding, sent a powerful force of the flower of his army into the river, where the Persians having joined battle with the Turks, either party without yielding as much as an inch of water or ground, fought bravely for more than three hours continuously, while both armies stood on the banks looking on and encouraging. At last, the Turks being repulsed by the Persians with great loss, were routed and driven from the sand-banks; many were drowned in the tumult, being carried away by the stream; and the Persians falling upon them persistently, caused a renewal of the battle more fiercely and cruelly than before; since, in this retreat Palæologus, carried away by the water, was nearly drowned, and the Turks wishing to assist him made desperate head again, regardless of their lives.[1] Thus the assault was renewed so fiercely that no advantage could be discerned on either side; however, the Persians at last obtaining the victory, again broke the enemy, and beat them back with great slaughter, Asmurat[2] remaining drowned in the waters.

[1] This battle took place near Malatia 1473.
[2] Knolles says that Mustafâ, Mahomet the Second's eldest son, and Amurath, Pasha of Roumania (the latter of whom was killed in the battle), commanded the Turks when they were defeated in 1473. He also mentions another battle the next year in which Mahomet was present in person and was defeated, one of his great Pashas being killed. Perhaps two battles were made out of this one, or more probably the battle previously mentioned (p. 20) was a Persian victory.

Mahomet Pasha, who was in array on a neighbouring sand-bank, seeing this, adroitly withdrew to the bank, where, on the arrival of the Persians pursuing the enemy, he a third time made head, and valorously sustained the Persian assault; and there would have been fiercer fighting than ever if the night had not come on and separated the combatants.

And there is an opinion that the closing in of the day robbed Ussun Cassano of a great victory; as, if Mahomet Pasha had been beaten, the Persians, to their great honour, would have made themselves masters of the other bank; and, as the Turk in the elevated country could not use his artillery or occupy an open space of ground with his cavalry, he would certainly have become a prey to the enemy; since, in the passage of arms in the river not more than five hundred Persians were killed, and from the Turkish army there were fifteen thousand missing in killed and drowned, and numberless prisoners.

On this account the Turk, harassed by a thousand conjectures, kept his army under arms all the night, fearing an attack. The next day he gave an extra donation to all the troops, liberated the slaves on the condition that they should return with the camp to Constantinople, and having arrayed the army, marched up the river, leaving it near the city of Braibret,[1] which he left on his right hand, across the mountains which separate Greater and Lesser Armenia, which road was towards the north-west in the direction of Trebizond.

The Turks being defeated at the fords of the Euphrates in the manner I have described, Ussun Cassano was incited by his sons and by the whole army to follow on, so as not to lose the fruits of so great a victory; since the Persians, who had proved the force of the enemy, despised them, and expected to come off victorious in every encounter. There-

---

[1] Baiboort, on the river Turak or Delchoroch Su, which flows into the Euxine near Batoum. It is situated nearly due north of Erzingan.

fore, the king followed the Turks on the other bank, to see what was their design; but when the Persians saw that they kept away from the Euphrates, they called on Ussun Cassano with great importunity, to cross the river, as they plainly saw the Turk was in flight. He gave way to this, although against his will (as, being a clever, practical, and veteran soldier, he remembered that noble precept of military science, " that one ought to pave the roads with gold and make bridges of silver for a flying enemy"), and acceded to the wishes of his men, to see how so much ardour and longing for battle would succeed. Thus, having chosen forty thousand of his most skilful and daring soldiers, he crossed the Euphrates, and began, with forced marches, to pursue the hostile army, having left Calul, his eldest son, on the other side of the river with all the Georgians, Tartars, and many other soldiers in charge of the baggage. By the end of August he reached the top of some mountains, from the summits of which he saw the Turkish army in the valley leading in the direction of Trebizond. Thinking, from his recent victory, that he could easily overcome them and put them to flight, he arrayed himself for battle.

The Turks, seeing the road closed to them, and knowing that they must either open it sword in hand or, to their great disgrace, be routed and cut to pieces, as happens when inspired by desperation, made a virtue of necessity, and also arrayed themselves with great ardour for the battle.[1] The Turk then having left Ustrefo with a considerable garrison in charge of his camp, set out to scale the mountain on another side, which was not occupied by the Persian troops. Ussun Cassano, seeing them leave the camp, sent Unghermaumet, his son, with a squadron of ten thousand cavalry to oppose Ustrefo, and to cut off all hope of safety from the Turk. And having made three other large divisions, he gave the right wing to Pirameto,[2] the Caramanian

[1] The battle of Tabcada. [2] Peer Ahmed.

Prince, and the left to Ezeinel, his son, commanding in person the centre with all the infantry, which was in magnificent condition. And the battle having begun at the fourteenth hour, the action lasted eight hours continuously, the Persians resisting that great army with such valour, that their personal prowess was wonderful to see; and if Mustafà, the son of the Turk, had not attacked with a fresh squadron the right flank of the Caramanian, the victory would have remained uncertain still longer; as, when the Caramanian gave way before the fresh assault of Mustafà, everything was thrown into confusion in that quarter.[1] Thus it was, that in his retreat he disordered the flank of the line of battle of Ussun Cassano, who, on account of the confusion of his troops and the attack of the enemy in front, saw himself so pressed that he was afraid of being surrounded. Therefore, seized with no small fear on account of the uncertainty of affairs, he jumped off his horse and mounted a swift mare, which he always kept ready for such emergencies; and seeing himself pressed more and more every hour and driven in on the right wing, he turned round and fled. His son Ezeinel seeing this, threw himself with great courage into the midst of the infantry and endeavoured to make head, so that the whole army might not be routed by one charge of the enemy; but, however much this gallant young man might sustain the fury of the Turks, being at length killed by them, the Persians were routed and put to flight. Unghermaumet, who had gone to attack the camp of the Turks guarded by Ustrefo, met with great resistance, but nevertheless hoped to have taken it in time; but, seeing the rout of his father, withdrew little by little, and was in great danger of being made prisoner; since, before his retreat, the Turks had occupied all the plain. However, by making great exertions, he escaped and rejoined his father. The

[1] Knolles says that the Turkish artillery did great mischief to the Persians, as in the battle of Schalderan.

latter not considering himself safe in his camp, which was ten miles distant from the field of battle, crossed the Euphrates, and retired with the rest of his men to the interior of his country. This fight took place in the year 1473, in which ten thousand Persians and fourteen thousand Turks fell.

Mahomet, thus remaining conqueror, decided to follow up this good fortune, and in the course of war to make himself master of some place of the enemy's. Therefore, having mustered his army, he marched a second time towards the city of Baibret,[1] and the Acangi[2] who preceded him were cut to pieces by the people of the country in great numbers. After this feat the inhabitants, warned by scouts, that the Turk was marching up in haste with the rest of his army, fled to the mountains, having, so to speak, given vent to their fury on their enemies. The Turks having arrived at the ford of the river Euphrates, where the first battle had taken place, crossed without any resistance, the Acangi still in advance.

Then marching towards Erscagan,[3] they found the country and towns everywhere abandoned; and four days after they reached Carascar,[4] a fortress posted on the top of a mountain; the Turks preparing to attack it, dragged some pieces of artillery up another mountain[5] which commanded the fortress, and thence bombarded it fifteen days continuously. At last a captain named Darap, a vassal of Ezeimel, the son of Ussun Cassano, who was in command, hearing of the death of his master, surrendered it. From Carascar, the army marched to Coliasar,[6] a city which, not wishing to essay its strength against so daring an enemy, also

[1] Baiboort. See p. 5.   [2] Ikindjis.
[3] Erzingan.   [4] Shebban Kara Hissar. See p. 23.
[5] After crossing the river the Turkish army evidently began to retreat to their own country. Why they went near Malatia is not very evident.
[6] Koili Hissar. See p. 23. According to Angiolello, it was near Erzingan that the Turks reached the Euphrates, and only the Acangi crossed on a foraging expedition, which is much more probable.

yielded. At that time news came to the Turk that Ussun Cassano was restoring his army with the design of driving, if possible, the enemy out of the country, and on this account he did not think it right to advance further, that he might not run into dangers from which he might not afterwards be able to extricate himself. Then, having faced about, he returned in great haste to Sevas, and thence to Tocat,[1] where was the ambassador of the King of Hungary, whom he had cajoled with many dissembling words in this way, saying to him that he wished first to free himself from the war with Persia, and that he would then conclude a peace with his king who was in treaty for one. All this he did with the object in this crisis not to be molested by the Hungarian arms. But after his victory he dismissed him without any conclusion of the affair, by which artifice the Hungarian king was deceived, to his great hurt and to that of all Christendom; as there is little reason to doubt that if he had availed himself of this opportunity, he would, even with very small forces, have driven the Turks from Greece, and also have terrified the whole of Asia.

And the Persian war having been concluded in the manner narrated above, the Turk returned in great triumph to Constantinople, leaving Mustafà in his Sangiacato,[2] where he soon afterwards died. And Acomat[3] Pasha went with a large army towards Laranto, a city of the Caramanian monarch, situated near Mount Taurus, where, pretending to have peaceable intentions towards the inhabitants, he gradually gained over the chiefs by inviting now this one and now that, with courtesy and familiarity, to eat with him. By using these arts for some time, so as to rid them of all suspicion of him and of the army, he fixed a certain day for his departure, before which he made a solemn feast for all these

---

[1] Tocat, fifty-six miles from Sivas, with a population of forty thousand, and a very extensive trade.

[2] Sanjak.   [3] Achmet.

lords, who, while they were eating and drinking merrily with him, were made prisoners by some of his men told off for the purpose, and strangled in some secret places; then, having entered the mountainous country without difficulty, he took away the people and sent them to Greece, putting others in their stead to inhabit the country. While these things came to pass in the Caramanian dominions, Ussun Cassano, who had had in a short space of time, first the best fortune and then the most adverse he had ever experienced, found himself in great distress of mind on account of his recent defeat; as the reputation of being invincible, which he had acquired in so many wars, seemed to disappear at one blow. For this reason, having at his court two ambassadors—one a Pole and the other an Hungarian—he dismissed them both, that they might not witness his misery, and, by so doing, increase it.[1]

And as his greatest hope was in the Christian princes, and as he saw that they had the same interests as himself, he despatched M. Caterino with letters written to all the kings of Europe, to beg assistance of them, urging the danger that both parties ran, and that he had taken up arms against the Ottoman, principally at the instigation of our Republic and the other Christian powers.

And thus all these ambassadors, setting out in company from the king, passed into Gorgora; and M. Caterino having left the other two to continue their journey, arrived at Salvatopolo on the Greater Sea, whence he crossed to Cafa[2] in a ship of Lugi da Pozzo, a Genoese; who, having heard on the voyage that he was ambassador to Ussun Cassano, wished to take him to Constantinople to the Turks, as Cafa obeyed

[1] It seems that the other Christian princes were not altogether so blind to the advantages of a Persian alliance as the Venetian writer would have us think.

[2] Caffa, anciently called Theodosia, situated in the Crimea, and then belonging to the Genoese, was a rich and busy port. It was subdued, with the rest of the Crimea, by Achmet Pasha in 1476.

the latter and paid tribute. Therefore, they sent a proclamation under severe penalties, that no one should lodge, receive, or assist him in any way. However, Andrea Scaranelli, an honest citizen of our Republic, without thinking of the penalties he would incur, esteeming the favour of our Government more than life or fortune, came alongside the ship secretly by night in a boat, and having told him wherefore he was come, took him off and brought him safely to land, hiding him in his house. M. Caterino not finding any money here was in great difficulty about his affairs, when a servant of his, named Martin, persuaded him with many words to sell him by auction, and to use the money. M. Caterino, although he admired the peculiar liberality and fidelity of Martin, still pressed by the want in which he found himself, had him sold, as he proposed, by auction, making use of the money he got for the sale: a rare example of a faithful servant, and worthy of being compared with any other in ancient times, when they say there were such devoted servants, that they would offer to be killed to save the lives of their masters. Nor did our Republic fail to recognise such a service done to so worthy a citizen, as, in addition to his ransom, they gave him a pension, on which he lived: an example for others to see of what value it is to serve the State faithfully.

From Cafa M. Caterino wrote letters to the most Illustrious Government, narrating in them all the events of the two recent battles, and how Ussun Cassano had despatched him with secret commissions to all the kings of Europe, to incite them to wage war with spirit against the common enemy, as he intended in the beginning of spring to take the field with all the forces of Persia, and to try afresh the fortune of battle. These letters were most acceptable to the Government on account of their news, none of which had yet reached them from any other source. But, hearing that M. Giosafat Barbaro had not yet arrived in

Persia, according to the commission he received when he accepted the embassy, they did not think it was consistent with their dignity to leave a most friendly king, and one most constant to his word, without an ambassador, now that M. Caterino had left him. For this reason, on the 10th September, in the year 1473, the Senate elected M. Ambrosio Contarini as ambassador to Persia, who set out on the 13th of February, as is narrated in his travels. This man, also going through Germany and Poland on the way to Cafa, at last crossed into Persia, where he found M. Giosafat Barbaro already arrived, but was not very well received by the king,—perhaps, because he had found in our other rulers promises and words enough, but few deeds. Our Republic had always kept inviolate all it had promised him, and was again most ready to join him in the same risks. Perhaps, also, because he found his soldiery inferior in strength to the Turkish, as it was not paid, but served the king in war when called out.[1] For this reason, he dismissed him with general words of being willing at some future time to wage war against the enemy; and, on his refusing to return, saying that that was not his commission from the Republic, compelled him by force to leave with another ambassador—the Duke of Burgundy's; and, M. Ambrosio being indignant with this king, on account of this slight, tried with many words to lower his reputation. M. Caterino, in the meanwhile, with the aid of S. Michele Aman, after having suffered many fatigues and gone through many great dangers, went to Poland, and found the King Casimir[2] waging a desperate war with the Hungarian king. Notwithstanding this, M. Caterino announced his mission from Ussun Cassano, and entreated him, in consideration of the great danger to Christendom, if after the conquest of the mighty sovereigns

---

[1] See note, p. 16.

[2] Casimir IV reigned from 1447 to 1492. He defeated the Teutonic knights and also the Hungarians.

of the East, Mahomet were to turn his arms towards the West, to make an alliance with this king, and to harass the enemy on his side, as he also would do on the East.

The king heard him graciously, and replied that, on account of the war with Hungary, he could not fight against the Turks with whom he was in league. M. Caterino perceiving from this answer the disposition of this monarch, and that he would not be able to get either ambassadors or a letter written to Ussun Cassano, exhorted him in a long speech to make peace with the Hungarians, saying that since he would not make war on the Turks, at least he ought not to be the reason of Hungary's not doing her duty by Christendom in this crisis, as she had been accustomed to do in so many other wars with the very same enemy; and so efficacious were his words, that Casimir having given an audience to the Hungarian ambassadors concluded and ratified a peace in three days.

While M. Caterino was in Poland he found M. Paolo Ognibene, who was going as Nuncio from our most Illustrious Government to Ussun Cassano, and gave him letters written to the king, full of encouragement and warm words, exhorting him to persevere boldly in the war he had begun, as, then at any rate, he would be seconded by the Christian princes, when they saw him really begin to act against the Ottoman; and that he himself would not fail by importunity, and all the pains in his power, to express all his commissions to the Europeans from him. With these letters he also wrote in the same tenor to the King of Gorgora and to Melico, King of Mingrelia; and having bidden Ognibene God speed, he set out for Hungary. Being honourably received there by the King Matthias Corvinus,[1] who was the most illustrious sovereign in arms and learning, not only of the Hungarians, but also of all the kings of Christendom, he discoursed

---

[1] Matthias Corvinus, son of the Great Huniades, the champion of Christendom against the Turks, reigned from 1458 to 1490.

to him so powerfully about the commissions he had from Ussun Cassano, that the king, who was of himself much inclined to go to war with the Turks, promised that he would never fail a king who deserved so much from the Christian commonwealth. Then, having conversed more intimately with M. Caterino, and having recognised his valour and virtue, he dubbed him knight with many honours, as may be seen in the special grant made at Buda on the 20th April, 1474, in which are related all his works and exertions in this enterprise.

M. Caterino left Hungary and came to Venice, where, as he had been in such distant regions, and as no Venetian in the memory of man had been a longer or more memorable journey in the service of his country, he was received by all the nobility and people with great acclamations, and his relations in particular looked upon him as a god come down from heaven. The Senate having afterwards heard the commissions of Ussun Cassano and the goodwill he had towards our Republic, elected four ambassadors to the Pope and the King of Naples, and sent with them M. Caterino as ambassador of the King of Persia, who was to take precedence of the others. They were despatched by the Senate on the 22nd of August, in the year one thousand four hundred and seventy-four. These embassies, however, produced no good effect, since, at that time, on account of the bitter discords existing among our princes, it seemed that a certain fatal jealousy prevented them from taking up arms with so great and valorous a king, and one who, moreover, had just exposed himself and his kingdom to the sport of Fortune, in order to show that he had this enterprise at heart against an enemy, who evidently aspired to make himself master of the world.

And before the departure of these ambassadors they wrote to M. Giosafat Barbaro, who was in Cyprus, that he should proceed to Ussun Cassano and not render his mission useless, as he had spent so long a time between Venice and the coast of Caramania (since, having been elected in the Senate on the 5th of January, 1471, he set out after having received this letter, which was written on the last day of January, 1473). Wherefore, having laid aside all care for his life, he at last set out for his destination to serve his country, and thus after having gone through many dangers he arrived at Tauris in the presence of Ussun Cassano, as he relates in his travels, in the year one thousand four hundred and seventy-four, where he was welcomed and favourably received by that sovereign. And this same M. Giosafat writes that he found him in the height of his grandeur and reputation, as at that time the Indian ambassadors, who were accustomed every year to bring certain gifts in sign of subjection, were received with the greatest pomp. But the war which broke out between him and Unghermaumet, his valiant son, was the occasion of taking from him all his reputation and of blunting the forces of his mind, which till that time had been considered invincible; so that on account of the grief he felt for the rebellion of so gallant a son, and one so famous for his prowess in Asia and Europe, he had to give up all the duties of a king, and more particularly to cast away all thought of the enterprise against the Ottoman.

The reason of this war between father and son was, that the Kurds, people of the mountains, being envious of Ussun Cassano and the grandeur of the Persian kingdom, in order to sow the seeds of discord in the midst of peace in that realm, spread a report around that Ussun Cassano was dead, to which rumour Unghermaumet gave ear readily, as after the death of his father he aspired to the throne of Persia. Thus, having collected the army his father had given him to guard Bagadet,[1] which was formerly Babylonia, and all the country of Biarbera,[2] he immediately seized Seras,[3] a city on the confines of Persia, gaining over almost all the Kurds

[1] Bagdad. [2] Diarbekr. [3] Shiraz.

to his party, as they, when they heard that Unghermaumet had made himself master of Seras, came together in great numbers and traversed and plundered the country up to Tauris. Hence Ussun Cassano took the field with the "porta", that is, the standing army, which he always kept as a guard about his person, and marched in great haste towards Seras. Unghermaumet being terrified at this, as he had already discovered the falsehood of the Kurds, and that his credulity had made him rashly endeavour, by force of arms, to complete a matter of such importance, left the territory, and by means of some chiefs, friendly both to him and to his father, tried to obtain forgiveness from him for his fault; but, hearing that Ussun Cassano was coming with a mind embittered against him, he considered that he had made a mistake, and therefore became apprehensive of being betrayed and losing his life. And his imagination coloured it so highly, that without even confronting the troops of his father, he fled, and reached the country of the Ottoman on the frontiers of the Sangiacato[1] of Bajazet, son of the Grand Turk, from whom with the consent of the latter, he obtained a safe conduct to allow him to seek an asylum under Turkish protection; and having sent his wife and sons to Amasia,[2] to give more assurance to Bajazet, he also rode in his direction, and was welcomed and greatly honoured by that prince. And since this gallant young man could not endure being thus, so to speak, deserted by fortune, desirous of trying his chance (which, as is said, often changes about from troublous to the most prosperous, provided one does not fail in duty to oneself), he passed on to Constantinople to incite, if possible, Mahomet, the Grand Turk, to give him some assistance, and was received with the greatest demonstrations of love and

[1] Sanjak.
[2] Amasia, the birthplace of Strabo and Mithridates, is now an important town with thirty thousand inhabitants and great trade in silk, situated on the Yekyl Irmak.

many promises, as Mahomet was a man of valour, and admired nobleness and bravery in illustrious men more than any of his predecessors among the Ottoman princes. Nor were his deeds less than his words, since Mahomet, wishing to take away Ussun Cassano's fame and reputation, and to gain such a friend that for the future the Persian arms might not oppose him in his full career of conquest, thought that he would do much for his advantage by assisting Unghermaumet in this enterprise, and by these discords between father and son exhaust the force of Persia, in order that in later times, either he or his descendants might subdue that country.

Unghermaumet having obtained these Turkish auxiliaries, entered the province of Sanga, on the confines of Persia, and thence damaged the country of his father by frequent inroads; the latter, although he sent several bands of cavalry and infantry to those frontiers to repulse his son who was thus at war with him, did not seem to wish to revenge himself for so many injuries, as both in public and in private he gave out that he felt such grief on this account, and so after a little feigned to have fallen ill, and gradually retiring with those he had most faith in, either on account of benefits he had done them or otherwise, caused it to be rumoured in Persia and Turkey that he was very ill, and at last published abroad his death through the same people. Hence letters and messages were quickly sent to Unghermaumet, furnishing him with information of the death of his father and the requests of the principal nobles of the kingdom to come in haste in order that his other brothers, namely, Calul and Giacuppo,[1] might not by chance take away his kingdom, which of right belonged to him, on account of his great valour, rather than to them; and, in order to hide the deceit better, they celebrated the obsequies of the dead king with great pomp in the city.

[1] Yakoob, who succeeded Ussun Cassano in 1478.

Thus the unfortunate Unghermaumet, who was led by his fate by the hair of his head to die, not recollecting that his too great credulity had already driven him from his home and exiled him to seek assistance from his enemies who favoured him outwardly, in order to gain a better opportunity for themselves to profit by his still lower fall, gave full credence to the matter, and having given the messages brought to him in charge to some of his people set out for Persia in such haste that in a few days he reached Tauris. Here, having sought out those who had written to him of the death of his father and given him hopes of gaining the kingdom, he was conducted by them to where his father was with such secrecy, that the unhappy wretch did not discover it till he found himself face to face with him; and being then received with severe words and threats, he was put in prison, and soon afterwards murdered. This was the end of Unghermaumet who, on account of his great courage, was always called by the Persians "The Valiant": a man without doubt most excellent in arms and worthy of his father's kingdom, if, attracted by the lust of power, he had not been so hasty of belief; as, if he had lived longer, the kingdom of Persia would have gained greatly in glory from him, and would have risen to greater fame than it afterwards did under Ismail, his nephew; nor after his death was Persia again molested by the Turks; nor did Ussun Cassano do anything remarkable until his decease.

And M. Caterino, also, after he had completed all the missions he had undertaken by the command of Ussun Cassano and of our Republic returned to Venice so well thought of and welcomed by all the nobles as well as people, that on account of the universal favour he was held in, all turned their eyes towards him, beholding a man who, through great dangers, had compassed not only Europe, but also a great part of Asia. And, as an example of the favour he was held in, at his election to the Council of Ten, what is most singular and a great honour in our Republic, he had only seventeen adverse votes in the great Council. But what is still more extraordinary is, that when he used to walk in the street, so many persons ran together to see him, that he could hardly proceed.

And thus it is true what is said, that the path of glory is narrow and difficult, and like Hercules[1] mentioned by Xenophon, who chose rather to become famous through great trials, than live at ease without a name in the world, the good M. Caterino, to serve his country, and to gain an honourable fame, never thought of dangers and difficulties; whence one may for certain conclude that sham honours paid by the common people are but dust and ashes in comparison with those meritoriously gained by a man's own exertions.

[1] It was Achilles, not Hercules, who is said to have preferred a short and famous career to a long life of inglorious ease.

END OF THE FIRST BOOK.

SECOND BOOK.

KNOWING well how universally people enjoy novelty in things, and above all, how acceptable an account of the deeds of illustrious kings is to those who are versed in history, I have thought fit to add to the above narration a short account of the other Persian wars which took place after the death of Ussun Cassano. From these few particulars they may see what wonderful things might be written about these kings if, in addition to civilisation in manners and valour in arms, they had a literature[1] to collect an account of their actions and hand them down to the admiration of posterity. And the kings of the East have no other thing to complain of, but that neither study nor polite literature flourished among them, as, if the love of learning were joined to that of military glory, the one would support the other, and their fame become greater than that of our kings. Since, in the same way that fine subjects draw out powers of composition, a fine writer will often enable lofty subjects to shine forth and to become models of splendour even among more illustrious ones.

Coming at length to the task I have prescribed for myself, I say that after the death of Unghermaumet, Ussun Cassano survived but a short time, and died on the eve of Epiphany in the year one thousand four hundred and seventy-eight, leaving four sons, three born from one mother, and one from Despina Caton,[2] the daughter of the Emperor of

[1] Persian literature at that time was in a most flourishing condition, the age comprising some of the most illustrious names in their annals. Vide p. 2.

[2] Caton-Khatoon, meaning " Madam" or " Lady", and so " Queen." Despina, Δεσποινα, means the same thing.

Trebizond,[1] which son on the very night of his father's death was killed by his three brothers. Between these three the desire of reigning they each had, produced great rivalry and hatred, so that the second assassinated his elder brother,[2] and reigned alone, being named Giacuppo Chiorzeinal.[3]

Despina had already been separated from her husband, and lived on the confines of Riarbera, in the city of Cavalleria,[4] where she died, and was buried in the town in the Church of St. George,[5] where even to this day her sepulchre[6] is greatly honoured. Ussun Cassano had three daughters by her: the first, named Marta, was married to Secheaidare,[7] Ruler of Arduil,[8] a town towards the north-east, three days' journey distant from Tauris. This chief was the head of the faction of the "Cacarineri"[9] (black sheep), which is the Sufi party, very powerful by the number of its partizans,[10] and the new doctrine, the whole of Persia being divided into two factions, one of which is called the White Cacari,[11] and the other the Black Cacari, which are like what the Guelphs and Ghibellines, the Bianchi and Neri used to be in Italy. And the other two daughters lived with their mother with great riches, and after her death still dwelt in Cavalleria; but hearing of the death of their father, and how cruelly their half-brothers had killed their full brother, fearing what might happen to them also, they collected their jewels and other valuables, and fled to Aleppo and thence to Damascus.

[1] Calo Johannes. See p. 9.   [2] Calul.   [3] Yakoob.
[4] From what appears in the other books this must be meant for Cartibiert Kharput, in the province of Diarbekr. See Angiolello, cap. 1.
[5] See *Travels of a Merchant*, cap. 3.
[6] She was buried in the town of Diarbekr.
[7] Sheikh Hyder.
[8] Ardebil, where are the tombs of Sheikh Hyder and Shah Ismael Sufi, is situated in the plain of Mogam. It has now entirely declined from its former importance.   [9] Kârâ Koyun.
[10] This was not the case, as the Suffavean family did not belong to either of the Toorkman tribes.   [11] Ak Koyun.

In this place one of them was living in the year one thousand five hundred and twelve, and saw M. Caterino, son of M. Pietro, the son of the M. Caterino who had been ambassador in Persia, which young merchant was then trading in Damascus, and having recognised him as a relation, she received him with the greatest demonstrations of love, and wishing to return to Persia, as she had heard of the good fortune of Ismail, her nephew, who had possessed himself of the kingdom of Persia, she endeavoured to take him with her, promising him great things and certain rank. But M. Caterino, who was restrained by the love of his country and further by affection for his relations, thanked her for her goodwill and kindness of disposition, but remained, excusing his not going on account of the importance of his affairs, and the affection he bore to his native country.

This Giacuppo, who had slain his elder brother, reigned a long time, and at last, as they say, was killed by an intrigue of his wife, who was not a *very* virtuous woman. After him Allamur,[1] his son, reigned, who, besides Persia, possessed Diarbec, and part of Greater Armenia, near the Euphrates; in his time the faction of the Black Cacari[2] was held in such credit, through Secheaidare, that the other of the White Cacari declined altogether. Secheaidare was a Saint or Master or Prophet,[3] as we should call him, who, by preaching a new Dogma in the Mahometan creed, that Ali was superior to Omar, obtained many disciples and people who favoured his doctrine. So great was his success, that at this time he was considered by all a Saint, and a man almost divine. He had by Marta, the daughter of Despina, and of Ussun Cassano, six children: three sons and three daughters;

---

[1] Also called Alumut or Eluanbeg; he was not left in undisturbed possession of the throne, as his brother Morad Khan disputed it with him, and established himself in Babylonia and Fars.

[2] Kárá Koinloo. See previous page.

[3] Follower of Ali, Alance.

and, although his wife was the daughter of a Christian lady, he nevertheless remained an enemy to our faith; as, having made himself captain[1] of a foraging party, he made frequent hostile inroads as far as Circassia, plundering everywhere and bringing back an immense number of slaves into Persia to Arduil,[2] his city. These incursions, in addition to the advantages he reaped from his booty, raised his reputation so high, that he soon had the support of all the chiefs of his faction, and having raised a large army marched on another similar invasion of Circassia, and passing Sumachi[3] in eight days' journey from Arduil, arrived at Berbento,[4] which is five days distant from Sumachi, having with him a force of between five and six thousand men, all warriors and brave, well-trained soldiers. Berbento is a city which was built in the passes of the Caspian Mountains by Alexander, to resist the incursions of the Scythians, where the pass is so narrow that one hundred resolute soldiers could bar with their pikes

---

[1] See Angiolello, cap. 12. [2] Ardebil.
[3] Shirvan, the largest and most important division of the Southern Caucasus, is watered by numberless rivers, the largest of which is the Kur. Its capital is Schamachi, under which name, according to Kinneir, there are two cities, the old and the new. He says: "New Schamachi is situated in a plain on the river Aksui, about fifty versts from the Kur, and the same distance from the sea. The form is quadrangular, each side being eight hundred paces in length. The walls are in tolerable repair, built of unburnt brick, and surrounded with a very deep and broad ditch. When this town was taken by Aga Mahomed Khan in 1795, the inhabitants were supposed to amount to six thousand souls; but the city, as well as the villages nearest the plain, were reduced to ruins by that relentless tyrant, who did not retire till the month of February of the following year. The ruins of the old Schamachi, once a large and populous city, are still extant, but they are almost hid from the view by thick brushwood. This is the Schamacha of the ancients and stands in a fine situation, in an angle formed by the southern branch of Mount Caucasus."

[4] Derbend, a strong fortress on the Caspian, the Peninsula of Apsheronon, near the Demir Kapoo or Iron Gates of the Caucasus. See note to Angiolello, cap. 16.

the passage of a million of men. Its site is considered the strongest of all the cities of the East, as it is situated on the summit of some mountains and has two walls[1] as far as the sea enclosing the town and the port, where the vessels lie, in a space not exceeding three hundred paces in extent; and this space is so strong and well fortified that, by keeping guard, no one can enter. It is the only pass by which one can enter Circassia, and the people of the country call it Amircarpi,[2] which signifies gates of iron, not because there are any, but because the place is so strong and secure against attack. For this reason, being safe themselves, the inhabitants would neither give free passage to Secheaidare,[3] nor let anyone enter, from fear of the men he had with him; then, immediately despatching letters and messages to the King Alamur to inform him of these things, they prepared to defend themselves, if Secheaidare tried to force a passage.

The king, greatly disturbed by these designs of Secheaidare, entertained no slight suspicion of him, as it seemed to him that he, by the esteem in which he was held, and his numerous followers whom he enriched from the great booty he made, might make himself so great in time as to be able to overthrow the kingdom, and establish a dynasty of his own firm and safe against any attack.

Secheaidare, seeing the passage barred to him, being greatly enraged against the people of Berbento, commenced attacking the country, and used all his power to get them into his hands. Alamur hearing this, did not think fit to hold back any longer, as too much procrastination might be productive of some misfortune. Therefore, having hastily collected an army, he advanced towards Berbento, and by marching quickly arrived in time for the support of his

---

[1] Compare the Long Walls at Athens.
[2] Demir Kapoo.
[3] Sheikh Hyder.

people. Secheaidare, when he heard of the approach of the army of Alamur, left off attacking the place, and set himself in array against him; and, the fray beginning fiercely on both sides, a stubborn fight was kept up for several hours before either side appeared to be getting the best of it. At length Secheaidare, overcome by the number of his enemies was cut to pieces, and his men, although but few, performed prodigies of valour, and there was not one who was not dead or mortally wounded. The head of Secheaidare, fixed on the point of a lance, was sent to Tauris and kept in a public place that it might be seen by everyone; and after rejoicing and celebrating the victory obtained over him, they threw him to the dogs. And this news being brought to Arduil, where the wife of Secheaidare and his children were, all those of the Sufi faction lamented greatly; nevertheless, they kept silence and dissimulated in order not to give the king cause for anger against them. But his sons, seized with fear for themselves and their lives, as in sudden emergencies one is afraid of everything, fled, one to Natolia, another to Aleppo, and the third to an island in the lake Attamar,[1] inhabited by Armenian Christians and called by the name of the Holy Mother of God, where he remained four years concealed in the house of a priest, without anything being known of it in Persia.[2]

This youth, who was called Ismail, was thirteen years old,[3] of noble presence and a truly royal bearing, as in his eyes and brow there was something, I know not what, so great and commanding, which plainly showed that he would yet some day become a great ruler. Nor did the virtues of his

[1] Aktamar or Van Lake, so called from the island of Ak Tamar, where the Catholicos of the Armenians resides.

[2] Knolles says he fled into Hyrcania to Pyrcales. See *Travels of a Merchant*. cap. 13, and next page.

[3] The accounts of authors vary as to Ismael's age (see *Travels of a Merchant*, cap. 13); but I believe this to be the correct statement.

mind disaccord with the beauty of his person, as he had an elevated genius, and such a lofty idea of things as seemed incredible at such a tender age. Therefore the good priest, who professed to be an astrologer and to know the course of events from the aspect of the heavens, cast his horoscope, and foresaw that he would yet become lord of all Asia. On this account he set himself with greater solicitude to serve him, and treated him to the extent of his power with every sort of indulgence and courtesy, thus laying up a debt of the greatest gratitude from him.

Ismail, longing to recover his paternal possessions, left this place before he had reached the age of eighteen years, and went to Carabac,[1] and then to Gillon,[2] finding out the house of a very old friend of his father's, named Pircale. He, moved with compassion for the condition of Ismail, as he had once seen his father a great ruler, wrote secretly to Arduil to all those of the Suffavean faction,[3] who he knew had lost fathers, brothers, or kinsmen in the battle of Derbent against the opposing faction of the white Cacari, in order that when they were reminded of all that Sechcaidare had done for them, they might assist his son Ismail, who had come to him from his place of concealment, both to gain his father's inheritance, and to restore the party. Also that, if ever one could expect great things from a young man as handsome and nobly-born as he was, he would promise wonderful things from him, as he saw that he had vigour of mind, quickness of perception, and a per-

---

[1] Kara Bagh, the country between the rivers Kur and Aras, the former river dividing it from Shirvan.

[2] Ghilan, a province along the south-west shore of the Caspian, is rich and populous, the soil exceedingly fertile, fruits, rice, and grain being cultivated with great success; but the cultivation of silk constitutes the principal trade, and quantities are exported annually to Astrakhan from Resht and Lankeroon, the two principal towns in the province. Its population amounts to about six hundred thousand.

[3] Followers of Ali, or rather of Sheikh Hyder, from the name of his

sonal valour which he had never yet seen equalled by any of his contemporaries.

Gained over by these letters, the people of Arduil offered for this object and for any other, which would help Ismail, all their power and influence. Therefore, he having sent secret orders as to what they would have to do, and having collected two hundred men of his faction in Gillon, and another two hundred given by the people of Arduil, with whom he was prepared to bring, by a prosperous start, his affairs to a happy termination, took up a position in a valley favourably situated for an ambush, whence at a favourable moment he hurried in the direction of the Castle Marmurlagi,[1] and having made a sudden assault cut to pieces all the garri-

ancestor Sheikh Suffee-u-deen Ishack. The family were lineally descended from Môossâh, the seventh Imaum.

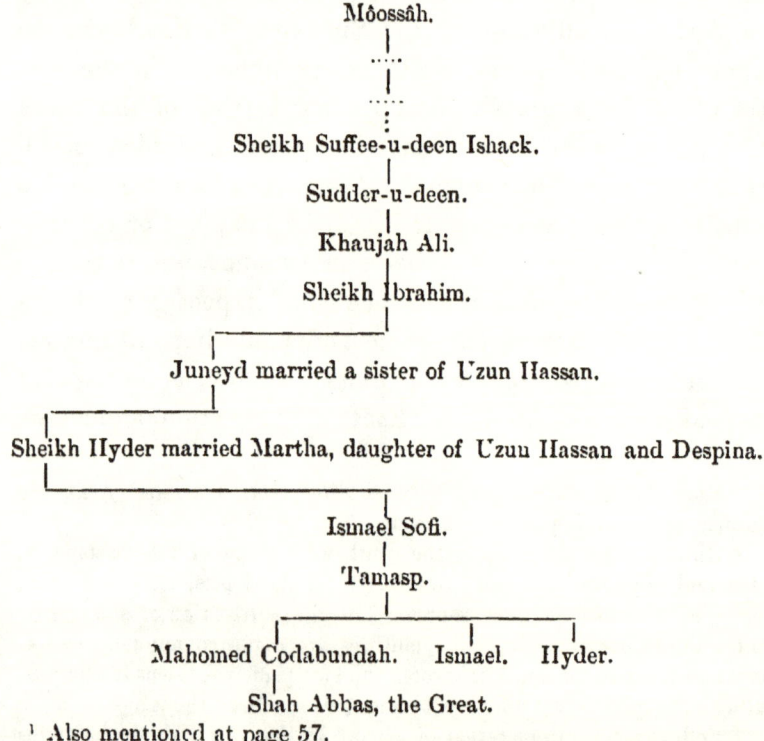

[1] Also mentioned at page 57.

son; then, having set it in order and left a better guard, he entered the town and gave it up to his soldiers to sack, putting all the inhabitants to the edge of the sword. This fortress was very rich from its position on a harbour of the sea of Baccu, eight days' journey distant from Tauris, and to this harbour came ships from Namiscaderem[1] and other places, laden with merchandise for Tauris, Sumachi, and the whole of Persia.

Having captured the fortress, Ismail caused the booty to be brought into it, and distributed freely among his soldiers, not keeping anything for himself from so many precious things, as he wished by this liberality to gain over as much as possible the affections of his men; knowing that in this devotion consists the whole stability of kingdoms and empires. Thus the fame of his liberality and boldness was quickly rumoured abroad, and the memory of his father, who was considered a saintly man, came out more bright and illustrious than ever, and the Suffavean faction, which since his death had been greatly reduced, began to agitate and rise, attracting adventurers in great numbers to it. Thus he, having assembled five thousand good soldiers, began to hope that he might safely attempt greater things than he had yet done.

Then seeing how easy it would be to make himself master of the town of Sumachi, as there was no suspicion of war in

---

[1] Mazenderan, part of ancient Hyrcania, is separated from Irak by the Elburz Mountains; in its soil and climate it resembles Ghilan, except in being more mountainous and wooded. Silk is not cultivated to so great an extent, though the commerce of the province is considerable. The inhabitants were regarded as the most warlike of the Persians, and even held out for a considerable time against the whole power of Tamerlane. The population is about one million five hundred thousand; the principal towns are Sari, the capital, Balfrush, with upwards of a hundred thousand inhabitants, Amol, Ferrabad, and Ashraff, famous for the palace of Shah Abbas the Great, who also executed that stupendous work named the Causeway of Mazenderan, which at present has been allowed to fall into disrepair.

the country,[1] and consequently few people in the garrison, he hurried towards it by forced marches. The King Sermendole, who ruled over it, hearing of this, and seeing that defence was hopeless against Ismail, fled to the impregnable fortress of Culifan,[2] in the same country of Sumachi. Thus Ismail found the city without defenders, took it without loss, and having cut to pieces the Sumachians all over the place, enriched himself with the immense treasure he found there; this was divided by him, and, as before, bestowed on his men, who thus became very rich.

This second enterprise, so successfully accomplished, raised him to the highest credit; so that the army being reinforced from all the neighbouring regions was greatly augmented in number.

For this reason Alamur, being more alarmed than he ever was in the time of his father, summoned all the great Persian lords to court, and, having collected fighting men, marched with his army against Ismail. The latter, finding his forces too weak to take the field, and, if an opportunity offered, to give battle to the king, sought the aid of some Georgian Christian chiefs whose land bordered on that country, whose names were Alexander Beg, Gurgurabet, and Mirabet. These, as they had an ancient enmity against Alamur, and wished to overthrow his power, availing themselves of the opportunity given by Ismail, decided to assist him against Alamur, and therefore each of them sent three thousand horse, so that they were altogether nine thousand excellent soldiers; these are the people who were anciently called Iberians, and as they then were, and still are, Christians, have continually waged war with the Turks on the frontiers of Trebizond. They were joyfully welcomed, and

---

[1] Alamur, or Eluan Beg, was not in sure possession of the throne, as he was engaged in a struggle with his brother Morad Khan, who ruled over Bagdad, Shiraz, etc. See page 43.

[2] Also mentioned at page 56.

received many presents from Ismail, who, with these Georgian auxiliaries, found himself with an excellent army of sixteen thousand men in the field.

Thence he advanced with the intention of giving battle to Alamur, if he had an opportunity, and thus both approached each other between Tauris and Sumachi, near a great river,[1] where Alamur, who had an army of thirty thousand men, infantry and cavalry, having placed himself on his guard, occupied the only two bridges by which Ismail could cross into the territory in which he was posted. He did it with the intention that the enemy, finding the passage barred to them, might not, with the daring which they say is often favoured by fortune, stake all on one throw, and force him to fight against his will.

But Ismail, who was fearful of losing his reputation by any check or loss of time, and the more so, as he saw that Alamur, by his occupation of the bridges, was safe in his position from any attack, and looked slightingly on any skirmish, having by great good luck found a ford of the river, crossed it silently by night, and forming into a heavy column attacked the enemy and caused great slaughter. This happened, as the king's men being half-naked, and not having time to seize their arms, were cut to pieces in immense numbers by armed and ferocious soldiers; and if here and there some bolder spirits made head, so fierce was the onset of the Suffaveans, that they were driven back in an instant by a continuous shower of blows, and forced to share the fortunes of the others. And never has a more horrible nocturnal struggle than this been recorded; because, in the greatest darkness of the night, the whole field of battle was lighted up with the flash of arms, and throughout the whole region were heard the clash and din and confusion caused by the rout and massacre of so large an army, which fled before the pursuit of the enemy. Alamur, having escaped with

---

[1] Either the Kur or the Aras, more probably the latter.

difficulty with a few friends, retired to Amir,[1] fortifying himself in that city.

And Ismail having, to his great reputation, put that great army to the edge of the sword, caused all the booty to be collected and divided among his men, without keeping a single thing for himself. The second day he appeared before Tauris,[2] and, meeting with no resistance, took it and gave it up to plunder, cutting to pieces those of the opposing faction; and then, in order to avenge his father on those captains and chiefs who were said to have opposed Secheaidare in the battle of Berbent, and to have had a hand in his death, he caused their bodies to be disinterred and burnt in the market-place. And, while they were carrying them there, he drew up a procession before them of two hundred harlots and four hundred thieves; and to show a greater indignity to those chiefs, he ordered the heads of the thieves and harlots to be cut off and burnt with the bodies. And, not satisfied with this, he had his stepmother brought before him, who after the death of his father had married a certain great lord, who was on the side of the king in the same action of Berbent, abused her to her face, insulted her in every possible way, and at last commanded that she should be decapitated as the vile and worthless woman she was, in revenge for the slight estimation she had held his father in.

All the people and neighbouring chieftains being terrified by the capture of Tauris and the rout of the king, sent in their allegiance to Ismail, except those of Alangiacalai, a fortress two days' distant above Tauris towards the north, which place, with ten adjacent towns, is inhabited by Catholic Christians, who at last, having remained faithful to Alamur for five years, hearing of his death, surrendered it on conditions to Ismail with its immense treasure. When he had gained possession of this castle, Ismail caused him-

---

[1] Diarbekr.
[2] Tauris, or Tabreez. See *Travels of a Merchant*, cap. 7.

self to be proclaimed sovereign of Persia under the new title of Sofi.

But Moratcan,[1] son of Alamur, having assembled an army of thirty thousand men with some Turkish auxiliaries, endeavoured to recover the throne which rightly belonged to him, with the design of regaining his father's dominions, and at the same time to avenge the defeat of his relative on the Suffavean faction. Ismail, hearing this, quickly assembled an army and advanced to meet Moratcan, when these two young princes came to blows in the plain of Tauris, and for a time both performed great feats with arms in their hands; but the Suffaveans were brave, and being veteran soldiers and accustomed to be victorious under the fortunate generalship of their commander, routed the soldiers of Moratcan with great slaughter, and this unhappy young man seeing no hope of re-establishing his affairs, fled to Diarbeca[2] with a few soldiers who escaped from the rout. These things happened in the year one thousand four hundred and ninety-nine, Ismail gaining a great reputation for good fortune, but more for courage, so that from that time he began to become a terror to all the East.

The following year Ismail made an enterprise against Diarbeca, which was still in the allegiance of Moratcan, and made himself master in that region of some important places. And since Aladuli[3] had assisted Moratcan from distrust of Ismail and his greatness, he collected an army of more than sixty thousand men and marched against him, not, however, without great fear of exciting against himself the Soldan and the Turk, as the country of Aladuli was situated between these two powers. Then, taking the road of Arsenga and Seras, he arrived in Maseria, through the dominions of the Turk, paying for provisions and tolls, without molesting the

[1] Morad Khan, brother, not son, of Eluan Beg, ruler of Fars, Babylonia, etc.
[2] Diarbekr. Eluan Beg had also taken refuge here.
[3] Allá-ed' Douleh.

inhabitants in any way, showing himself desirous of being on a good footing with the Ottoman. Thus, having arrived in Aladuli's country, at the town of Alessat,[1] he crossed some mountains in one day, in this way reaching Amaras,[2] putting all the country to fire and sword and rapine. But Aladuli, who had escaped to the mountains of Catarac,[3] and fortified himself there, not wishing to stake all his power at once, took particular care not to give battle to Ismail. Instead, he sent out some bands of good cavalry and, by attacking the Suffaveans, sometimes by day and sometimes by night, and retiring to the mountains, kept continually harassing the hostile army, wherefore Ismail having remained from the twenty-ninth of July to the middle of November, without succeeding in his undertaking, was forced to retreat from want of supplies, the winter, and dearth, to Malatia, a city of the Soldan's, from whence he passed on to Tauris, having lost on the road many soldiers and an almost countless number of his horses and camels, through the bitterness of the cold and the quantity of the snow.

But, not being in the least cast down by this repulse, the following year, assembling an army of forty thousand men, he attacked Casan, a town in Babylonia belonging to Moratcan, to free himself from all apprehension of his ever doing him any harm. On this account, Moratcan having collected an army of thirty-six thousand infantry and cavalry, advanced to Sevas,[4] to draw the enemy off from attacking Casan; then Ismail following him, advanced to Spaám[5] to join battle with Moratcan, staking the whole of his fortune on this battle, knowing well the valour of his men, and that already the Persians and all the others who had been under the sway of Alamur began to desire that he should rule over

---

[1] Albistan, sixty miles from Marash; ten thousand inhabitants.
[2] Marash, sixty miles from Iskenderoon; ancient capital of Karamania.
[3] Kara Dagh, or Black Mountain.
[4] Shiraz in this case, not Sivas.   [5] Ispahan.

them. This move of Ismail's cast such terror into the hostile army, that gradually they began to desert and to escape into the Suffavean camp; hence, Moratcan being thrown into consternation, attempted to make peace with Ismail, and sent ambassadors to announce his willing submission, if he would only leave him Bagadet;[1] but, as neither the ambassadors nor the conditions of peace were received by Ismail, who aspired to become sole master, Moratcan, despairing of his life if he fell into his hands, fled with a squadron of three thousand cavalry towards Aleppo. As he was not received here from the fear the Soldan had of irritating Ismail, he went on to Aladuli, and was most graciously received by that lord, who had formerly been his great friend and who gave him hopes of re-establishing him in his power, if an opportunity showed itself; and, in order to increase his hopes, gave him one of his daughters as his wife.

Ismail having in the manner related, defeated Moratcan, came with his whole army to Bierbeca,[2] and made himself master of Bagadet and Seras,[3] cutting to pieces many of the opposing sect in that region, and then having established laws and settled a garrison, returned to Tauris. The following year, which was 1508, after making great preparations for war, he advanced in person against the Tartar Leasilbas,[4] ruler of Samarcant, whose subjects are the Zagatai, otherwise called the Green Caftans.[5] This chief was at that time on the frontier of Persia with a victorious army, having performed many feats of arms in the vicinity, as, after seizing the country of the Saracens, he had then taken the great

---

[1] Bagdad. [2] Diarbekr. [3] Shiraz.
[4] Sheibani Khan, or Shahabeg Khan, a descendant of the Great Zengis, the enemy of Baber the first of the Moguls, was the founder of the Usbeg power on the ruins of that of Timour, in Central Asia. He was defeated and killed by Shah Ismael Sofi at the battle of Merv Shah Jehan in 1514. See Baber's *Memoirs*, translated by Mr. Erskine.
[5] Sunnees.

town of Eri[1] and Caradisca, and Cara,[2] and, last of all, Sanderem[3] and Sari,[4] two large cities situated on the Sea of Baccu,[5] and close to the dominions of Ismail; by these conquests he had thrown all the East into the greatest alarm, and particularly raised great apprehension in the Sofi, who was an enemy of those of the Green Caftans. On this account he retired to Spaàm,[6] and encamped with his whole army, but the victorious Lasilbas,[7] in order to gain a pretext for coming to blows with the Suffaveans, demanded a free passage from Ismail, in order that he might pay his vows at Mecca. This demand made Ismail still more apprehensive; therefore, having refused point blank, he strengthened all the region on the frontiers of Lasilbas with a strong force of cavalry, keeping his army the whole year, 1509, in those parts with the intention of opposing the Tartar if he attempted to force a passage. At length, by the intervention of some Tartar and Persian lords friendly to both, they concluded a peace between them.

And Ismail, who, from one war was urged on to another, in the following year went against the Ruler of Siraan,[8] who had refused the tribute which he paid every year, and having entered the plains of Carabac,[9] which are more than one thousand miles in extent, in the midst of which is the territory of Chianer,[10] whence come the Canary silks, he sent to take Sumachi, and having attacked Culofan,[11] a very strong

[1] Herat, a city of great importance in the history of Persia, and the key or gate of India, as it has been aptly described; it is well fortified, and the emporium of commerce between Cabul, Bokhara, Hindostan, and Persia, with a population of forty thousand; it is now subject to Affghanistan.   [2] Khaf.

[3] Sanderem, probably Amol or Balfrush, in Mazanderan.

[4] Sari, the capital of Mazanderan, a well fortified town of fifteen thousand inhabitants, with a brisk trade with Astrakhan and the interior of Persia, twenty miles from Balfrush.

[5] The Caspian.   [6] Ispahan.   [7] Sheibani Khan.
[8] Shirvan.   [9] Kara Bagh.
[10] Canar.   [11] See page 50.

fortress situated in the same region as Sumachi, he reduced it, together with Mamurcagi,[1] a castle of great importance in those parts, from its strength. And then, marching by the shores of the Sea of Baccù, he took many other strong castles, since the country of Servan is seven days' journey in extent along the coast of this same sea, beginning at Mamurcagi as far as Berbento, in which tract there are three large cities and three castles. With this conquest he returned in triumph to Persia, and feasted several days in honour of the victory he had obtained, with almost all the great lords and princes of the realm.

And a short time after there broke out a fierce war with the above-mentioned Tartar Lasilbas, from a certain ambition and rivalry which existed between them; when Lasilbas came with a great army against the Suffaveans, and, joining in a fierce and sanguinary contest,[2] bore himself as a valiant man for many hours; nevertheless, the forces of the enemy prevailing, he was repulsed and routed, and saved[3] himself by flight to Samarcant.

This victory was the most illustrious that Ismail ever obtained, as he fought against enemies who were great warriors and famous in all the East. For this reason the Turk and the Soldan became greatly apprehensive of the power of Ismail, both considering, that if after all the Tartar happened to be conquered, the road would be opened for Ismail to acquire Asia and Egypt, as in all the East there were no princes more powerful than they, but the Tartar Lasilbas.

---

[1] See page 48.

[2] The great battle of Merv Shah Jehan, 1514. The city of Merv, the ancient capital of Margiana, was founded by Alexander the Great, and embellished by Antiochus Nicator, who gave it the name of Antiochia. It was long the seat of the Seljooks and also of the great Alp Arslan, whose tomb is there. It has now declined in importance, having been repeatedly sacked by the Usbegs.

[3] He was killed in the battle.

On this account Selim, the Grand Turk, having heard that Ismail was engaged with the war waged against the city of Samarcant,[1] which was the largest in the possession of the Tartar prince, brought together an immense army of Turks, and advanced in person against Persia, in the year 1514; he marched towards the river of Sivas,[2] which is six hundred miles distant from Constantinople and six hundred and forty from Tauris: so that one may say that it is about half way between the two cities, and having passed the river Lai,[3] he marched forward quickly through the country of Arsenga.[4] Ismail, who was in Tauris without his regular troops, who were engaged in besieging Samarcant, hearing of this, began to levy other forces in haste, and having collected a tolerably good army placed it under two of his most valiant captains, one named Stàcàlu Amarbei and the other Aurbec Samper, and sent them against Selim, in order, by skirmishing, to retard his advance until he had assembled sufficient men to oppose his enemy openly in the field. This army consisted of fifteen thousand horsemen, all good soldiers, and, so to speak, the flower of the Persian people, as the kings of Persia are not accustomed to give pay on the occasion of war, but to a standing force, which is called the "porta" of the king. Thus it is that the Persian gentlemen, to be well brought up, pay great attention to horsemanship, and when necessity calls, go willingly to war, and bring with them, according to their means, a certain number of servants as well armed and mounted as themselves; nevertheless, they do not come out except for the defence of the country; so that, if the Persian soldiery were paid, as is the Turkish, there is no doubt but that it would be far superior

---

[1] Samarcand, a city once almost the capital of the world, being well known as the seat of Timour, but now greatly declined in importance. It is a hundred and thirty miles from Bokhara, and is still the *entrepôt* for a caravan trade, with ten thousand inhabitants.

[2] The Iris, present Kizzil Irmak.   [3] Iris.   [4] Erzingan.

to that of the Ottoman princes. This thing has been observed by all those who have had anything to do with both these nations.

The Persian ladies themselves follow in arms the same fortunes as their husbands, and fight like men, in the same way as those ancient Amazons who performed such feats of arms in their time.

Now, the two captains, Amarbei and Samper, marched ahead, and hearing that Selim had crossed the Euphrates and was advancing by forced marches, retreated to Coi,[1] where Ismail, who had come from Tauris, was in person. Being informed of the large forces Selim was bringing with him on this enterprise, he caused his army to be strongly entrenched, and returned to Tauris to collect more troops, and then to show front to the enemy.[2] Coi is a city which

---

[1] Khoi, the capital of a rich district, with a considerable trade between Turkey and Persia; it has a population of twenty-five thousand, and is a well-built, handsome town, on the Ak Schai, a tributary of the Aras.

[2] Battle of Schalderan, fought, according to Knolles, on the 7th August, 1514. He says that Ismael himself was present in the battle and did wonders in arms, as, with only thirty thousand men he attacked the Turkish army three hundred thousand strong. The Persian cavalry bore down the Turks on every side, though with the loss of one of their great chiefs, Usta-ogli. "The Persians were now ready on everic side to have assailed Selymus in his greatest strength; when Sinan Bassa, although the wing he led was sore rent and weakened, yet following the Persians through the middest of the heaps of the slaine footmen, came in, in good time for Selymus, and with certaine fresh troups which had escaped from the furie of Usta-ogli restored the battell before almost lost; but, especially by the invincible courage of Alisbeg and Mahomet his brother, descended of the honourable familie of the Molcozzii, which for nobilitie among the Turks is accounted next unto the Ottomans; both of them for courage resembling their warlike father Molcozzius, famous for that wofull expedition he made into Friuli against the Venetians in the raigne of Baiazet. Selymus, also not yet discouraged, but still in hope, commaunded all the great ordinance wherewith he was environed which he had reserved as his last refuge, to be discharged; by the violence whereof such slaughter was made as well of his owne men

they say was built on the ruins of the ancient Artasata,[1] not more than three days' journey distant from Tauris; on this account, it appeared likely to Ismail, from its proximity, that he might in a very short time find himself engaged in a battle, and therefore expressly commanded the above-mentioned captains to wait, and when he arrived with fresh forces they would drive back the enemy together. However, shortly after the departure of Ismail, the Turkish army came up in array, on the 24th of August, and spread itself over the plains called Calderane, where the Persians also had their encampment.

The latter, seeing the enemy behave with such audacity and provoke them to battle, could not refrain from attacking them, as they had been victorious in so many past wars under the auspices of the greatest monarch of the East: hence, having been joined the night before by some bands of horse from Tauris, making them in all twenty-four thousand men, divided in two deep columns, of which one was led by Stacalù Amarbei and the other by Aurbec Samper, signal of battle being given, they attacked the enemy bravely. Amarbei, who was foremost, assaulted the troops of Natolia with such a terrific rush, that he broke and routed them utterly, and the Persians made such a slaughter of the Turks, that in that quarter they already had the victory in their hands, if it had not been that Sinan Pasha, to aid that side of the conflict advanced the Caramanian troops, and, taking the Persian force in flank, enabled those who were routed

as of his enemies, mingled togither, that what for dust, what for smoake, and thundering of the artillerie, having on both sides almost lost the use of sight and hearing; and their horses being so terrified with the thundering report of the great ordinance that they were not now to be ruled, the battell was broken off, the victorie yet doubtfull." He goes on to say that Ismael was slightly wounded, and had to retire from the field, which gave the Turks breathing time.

[1] The site of the ancient Artaxarta is fixed on the Aras, a little to the south of Erivan.

and preparing to fly to make head again. The Persians, resisting Sinan, bore themselves as valiantly as, before; nor even when Amarbei was cut to pieces did they fail to keep up the fight courageously.

Samper, seeing the Caramanians change their positions and attack Amarbei, also closed his column and attacked Sinan on his flank, routed the Caramanians, and in a moment was on the royal forces, and the cavalry, though in disorder and badly led, cut to pieces the foremost ranks of the janissaries, and cast into confusion that famous infantry, so that it appeared a thunderbolt cleaving that large and mighty army. The monarch, seeing the slaughter, began to retreat, and to turn about, and was about to fly, when Sinan, coming to the rescue at the time of need, caused the artillery to be brought up and fired on both the janissaries and Persians. The Persian horses hearing the thunder of those infernal machines, scattered and divided themselves over the plain, not obeying their riders' bit or spur any more, from the terror they were in. Sinan, seeing this, made up one squadron of cavalry from all that which had been routed by the Persians, and began to cut them to pieces everywhere, so that, by his activity, Selim, even when he thought all lost, came off the victor. It is certainly said, that if it had not been for the artillery, which terrified in the manner related the Persian horses which had never before heard such a din, all his forces would have been routed and put to the edge of the sword; and if the Turk had been beaten, the power of Ismail would have become greater than that of Tamerlane, as by the fame alone of such a victory he would have made himself absolute lord of the East.

As it happened, the Persians being discomfited, in the manner related, by Selim, not without great loss on his side, Aurbec Samper was led before him covered with wounds, and on his hearing that Ismail had not been in the action, he said to him, full of indignation, "Dog that thou art, thou hast had the audacity to come against me, who am in the place of a prophet, and hold the post of God on earth." To this, without any sign of fear, Samper replied, "If you held the post of God on earth, you would not come against my master; but God has saved you from our hands, that you may fall alive into his, and then he will avenge his and our wrongs." Selim, being greatly enraged by his words, said, "Go and kill this dog." And he replied, "I know that this is my hour; but do you prepare your soul to pay the sacrifice of mine; since my master will meet you in a year, and will do the same to you, which you order to be done to me"; whereupon he was immediately cut to pieces. Having done this, Selim raised the camp and came to Coi, in which city he rested with his whole army some days; he then published abroad, and wrote in many letters sent to different places, that he had gained the victory, and that Ismail had been in person in the battle which had taken place in the Calderani[1] plains. This, however, was written falsely, as

[1] Knolles says:—"This was that notable battell fought in the Calderan fields neare unto the city of Coy, betwixt these two great princes, the 7th day of August, in the yeare of our Lord 1514. In which battell Selymus lost above thirtie thousand men, amongst whom was Casan Bassa, his great lieutenant in Europe; seaven Sanzackes, in which were the two Malcozzian brethren, who, labouring the one to rescue the other, were both togither slaine. Beside his common footmen, of whom he made least reckoning, he lost most part of his Illirian, Macedonian, Servian, Epirot, Thessalian, and Thracian horsemen, the undoubted flower and strength of his army, which were in that mortall battell almost all slaine or grievously wounded. Selymus, for all this great losse, by the confession of his enemies having gotten the victorie, and receiving embassadours from Coy and the cities thereabout, and the great citie of Tauris, promising to relieve him with whatsoever he needed, and to doe what else he should commaund, marched directly to Tauris, desiring both to see and possesse himself of that citie as one of the chiefe pallaces of the Persian kings. This citie is two daies' journey distant from Coy, where the battell was fought, and is probably supposed to be the famous citie called in auntient time Ecbatana, about an hundred and fiftie miles distant from the Caspian Sea. The citizens were readie at the comming of the Turks, and brought them great store of victuals out of the gates

Ismail was not there in person, nor even the corps of his veteran soldiers, who were then round Samarcant, investing that city. Ismail, hearing the news of the rout of his army, collected some of the men who had escaped from the action and had made head in Tauris. With his wife and all his riches he left the city and went to Caseria,[1] which is six days' journey distant from Tauris towards the East, assembling another army to try again in person the fortune of battle.

After his departure the Turk leaving Coi, arrived at Tauris, and was received with favourable and courteous demonstrations by those of the city, because it did not seem fit to them to peril their lives, as they had no chance against the enemy, before whom so many valiant men who had armed in defence of Persia had not been able to make head; and remaining there only three days, and not seeing that any of the people or neighbouring chiefs came to give in their submission to him,[2] Selim began to be apprehensive lest Ismail should be more powerful than he had thought him, as he in truth was, since all the principal men of Persia began to join him with their forces for the safety of the kingdom. Therefore, taking with him different men skilled in arts and five hundred loads of treasure, without injuring the city in any other way, he left it and marched towards the Euphrates, being continually harassed on the road by the Georgians,[3] who, with some troops of light cavalry, pillaged

---

of the citie, where Selymus had lodged his army in the suburbs, thinking it no safetie to lodge within that great and populous citie, contenting himselfe to have the gates thereof delivered unto him, which he kept with strong guard."

[1] Caseria, probably Casbin.

[2] The janissaries mutinied, according to Knolles.

[3] Knolles says:—" Yet for all the speed he could make, the Georgian horsemen, the forerunners of Hysmaell, his armie being come within sight before the Turkes were all got over, raised such a feare and a stirre all alongt that side of the river that two thousand of the Turkes were in their hastie passage there drowned, divers field pieces left stick-

the baggage of the army, and cut to pieces all those who quitted the ranks ever so short a way. Their assaults were so frequent, that the Acangi[1] who were accustomed to range forty or fifty miles at least from the army, did not dare to forsake it as these fierce guerilla foes made a great slaughter of them everywhere; nor did they fall by the sword alone, but also by hunger; since, as they were accustomed to forage for the army, and not being able to perform this office from fear, it followed that in avoiding one miserable death, they perished by another still more wretched one.

Ismail, in the meanwhile, had greatly strengthened his army, and therefore, hoping soon to fall in with the enemy, advanced to Tauris, where, hearing that the Turk had departed, and was retreating in such haste that he would not be able to overtake him, thought fit to remain and to take steps with more caution in this enterprise. He therefore wrote letters and sent ambassadors to the Soldan, to Prince Aladuli, and to the King of Gorgora, to show them the great peril they ran if they did not take up arms with him against Selim, since if Persia were subdued, all their States would become a prey to the enemy. These ambassadors were willingly listened to, from the fear these princes entertained on account of Selim's victory over the Suffaveans. On this account they formed a league, into which Ismail, the King of Gorgora, the Soldan,[2] and Aladuli entered, these monarchs promising to aid one another in case of need against the Ottoman, with the express condition that they should not receive any ambassador from the Turk; this condition not being observed by the Soldan, was afterwards his ruin, and that of all the power of the Mamelukes. As, the Turk having sent an ambassador a short time later,

---

ing in the mud, and much of their baggage carried away with the force of the river. The Georgians contenting themselves with such things as were left, pursued them no farther."

[1] Ikindjis.   [2] Khafour el Ghouri.

he received and heard him against the condition of the league; therefore, when Selim entered Soria[1] to fight against the Soldan, Ismail would not give him his assistance from fear of being left in the lurch.[2]

The league being concluded in the manner related, Ismail, who was fully prepared for the enterprise against the Turks, sent ambassadors to Selim, who was then in Amasia,[3] with presents, a *bâton* of massive gold, a saddle and richly-mounted sword, with a letter to this effect:—"Ismail, great Sovereign of the Persians, sends to you Selim these gifts, quite equal to your greatness, as they are worth as much as your kingdom; if you are a brave man, keep them well, because I will come and take them from you, together with your head and kingdom, which you possess against all right, as it is not proper that the offspring of peasants should bear rule over so many provinces." This letter so enraged the haughty spirit of Selim, that he wished to kill the ambassadors, but refrained, being kept back by his Bashas. However, in his rage he could not restrain himself from having their ears and noses cut off, and sent them back in this state with a letter written to Ismail, saying:—Selim, great Sovereign of the Turks, replies to a dog without taking the least notice of his baying; telling him that if he will show himself, he will find that I will do to him what my predecessor Mahomet did to his predecessor Ussun Cassano."

[1] Syria.
[2] Knolles gives a different reason, namely, that the Persian soldiery were well suited for defending, but not for fighting out of their own country: so Ismael would not risk an invasion.
[3] Amasia, birthplace of Strabo. See page 37.

DISCOURSE OF
MESSER GIOVAN BATTISTA RAMUSIO

ON THE

WRITINGS OF GIOVAN MARIA ANGIOLELLO AND OF A MERCHANT WHO WENT THROUGH THE WHOLE OF PERSIA; IN WHICH ARE NARRATED THE LIFE AND DEEDS OF USSUN CASSANO.

DISCOURSE OF
MESSER GIOVAN BATTISTA RAMUSIO.

INTRODUCTION.

EVERYONE who considers the various changes brought by the course of events to human affairs, will, on reflection, be filled with wonder; but I think that those who read ancient history have greater reason to be so, seeing many republics and many great and powerful kingdoms, so to speak, collapse without, in certain cases, leaving even a name, or any memorial behind. The same course of events has caused many races to leave their native countries, and, like proud and rapid rivers, invade those of others, chasing away the ancient inhabitants, and, not content with that, even change their names. So it happens that, nowadays, there are many races whose origin is not known, of which miserable Italy is an example, as, after the ruin of the Roman empire, a multitude of strange and barbarous nations entered from the North, ousted the inhabitants, changed the vulgar tongue, the names of the provinces, rivers, and mountains, moved the towns from their proper sites, and built them up afterwards at a distance from the spots where they first stood. This has not happened to Italy alone, but also to the province of Gallia, which, on its occupation by the fierce nation of the Franks, lost its name as well as its inhabitants. The same happened to Britain, now called England; to Pannonia, which is now Hungary; and to many other countries which it would be tedious to enumerate; But I cannot hold my peace about poor, afflicted Greece, celebrated by all classic writers, which was anciently the home of science and the example of humanity, but now fallen low indeed, being subjected to the empire of the Turks, and inhabited only by barbarous and unlettered tribes. This same calamity has fallen also on the whole of Asia, since (as one reads in the books of M. Marco Polo and the Armenian), great hordes of Tartars issued from the regions of Cathay and overran the countries, and, having settled in their new abodes, changed the names of the provinces to others familiar to the conquerors. Thus Margiana, Bactriana, and Sodiana, provinces near the Caspian Sea, being taken by Zacatai, brother of the Great Can, were called instead the country of Zacatai, from the province of Turquestan, which is beyond the rivers Jaxartes and Oxus.

There came another great multitude of people, who settled themselves in Asia Minor,—that is, in Bithynia, Phrygia, Cappadocia, and Paphagonia, and called it Turkey. At the same time, Hoccota Can[1] having made himself master of the provinces of Media, Parthia, and Persia, now named Azemia;[2] his successors gave them different names; and even in our times the Sophi, who was the son of a daughter of Ussun Cassano, King of Persia, had these provinces named after him. As there have come into my hands some carefully composed writings, in which are narrated the life and acts of the above-mentioned Ussun Cassano, or Assambei,[3] which are synonymous, and of Sheikh Ismail, who is the Sophi, I thought them suitable to follow the books of M. Marco Polo, and of the Armenian. Moreover, they treat of the same matter, and though agreeing, are different versions, so I think they will greatly amuse my readers. I find that the first author, who speaks of the life of Ussun Cassano, was named Giovan Maria Angiolello, who relates in his history that he served Mustafà, son of Mahomet II, Grand Turk, and that he was in the action[4] with the same Grand Turk, in which he was routed on the

[1] Hulakoo Khan, son and successor of the great Zingis, and the conqueror of Bagdad.   [2] Ajemi.   [3] Hassan Beg.
[4] This action was fought near Malatia, at a point previous to the

islands in the bed of the river Euphrates by the army of
Ussun Cassano. The name of the second author is not
known; but it is evident that he was of a cultivated intellect, and that in the course of his business he went through
almost the whole of Persia. To these two authors we have
added two Travels, one of the Illustrious M. Josapha Barbaro, and the other of the Illustrious M. Ambrosio Contarini,
Venetian gentlemen, who treat of the same matters; so that
of the affairs of Persia of late times, we have a history, if
not continuous, at least leaving little to be desired. I wish
that fortune had been favourable enough to allow me to get
into my hands the Travels of the Illustrious M. Caterino Zeno,
knight, who was the first ambassador who went into that
region to the monarch Ussun Cassano; but, although printed,
it has been lost, owing to the length of time that has elapsed.
And truly the above-mentioned M. Caterino was one of the
rare and worthy gentlemen who existed at that time in this
most excellent Republic. Therefore, in the year 1471 he
was elected ambassador to the King Ussun Cassano, to incite him to attack the Turk, with whom the Republic was
then engaged in the fiercest war. He, moved by the love
he bore to his country, like a good citizen, not considering
the length or danger of the journey, accepted the charge
cheerfully, and went the more willingly as he hoped to be
a more fitting instrument for good than anyone else. Since
Caloianni,[1] Emperor of Trebizond, having given one of his
daughters, named Despinacaton,[2] in marriage to Ussun Cassano, King of Persia, married another of them called Valenza
to the Duke of the Archipelago, named the Lord Nicolo
Crespo, by whom the duke had four daughters and a son,
Francesco, who succeeded his father, and whose descendant,

Euphrates entering the Gerger Gorge (Elegia). The islands do not now
exist, and they were probably (considering the time of year) only sandbanks left by the fall of the river.

[1] Calo Johannes. See Zeno, p. 9.
[2] Despina Khatoon; *i.e.*, " Lady" or " Queen" Despina.

Giacomo Crespo, the twenty-first Duke of Naxo, is still living. The daughters were all honourably married at Venice: one named Firunza was mother of the Queen of Cyprus and of the most Illustrious M. Giorgio Cornaro, knight, and his brother, the Procurator, from whom are descended many reverend Cardinals. Another named Lucretia was married to the noble M. Jacomo Prioli, who was the father of M. Nicolo Prioli, the Procurator. Valenza, the third, was the wife of the noble M. Gio. Loredano, and Violante, the fourth, was the wife of the above-mentioned M. Catharin Zeno. Now this Despinacaton, though she was in Persia and at a distance, continually kept up the remembrance of her relatives, her affection for her sister Valenza, wife of the Duke of the Archipelago, and her nieces at Venice. For this reason, this gentleman went readily and was not deceived in his opinion, as, after many hardships and dangers, when he arrived at Tauris in the presence of Ussun Cassano and Despinacaton his wife, he was recognised by her as her nephew, and had great honours and favours paid him; and by the influence he acquired with that monarch he was able to perform many things for his Republic, described in his book, which, as we have said above, we have not been able to get into our hands. King Ussun Cassano, to do greater honour to the noble M. Catharin, chose him for his ambassador to the Christian princes, to incite them against the Turk, and principally to the Kings of Poland and Hungary; but, when he came to them and found them at war with each other, he passed on to others. At this time, the most Illustrious Government hearing of the departure of M. Catharino, elected in his place M. Josapha Barbaro, and after him M. Ambrosio Contarini, whose travels, on his return journey to Venice, by the Caspian Sea, the river Volga, and the country of Tartars, I think will greatly amuse his readers from their novelty and the account of the various accidents that befel him from day to day.

A SHORT NARRATIVE OF THE LIFE AND ACTS OF THE KING USSUN CASSANO.

BY

GIOVAN MARIA ANGIOLELLO.

CHAP. I.—Assambei, King of Persia, takes as wife the daughter of the Christian Emperor of Trebizond, and after he has had sons by her, she, with two daughters, goes to lead a solitary life in the Christian faith; her father is taken prisoner to Constantinople.

ASSAMBEI,[1] the most powerful King of Tauris and Persia, had several women as his wives; and, among others, one named Despinacaton, who was the daughter of an Emperor of Trebizond, named Caloianni, who feared the might of the Ottoman, Mahomet II, and hoped in this way to strengthen himself, with the assistance of Assambei, in case of need, so gave her to him as his wife, with the condition that she might hold to the Christian faith, employing chaplains to perform the sacred offices. By this lady Assambei had one male and three female children. The first of these daughters, named Marta, was married to Sachaidar,[2] father of Ismail Sophi. The other two remained with their mother, who, after a certain time, determined to lead a solitary life apart from her husband, who consented and gave her a large income, assigning as a residence a city named Iscartibiert,[3] on the frontiers of the land of Diarbet.[4] This lady remained in this place a long time, and with her her two daughters,

---

[1] Hassan Beg.   [2] Sheikh Hyder. See Zeno, p. 48.
[3] Present Kharput. See *Travels of a Merchant*, cap. 3; and Zeno, p. 42.
[4] Diarbekr.

leading a Christian life, and after her death was buried in the city of Amit,[1] in the church of San Giorgio, where her tomb is to be seen even to this day. The son, Jacob or Juibic, remained with his father, Assambei, and, when about twenty years of age, the very night on which his father died, was strangled by three other brothers by another mother. His sisters, named the one Eliel and the other Eziel, hearing of their brother's death, decided to fly; and, after packing up their goods, went to Aleppo, and thence to Damascus; where they have been often seen by our countrymen, one of them being still alive. Now, to return to Caloianni, who thought, by giving his daughter as wife to Assambei, that he would strengthen his country against the enemy and remain in possession of Trebizond, I will mention that the Turk quickly came down upon him with his army, before he could obtain succour. The unhappy monarch,[2] not finding help on any side, was constrained to give himself up to the enemy. Thence he was taken to Constantinople and treated honourably enough, but died before a year was over, in 1462.[3]

CHAP. II.—Pirahomat makes war on Abrain, his brother, in order to take from him the kingdom of Caramania, and obtains his end by the aid of the Grand Turk, against whom he afterwards rebels, and flies to Persia.

The King Assambei afterwards had a war with the Ottoman monarch on account of the kingdom of Caramania, to which both preferred a claim. This kingdom was anciently called Cilicia, but afterwards, and to the present time, called

---

[1] Amid (Diarbekr.) The Church of San Giorgio, or Mar Jurjees, was an old Jacobite church, but is now in ruins. See Zeno, p. 42.

[2] It was David Comnenus who was the last Emperor of Trebizond. Calo Johannes, his elder brother, having died before the Turkish invasion. [3] Trebizond was taken by Mahomet II in 1461.

Caramania, from an Arab chief named Caraman, who, in course of time, had a descendant named Turuan, who had seven sons. After his death these sons came to blows amongst themselves, and five of them dying, there were two left, Abrain and Pirahomat. Abrain,[1] by having more adherents, made himself master, and Pirahomat[2] fled to the Grand Turk, who claimed relationship with them. Pirahomat, while in Constantinople, continually solicited the Turkish monarch to give him aid to oust his brother and to make him king, offering, in return, to be his subject. The Ottoman monarch, seeing that this offer suited his purpose, agreed, and gave him sufficient forces. Abrain, Prince of Caramania, hearing this, made preparations to defend his State. In the year 1467 the two armies met between Carasar[3] and a city called Aessar,[4] a great slaughter taking place on both sides. However, at length Pirahomat gained the victory, and remained master of the country without any opposition; his brother turning to fly, fell from his horse, and breaking his ribs, died from it. Pirahomat, however, remained in peaceable possession of the throne for two years only; for it being the custom for all the Turkish barons to go to visit the monarch once a year and to kiss his hand, giving him presents in proportion to their incomes and dignity, and for the monarch to caress them, and to give them many presents, Pirahomat, not caring to observe this custom like the others, the Turk sent to tell him to come to his assistance with part of his forces, as he wished to march against the Christians. But Pirahomat would not obey; wherefore the Turk, enraged at his disobedience, went in person to attack him, and took from him part of the country as far as the Cogno,[5] putting in command his second son,

---

[1] Ibrahim. [2] Peer Ahmed. See Zeno, p. 15.
[3] Shebban Kara Hissar. See Zeno, p. 23. [4] Niksar?
[5] The city of Konieh; but the text denotes a river rather, probably the Iris.

named Mustafà Celebi,[1] leaving a large force with him and sending a good commander with a number of men to go on occupying the rest of the country. Pirahomat, seeing that he could not resist the Turkish forces, left some governors in certain fortresses, departed from the country, and went to Persia to the King Assambei. On his arrival in Tauris he was greatly welcomed, and his prayers for aid against the enemy being favourably listened to, a force of about forty thousand men was set in order. The commander was named Yusuf,[2] a man of great reputation, ability, and courage, who, taking the field with the army, soon arrived at the city of Toccat,[3] and put the whole country to fire and sword, burning the towns belonging to that city, not delaying to attack fortresses, but went plundering and devastating the country, so that every one fled to the fortresses. At this time Mustafà, the son of the Turk, was sent with one of his father's generals, named Agmat Bassa,[4] to take the fortresses of Caramania, and was encamped before a strong city named Lula, the inhabitants of which, unaccustomed to hear the terrible sound of artillery, surrendered, and were cruelly treated by Mustafà. Having placed a garrison in the city and hearing that the Persian camp was in the neighbourhood, but that Ussun Cassano was not there in person, he retired to the Cogno, and sent his women and goods away for safety, to a place four days' journey to the west, towards Constantinople, named Sabi Carrahasar,[5] situated on a high mountain. The camp remained some days at the Cogno, when they, hearing of the approach of the Persians, and not considering themselves strong enough for resistance, retired to the city of Cuthey,[6] where Daut[7] Bassa, Beglerbeg of Natolia, happened to be collecting

---

[1] Tchelebee or the noble, a common title among the Ottoman princes.
[2] Yusuf Khan.   [3] Tocat.   [4] Achmet Pasha.
[5] Afioom Kara Hissar. Zeno, p. 19.
[6] Cutaych.   [7] Daoud.

men to resist the Persians. The Grand Turk also had crossed the strait with all his court and part of the Rouman troops to join his other camp, being deceived as to the strength of the enemy, who had been joined by some Caramanians and were marching boldly through the country.

CHAP. III.—Mustafà comes to an engagement with the Persians who had come with Pirahomat to defend Caramania, and routs them. Ussun Cassano exhorts the Venetians to make war on the Turk and to send him artillery.

Mustafà, hearing that Ussun Cassano was not there in person, and that in all, both cavalry and infantry, there were about fifty thousand men, taking leave of his father with Agmat Bassà,[1] and a force of sixty thousand men, the greater part cavalry, set out against the Persians. The enemy, hearing of this movement, advanced no further, but retired to the country of Caramania to get reinforcements and provisions. Now, the Turkish army riding forward in great haste for several days, arrived not very far from where the enemy were encamped. A force of four thousand cavalry under a captain named Arnaut was sent in advance, and at the dawn of day attacked the Persian camp, and during the engagement the rest of the Turkish army came up to the aid of the four thousand horse who had already been roughly handled, Arnaut and more than two thousand of his men being slain. The Persians, seeing their advantage met the Turkish squadron boldly and showed great courage in the contest. But after a great number had been slain on both sides, about the third hour the Persians began to yield, and were routed by the Turks; Yusuf, the commander, and other chiefs, were taken prisoners, while many others were slain. The tents and baggage were captured with a great booty in horses, camels, and other plunder. Pirahomat,

[1] Achmet Pasha.

Prince of Caramania, having the country in his favour, found means to escape, but not feeling safe in his own dominions, returned to Ussun Cassano in Persia. The Turkish sovereign, hearing of this victory, caused great feasts and rejoicings to be held in Constantinople, sending many presents to his son Mustafà and his captains. After this defeat the King Assambei sent an ambassador to persuade the Venetian rulers to make war on the Turk, since the latter was coming in person against him. And, in addition, he requested artillery from them, which a short time after was sent to Cyprus with their fleet, but arrived too late, after Assambei had come to blows with the Turks, in which action he had suffered a defeat and retired to Tauris, where he was followed by Messer Josaphat Barbaro and the artillery.

CHAP. IV.—The preparations made by the Turk to go in person against Ussun Cassano and the array of his army in the camp and on the march.

The Turk having gained the victory and made himself master of Caramania, perceiving that Ussun Cassano was hostile to him, by giving aid to Pirahomat, in the year 1473 determined to show him that he was not in the least afraid of him. This he had already done in the battle, but he resolved to do more, and make him feel his immense power. Therefore, the following spring, he made preparations for going in person against Ussun Cassano, ordering great musters of men to be made. And when the time for opening the campaign was come, in the above-mentioned year he crossed the Strait of Constantinople, with his whole court, into Asia. On arriving in Cappadocia he halted in a plain near a city called Amasia,[1] the residence of Baiesit[2] Celebi,

---

[1] Amasia. See Zeno, p. 37.   [2] Bajazet Tchelebee.

the eldest son of the Turk. This plain is called Casouasi,[1] which, in our language, signifies the plain of the goose; it can support great armies, and has great resources of water and forage, as there are many towns round it. As this was on the route the Sultan intended to take, it was determined on as the rendezvous for the grand army. Having (as we have already mentioned) ordered all his generals and captains to be prepared, and at the appointed time, with everything in readiness, to appear in this place,—it was done as he commanded. But the Turkish monarch, knowing that this enterprise was of the greatest importance, determined to make all the preparations that the number of his men, the scarcity of necessaries, and the safety of his country and himself required. Therefore, of his three sons, he wished the two elder ones to come on this enterprise, namely, Baiesit the eldest, and Mustafà his second son; the third, by name Gien,[2] remained at Constantinople with good advisers to watch over the safety of his realm. The army being mustered and arranged in this plain of the goose, he resolved on the order it was to hold in the camps and on the road, and the means by which there might be no want of any necessaries or comforts.

It was first resolved to make five principal commanders, one of whom was the Turkish monarch at the head of his court, and other troops to the number of thirty thousand infantry and cavalry. The second was his eldest son, Baiesit, who had a following of another thirty thousand, with his position on the right of his father. The third was his second son, Mustafà, who also had thirty thousand men, among whom were twelve thousand Wallachians from the Basha of Wallachia, under a chief named Bataraba, and this column had its position on the left of the Turk. The fourth was the Beglerbeg of Roumania, named

[1] Quzbvassi. The Goose's Plain.
[2] Djim or Zizim. See Zeno, p. 22.

Asmurat,[1] of the family of the Palæologi; and, as he was young, Maumet Bassà was given him as an adviser, as he was the first, and considered the most prudent man of the whole empire of the Turk; he was a counsellor of the sovereign, as he had also been of Amurat, the father of the present monarch. This column was sixty thousand strong, comprising many Christians, Greeks, Albanians, and Sorians in their number; and this column had its post in front of the Turk. The fifth commander was the Beglerbeg of Natolia, named Daut Bassà, a man of authority and mature discretion. The column was forty thousand strong, including Mussulman infantry and cavalry, and their post was behind the Grand Turk; so that the Sultan, with his court, remained in the midst surrounded by the four abovementioned columns. And the commands were that they should pitch their tents, which are very numerous, according to their rank, but without disturbing the order of the march, or leaving their own divisions, arranging close together like a fortified place; but, that they should always leave roads for passage in the camp, and in the middle of each column a large space for a square, since in each column was a market for cooked foods, forage, and other comforts. There were besides in each column seneschals and marshals with full powers for keeping order and providing against disturbances. Each of these four commanders was obliged to send out sentinels and to keep guard in his division. Besides the five columns we have mentioned, there was also another of the Aganzi,[2] who are not paid, except by the booty they may gain in guerilla warfare. These men do not encamp with the rest of the army, but go traversing, pillaging, and wasting the country of the enemy on every side, and yet keep up a great and excellent discipline among themselves, both in the division of the plunder and in the execution of all their enterprises. In this

---

[1] Amurath. [2] Ikindjis.

division were thirty thousand men, remarkably well mounted, and as a commander they had given them a valiant chief named Maumut Aga.

CHAP. V.—The supplies of provisions made by the chief, Arphaemiler, that the army might be in plenty.

In the matter of provisions great care and diligence were required to keep the army in plenty, and for this, two Arphaemiler (as the chief commissariat officers are called, who have two hundred and fifty men under each) were appointed. Their duty is, when the Grand Turk takes the field to send word on a day in advance, to let the people know that the army is about to encamp in that region. And the governors and rulers of those districts provide abundant provisions for the army; and people of every condition come willingly in order to find a market for their produce, as well as for the sake of fellowship and a welcome, being perfectly sure that no violence will be offered them; and woe to anyone who dares to do them violence, as he would be severely punished. There also follow the camp many sutlers, as butchers, bakers, cooks, and many others, who go about buying goods, and bringing them to the camp to make a profit, and in this traffic great and rich men also engage. And those who pursue this trade are favoured and protected by the authorities in all the things they do for the accommodation of the camp; so that at all times when the army is in the field, if the roads are not blocked up by the enemy, there is the greatest abundance.

When the Turkish monarch wishes to go against the enemy and begins to leave his territories, and plenty of provisions are not easily obtained, they determine on the road they are to take, as when in this case against Ussun Cassano we entered the country and advanced ten days' journey from the Turkish frontiers. All safe communication with the frontiers was cut off for three months; so that Gien Sultan, his son, to whom was left the Government of the State at Constantinople, remained more than forty days without news of his father or of the army. At length it was rumoured that we were all routed and cut to pieces, which he believed, and endeavoured to gain over to his allegiance the governors of the fortresses as well as the other magistrates, with which the Turk became so indignant, that he put to death the counsellors who had advised Gien to do so. One of these was named Carestra Solciman and the other Nasufabege. Now, when it happens that the army is past the frontiers and in the enemy's country, and there is need of provisions, these Arphaemiler have the charge of sending to all parts of their sovereign's dominions, where they know there is plenty of grain, and of ordering each city to send so many camel loads of corn and barley. The cities, with their territories, are bound to obey and to furnish their overseers with the quantity of corn and barley which has been imposed upon them. Besides, they must send sufficient provisions for the use of the men and animals, who convey it on the way, so that the victuals ordered by these lords for the army be not aught diminished, but that at the time of distribution there be found as much as was ordered, otherwise, the communities would suffer reproofs and loss. When these overseers arrive in the camp at their appointed time, they present themselves to the officials of the abovementioned masters of the camp, who, taking note of their arrival, assign to them their places of encampment. Similarly, they take note of all the loads of provisions, and do not touch them without the order of these Arphaemiler, and do not distribute them while they can obtain provisions in any other way. And when the roads are blocked up, and there is a want of provisions, the seneschals of the camp go to these Saraphaemiler masters of the camp, and mention that such and such districts are in want of corn and barley, and these lords consign one or more of the overseers with his convoy to them, sending one of their clerks with them, while sometimes a commissary of the seneschals of the camp accompanies them, when, putting the provisions into the market with prices set upon them, they thus sell them, taking equally good reckoning of the quantity of grain as of the money received, lest they should be cheated. After the sale, the money is handed over to the overseer in the name of the community, and receipts taken for the quantity of supplies sold, and of the money consigned. When the overseer arrives at his home he hands over the money to the community, which is distributed in proportion to the quantity of supplies each man has forwarded to the camp, and as such good order reigns, the supply of necessaries is easy. And it is a thing almost incredible to those who have not witnessed it, to see the vast numbers of camels carrying provisions, more especially in this expedition against Ussun Cassano; in which the Turk, in addition to the ordinary pay, gave an advance of three months, that is, one quarter, according to the person's rank. He also gave assistance to the paymasters, as they have the payment of the incomes assigned to them.

CHAP. VI.—The Grand Turk holds a consultation as to the route to be followed by the army on leaving Amasia; of the places passed on the way; and of the dromedaries bringing presents from the Lord of Sit and the Soldan.

Everything necessary for the journey being got ready, they held a consultation about the route to be followed in going against Ussun Cassano. There was at this consultation the great chief, Jussuf, with other great captains of Ussun Cassano, who, as I have mentioned before, were taken prisoners the previous year, 1472, when the army was routed at Begisar; the Grand Turk had promised to liberate them, if he found that they told the truth about the things that were asked them of the route to be pursued; nevertheless, they were conducted with the army under a safe escort, and were often questioned about the passes, provisions, water, and encampments. The Turk, also by means of his attendants, treated with and brought to his camp some merchants and other persons accustomed to this journey; and they also were examined separately on these matters. Similarly, the Aganzi,[1] scouring the country and making prisoners of people well acquainted with the country, sent them to the court, where they were likewise examined, and the information given by all being then weighed, they advanced with the greatest caution.

All the necessary preparations being made, the Grand Turk moved the army from the Plain of the Goose and from the city of Amasia,[2] and advanced towards Toccat, a city of Cappadocia; and the army following its route arrived at the city of Civas,[3] situated near the mountains, and near it crossed a large river named the Lais,[4] flowing from the mountains of Trebizond, over which is an immense stone bridge. Leaving this city on the left, and having crossed this river, we entered a valley of Mount Taurus and arrived at a fortress called Nicher,[5] belonging to King Ussun Cassano. Here the Aganzi were attacked by the enemy, and a small skirmish took place, in which as many were killed on one side as on the other, and twelve prisoners were brought to the headquarters of the Turk. The rest of the garrison, not waiting to be attacked, departed, leaving the castle undamaged, where the army arrived, but not delaying to besiege fortified places, proceeded on its way, leaving on the left not very far distant a city called Coiliuasar,[6] situated among mountains in a valley surrounded by many villages. Still advancing, we

[1] The Ikindjis. irregular troops.
[2] Amasia, birthplace of Strabo and Mithridates.
[3] Sivas. See Zeno, p. 23.
[4] The Iris or Kizzil Irmak.
[5] Niksar.
[6] Koili Hissar. See Zeno, p. 23.

arrived on the slope of a high mountain at another city named Careafar,[1] where alum is found; the army encamped half a mile from this city, and the cavalry scoured and ravaged the country, so that the greater part of the peasants, with their cattle and goods, fled to the strongholds in the mountains and other safe places. Having raised the camp and continued our march, we arrived at a large plain, in which is the city of Argian,[2] on a site a little elevated above the plain, which is called the country of Arsingan.[3] But, as the city was not fortified, the inhabitants had fled across the river Euphrates. Nevertheless, some few remained, among whom was found, on the arrival of the Aganzi, an aged Armenian, in a church, surrounded by many books; and, although those who found him called to him several times, he did not answer, but continued most attentively reading the books before him, and the anger of the soldiers being aroused, he was killed and the church burnt over him, with which the Grand Turk, on hearing it, was very indignant; as it was said that this man was a great philosopher.

Continuing our journey through this country of Arsingan, which is a part of Lesser Armenia, and approaching the river Euphrates not very far from Malacia,[4] which journey we performed in eight days, and the army having already halted about the hour of nine, behold there arrived eleven dromedaries coming with presents from the lord of Sit, and from the Soldan, and on these dromedaries were men closely wrapped up in white cloth, as otherwise they could not bear riding these animals, as the great pace would shake their persons too much. Of these eleven men some were white, and others black, and the first of them had in his hand an arrow, on the point of which was fixed a note; all the others had

---

[1] Shebban Kara Hissar. The alum mines are still worked, but yield little revenue. See Zeno, p. 23.

[2] Probably Egin. See Zeno, p. 23.

[3] Erzingan. [4] Malatia.

before them a covered box, with various sweetmeats inside; others carried bread and cooked meat, which was still hot. When they arrived at the pavilion of the Turk, without alighting or stopping, they put down the note and the boxes, and said that they had come ninety miles in six hours. Their answer was given them without speaking, in another note fixed on the same arrow; and when they departed, it seemed as if they disappeared before our eyes, so marvellous is the speed of those animals.

CHAP. VII.—The Grand Turk, arriving at the river Euphrates, determines to cross, and orders Asmurat to force a passage with his men, whereupon he is defeated by the Persians.

Now on arriving at the river Euphrates, and marching north-east along its bank, we perceived that Ussuncassano had arrived with his army on the other side, at the spot where he thought that the Turk would cross. The river was wider in this place—divided into many streams by banks of mud; here the armies encamped opposite each other, with the stream separating them. Ussuncassano had an immense army, and with him were three of his sons, the first named Calul,[1] the second Ugurlimehemet,[2] and the third Zeinel, and also Pirahomat, the prince of Caramania, and many other lords and men of various nationalities, namely, Persians, Parthians, Albanians (?), Georgians, and Tartars. On Ussuncassano's seeing the Turkish army encamped, he was quite astonished at the multitude, and stood some time without speaking, and then said in the Persian language, "Baycabexen nede riadir," which means, " O, son of a whore, what a sea!" comparing the Turkish army to an ocean. On the same day that the armies encamped in this place, about nine, it was decided to attempt a passage and to attack the

[1] Khalul.   [2] Called Unghermaumet in Zeno.

enemy, and that Asmurat,[1] Beglerbeg of Romania should attempt it with all his men, and, as he was young, Mahumut Bassa was given him as a colleague. Then having raised the standards, sounded the drums, the naccare, and other warlike instruments, they began to cross, swimming over certain streams, and going from sandbank to sandbank, and so arrived nearly at the other side of the river.

Ussuncassano, seeing that the Turkish troops began to cross, and were already near his bank, sent a body of his own men against them, who also entered a good way into the river; but as a deep stream separated them, they began the fight with arrows. Still the Turks, wishing to cross, made great exertions; and a part of them crossing the stream, came to blows with the Persians, the fight lasting more than three hours, with great slaughter on both sides. The Persians being nearest their bank of the river, easily received support from their own people; while the Turks, being only able to cross by a narrow ford, arrived a few at a time, swimming over with their horses, many also being drowned by the rush of water which carried them away from the ford. At length the Turks were overcome by the Persians, and made to retreat, recrossing the stream in their flight. Mahumut Bassa, who was on a bank, half a mile distant from the place where they were fighting, not only did not give them assistance, but retreated across several streams to another sandbank. The Persians pursued the Turks, killing and taking prisoners; and the Turks in their flight got into disorder, and blocked up the passage, many being drowned by falling into the whirlpools of which there are a great many in this river, and among others Asmurat, Beglerbeg of Romania. When he, with many others, fell into a large whirlpool, the Turks, and in particular his slaves and retainers, endeavouring to assist him, made head, and attacked the Persians again. And numbers of them being

[1] Amurath Palæologus.

killed and drowned, the Persians crossing several streams in pursuit of the Turks, arrived at a muddy bank on which Mahumut Bassa had formed many squadrons, and where the contest was renewed.

But the Persians, with all their efforts, could gain no ground in the hand to hand fight that ensued with the troops of Mahumut, neither party gaining the least advantage. And as the evening began to come on, and the day to close, the Turk, who the whole time with all the rest of the army had been under arms on the bank of the river, sounded a retreat, and Ussuncassano, who had been also under arms on the other bank, did the same. And the retreat being sounded on both sides, each withdrew without any further attack; still Ussuncassano had the best of the fight, as of his men fewer were killed, but few drowned, and not one taken prisoner. But on our side, when the muster was made, there were twelve thousand men missing, among whom were several persons of note. Sentinels were posted on the banks of the river, the Persians doing the same, as both parties were apprehensive of an attack.

The Turkish monarch was very indignant that Mahumut Bassa had retired from one bank to another instead of giving assistance to Asmurat, and suspected that he had done so on purpose, not being very friendly with him. Nevertheless, the Turk did not at this time show ill-will towards Mahumut, as neither the time nor place appeared convenient, but principally because this Mahumut[1] was beloved by all; dissimulating now, he awaited the time that he could punish him without risk to himself, which happened six months later, when he caused him to be strangled with a bowstring.

[1] Knolles, in his *History of the Turks*, says that a great Pasha Mahomet was assassinated by the janissaries on the accession of Bajazet II to the throne, but makes no mention of this incident.

Chap. VIII.—Ussun Cassano pursues the Turk, who, after his defeat, returns to his country, and a battle takes place, in which, by the flight of Ussun Cassano from the army, the Persians are routed, and the Grand Turk remains victorious.

Having suffered this defeat, the Turk became very apprehensive, and determined to lead his army back to his country by the shortest route; and, to console his soldiers, besides their usual pay, he gave them another advance, making them a present of the former one which he had given at his departure. Also he liberated all his slaves that were in the camp, on the condition that none should abandon him, but should serve him like the other troops, who are not slaves, and who can do what they like with their own; he made many other concessions to the captains. The army having started, we marched along the bank of the river, and the Persians did the same on the other side, not attempting to cross, but keeping on their guard, seeing that the Turkish army was still larger than theirs; nevertheless, as was afterwards reported, Ussuncassano was incited by his sons and the other commanders to cross the river and attack us, as we were in flight in consequence of the defeat we had sustained, many consultations being held about it. At the end of about ten days the Turkish forces, having turned away from the river, with the city of Baybret[1] on their right, among the mountains which separate Greater and Lesser Armenia, took their way towards the north-west, entering a valley on the route to Trebizond. At the second halt we made after entering the valley, at the end of August, at the fourteenth hour of the day, behold the Persians appeared on the mountains on our right.[2]

Then the Turk faced round towards the enemy, and gained the heights, but first fortified the camp, leaving the brother of the ruler of Scandeloro, named Eustraf, to guard it and

---

[1] Baiboort. See Zeno, p. 26. [2] Tabeada.

the baggage-waggons. All the arrangements being made, he marched by the mountains towards the enemy, placing Daut Bassa Beglerbeg of Natolia, with his whole column, and all those of Romania who remained from the first rout in the van, Bajesit, the Grand Turk's eldest son, being on the right of his father, and Mustafa, the second, on the left. Thus marching over mountains and rocky ground, we arrived at a valley on the other side of which the Persians were drawn up, with a very extended line, opposite which the Grand Turk had his men arrayed. Then both sides sounded a countless number of naccare, drums, and other warlike instruments, the noise and din being so great that one had to hear it to imagine it. The slopes of the valley where the armies fronted each other were easy of ascent and descent; it was a quarter of a mile wide and rather long, in a wild situation among mountains.

Here began a stubborn contest, first one party and then the other repulsing the enemy, each giving assistance to their own side wherever the need was greatest, until Pirahomat, prince of Caramania, who was on Ussuncassano's right, after a fierce resistance, was defeated by Mustafa, son of the Grand Turk, and recoiling on the flank of Ussuncassano, who, fearing to be surrounded, which might easily have happened, from the superiority of the Turks on every side, and principally on the right, where the great captain Mustafa fought, began to get very much afraid, mounted an Arab mare, and in a very short time took to flight. In this way they were routed and chased as far as the tents, which were nearly ten miles off in a plain, and some of the prisoners taken at the rout of the fords were rescued.[1] The tents were also plundered and an immense booty taken, and among the slain was a son of Ussuncassano named Zeinel, whose head was presented to the Turk by a foot-soldier

[1] How this happened it is not easy to understand, as Zeno says the Persian king pursued the Turks with only a flying column.

who had killed him in the battle; since this prince Zeinel, leaving his father when he mounted the mare, entered among the infantry, and was surrounded and slain with many of his followers. This was a great rout, about ten thousand of the Persians being killed, and many more taken prisoners, of whom some were put to death each day.

The night was all spent in rejoicing, with bonfires, and music, and shouting. But because Mustafà the Sultan's son had pursued Ussun Cassano, and it was now the second hour of the night, the Turk became anxious, and sent some couriers after him, with whom he returned. His father came out of his tent with a cup of gold full of julep, which he presented to him with his own hand, kissing him and commending him greatly for his bearing and valour. This battle lasted eight continuous hours before the Persians were put to rout, and if it had not been for Mustafà and Ussun Cassano's cowardly flight, they might not have lost. In this battle, of Turks there were in all about one thousand killed.[1] There were found in the baggage-waggons of Ussun Cassano some vases of gold, with their sheaths covered with copper, and other vases of gold and silver; there were also some fine suits of armour, made at Syras,[2] quite masterpieces, like mirrors, with gilt borders wonderfully polished and a marvel to behold. They also captured a thousand horses and a great number of camels. I must not omit to mention that in this battle Ugurlimehemet, Ussun Cassano's second son, came with a great number of men to assail our camp, but he also was repulsed by the lord Cusers[3] and the rest of the garrison, and so much so that he narrowly escaped being taken prisoner, but got away through his acquaintance with the country. Thus if Ussun Cassano had remained content with his first victory, the Turk would have gone

---

[1] Zeno says fourteen thousand.
[2] Shiraz; it has still a great manufacture of sword-blades and armour.
[3] See p. 89. Eustraf?

away ignominiously, and he would not have lost the territories he did.

Having rested the army for three days, the Turk resolved to go back again by the way he had come. Therefore, raising his camp, he marched towards Baibret,[1] where, on account of the rout of Ussun Cassano, he found that the inhabitants of this city and of the surrounding country had fled to the strongholds in the mountains. Nevertheless, the Aganzi took some prisoners and plunder, and some of these Aganzi were assailed by the Persians, and the prisoners and booty recaptured. On being pursued they retired to the city of Baibret. And the Persians following in pursuit, the Aganzi defended the place, the whole of one night and half of the following day, until the news came to the army, when relief was sent to them. The Persians hearing this, went off, not wishing to await the attack. Proceeding on the march, we arrived on the banks of the great river Euphrates, finding the castles and villages all abandoned, and a good many of them burnt. Coming to the ford, the Aganzi crossed without opposition, and traversed the country on the opposite shore for one day's journey in distance, seizing some small flocks as booty. When they returned to the camp we directed our route towards Erfonia,[2] a city in front, which had been abandoned; here we fixed our camp for one night, and four days after leaving it we arrived at Carassar,[3] which is situated on a black mountain, and has a very strong natural position, from having high precipices all round, except on one side, where there is one place that one can get up to the gate by a tortuous and rocky path. Having encamped here, the people of the place stood silently on the walls provided with sharp pikes and many bows; at first they would not listen or speak to any one, but fired and hit everyone who approached, so that they were obliged to

---

[1] Baiboort. [2] Erzeroum or Erzingan.
[3] Shebhan Kara Hissar.

direct five cannon against them. Two of these were drawn up a hill not very far from the city, and did great harm. And after they had bombarded it fifteen days, and killed a considerable number of the people of the place, the latter were obliged to capitulate. The governor of it was named Aarap,[1] a retainer of prince Zeinel, the son of Ussun Cassano, who was killed in the above-mentioned battle, and who possessed this Sangiacato[2] or territory. Aarap, hearing that his master was dead and his head being shown him, wept bitterly, and then, with some of the inhabitants, determined to make sure of his life and property. The Turk promised him the conditions, and the seventeenth day after we encamped they surrendered the place, and we returned, taking Aarap with us, who, however, was shortly afterwards restored to liberty, the Turk giving him a Sangiaccato on the borders of Hungary. In fact, if he had held out eight days longer, we should have been forced to raise the siege from want of provisions, and principally of fodder for the horses, which had to be fed on oak leaves and twigs cut small.

The army, marching thence, came to the city of Coliasar[3], which town, hearing that the strong fortress of Carcasar had surrendered, and that prince Zeinel had been killed, sent ambassadors and surrendered to the Turk, while Nieser[4] did the same. All necessary provisions having been made for their government, the army proceeded and arrived at Sivas.

CHAP. IX.—Assambei, being defeated, returns to Tauris; the following year he goes into the country; his son rebels, and flies to the Grand Turk; but Ussun Cassano, causing a report to be spread of his death, induces him to return to Tauris, where he causes him to be put to death.

After this defeat Assambei returned to Tauris. In 1473 M. Josaphat Barbaro arrived, who relates that the lord

[1] Called Darap by Zeno. [2] Sanjak.
[3] Koili, or Koyumlu Hissar. [4] Niksar.

Assambei, after remaining quiet that year, in the following year, 1474, determined to go with his people into the country, as was his wont. He accordingly asked this M. Josaphat if he would accompany him, and as he said he would, they therefore set out together. In the month of May, therefore, the lord Ussun Cassano set out with his troops, the number being twenty-five thousand foot-soldiers, eighteen thousand country-people, three thousand tents, six thousand camels, thirty thousand baggage mules, five thousand riding mules, two thousand baggage horses, five thousand women, three thousand boys and maid-servants, and many animals of different kinds. These all went into the country, and found plenty of pasture. This was his standing army; I leave you to judge of the number he could levy on an emergency.

While the lord Assambei was in the country near Sultania, the news came to him that Ugurlimehemet, his son, had seized Syras. The king Assambei having heard this, immediately raised his camp and marched towards Syras. His son, hearing that his father was coming against him with a large army, fled, and leaving his dominions, escaped with his wife and all his family into the Turkish territory, where he sent messengers to beg a safe-conduct from the Sultan Baiesit, who had his residence not far from Ussun Cassano's frontiers. Baiesit immediately sent to let his father know, who approved of giving the safe-conduct, but told him that by no means should he go out of the territory of Amasia to meet him, but should show him every other honour, while still keeping an eye upon his actions, from fear of Persian treachery. And you may know that the city of Syras,[1] which this same Ugurlimehemet had taken from his father, is the most important city of Persia on the frontiers near Chirmas,[2] and is walled with stone. It is twenty

[1] Shiraz, a far more important town then than it is now.
[2] Kerman.

miles in circumference, and has two hundred thousand inhabitants. It has a great trade, with manufactures of arms, saddles, bridles, and all equipments of men, as well as horses, and supplying Soria,[1] Constantinople, and all the East with them. Ugurlimehemet having thus escaped to Sivas, sent his wife with his small family in advance, to avert every suspicion his coming might awaken, while he himself followed with three hundred horsemen. He was favourably received by Baiesit, who embraced him and made sumptuous feasts in his honour. Some days after, Ugurlimehemet left with his troop, and having arrived at Usuhuder, the Grand Turk sent a guard of honour to meet him, with whom he proceeded to Constantinople. Here he was honourably lodged, and provided with sustenance both for himself and suite at the expense of the Grand Turk, who then opened his court, and arriving at the place in which he was accustomed to give audiences, Ugurlimehemet came to the court to visit the monarch whom he had not yet seen. The Grand Turk sent councillors and captains to meet him, and commanded that he should be permitted to come on horseback into the second seraglio, which it is the custom for no one to enter except the monarch; and that when he dismounted he should be admitted to his presence girt with his sword, which no one is permitted to wear, however great a lord he may be, not even the princes themselves. On the entry of Ugurlimehemet, the Grand Turk rose from his seat, and greeted him kindly, and made him sit down beside him, where they conversed on different subjects for the space of an hour, Mahomet calling him "son", and making many proposals to him. On this occasion he left without asking any safe-conduct or any other favour; but after visiting the monarch several times, he thought fit to ask for a command on the Hungarian frontiers, promising to be always a good and faithful subject. The Grand Turk replied that he would

[1] Syria.

make him King of Persia in the room of his father, who was his enemy; and giving him troops and means of commencing operations, sent him to Sivas, on the boundary between the Grand Turk and Ussun Cassano. Ugurlimehemet having arrived on the frontiers, was but a short time before he began to make inroads and forays, doing great damage to his father's territory, who sent troops to protect his dominions, without, however, showing much interest in this expedition against his son. On the contrary, he feigned great grief and mortification on account of his rebellion, and then gave out that he had fallen ill. He then retired to his apartments for some days, and would not allow himself to be visited by anybody but those in whom he could trust. While thus dissembling, a report was spread abroad to Constantinople, that Ussun Cassano had fallen dangerously ill from melancholy, on account of the rebellion of his son, and a rumour of his having got worse being whispered about, some of his most faithful adherents, as had been arranged, announced his death, while messengers were sent to Ugurlimehemet with letters and tokens, as is customary, giving information of the death of his father, and begging him to return and take possession of the throne, before either of his brothers, Halul or Jacob,[1] could do so. And in order to give greater semblance to the affair, funeral rites were paid, and his death was really believed in throughout the country. Ugurlimehemet having received three different messages, with secret pledges such as are used in affairs of state, thought it safe to go to Tauris. He arrived there in a few days with a small escort, and on going to the palace to make himself sovereign, was taken to where his father was in perfect health, who ordered him to be confined, and afterwards put to death, without showing any consideration for his being his son.

[1] Khaleel and Yakoob.

Chap. X.—Assambei goes to ravage the country of the Georgians, and having made them pay tribute, returns to Tauris, where he dies. One of his captains defeats the Mamelukes.

These things happening in the year 1475, Assambei remained at peace till 1477, when he assembled a large army, giving out that he was going to attack the Ottoman, when in fact he meant to ravage Georgia. His troops consisted of about twenty or four and twenty thousand horsemen, and about eleven thousand foot soldiers. I have already made mention of the numbers of women, children, camp-followers, and others; so I shall say nothing about them. Marching for seven days in a westerly direction, they turned off to the right towards Georgia, which country the king wished to plunder, because the Georgians had given him no assistance in his war with the Turk. According to their custom, he sent forward his light cavalry, about five thousand strong, who on their march went burning and cutting down the woods, as they had to cross mountains and pass through immense forests. After two days' journey through Georgia[1] we found a castle named Tiflis, commanding a pass, but deserted, which we took without any resistance. And advancing to Geri[2] and other places in the vicinity, he sacked them and also ravaged a great part of the country. The chief, Pancratio, with the King of Congiurre, which borders on Georgia, and seven other lords, sent to sue for peace, and agreed to pay a tribute of sixteen thousand ducats, while Assambei promised to leave the country free, except Tiflis,[3] which he wished to keep from the importance of its position. The prisoners taken were about five thousand. The peace being made, and the payment of tribute being

[1] Angiolello had evidently by this time left the Turkish camp and joined the Persians.   [2] Gori.
[3] Tiflis, the present capital Russian Trans-Caucasia, on the river Kur, was founded in 1063. It has a population of fifty thousand, and, under the Russian sway, has become almost like a European town.

settled, Assambei returned to Tauris, and died in the year 1478, leaving four sons: three by one mother and one by the Princess of Trebizond. This prince, who was twenty years of age, was strangled by his three brothers, who divided the realm among them, after which the second, named Jacob Patissa,[1] made a coalition with the eldest, named Marco;[2] whereupon the youngest fled, and Jacob made himself sovereign, ascending the throne in 1479.

In the year 1482 (?) it happened that the people of Amit,[3] the principal city of Diarbec, heard that the Mamelukes had seized and plundered Orfà,[4] doing great damage to all the country. The general of Assambei determined to go against them, crossed with his troops some mountains between Amit and Orfà, and entered the plains of Orfà, three days' journey from Amit. The Mamelukes hearing this put themselves in order of battle, and the two armies marching to meet each other, at length joined battle, the contest lasting till midday. Though both armies in turn repulsed the enemy, the Persians came off victors, cutting to pieces more than half of the Mamelukes, with many lords. The Persians following up their victory, advanced to Albir,[5] and took it with many other fortresses, finding immense booty; they then returned to Tauris, where they found that the King Assambei had died on the eve of Epiphany in the year 1487 (1478).

CHAP. XI.—Jacob, the son of Assambei, on ascending the throne takes a wife of a wicked disposition, who, to raise her paramour to the throne, gives the king poison, which also causes her own death and that of her son.

Jacob Patissa, as I have already mentioned, after the death of his father, made himself master of Tauris and

[1] Padishah.
[2] Khaleel is generally called the eldest of Uzun Hassan's sons.
[3] Amida, present Diarbekr.
[4] Orfa. See *Travels of a Merchant*, cap. 2.
[5] Birjik, or Bir, ancient Apamea. See *Travels of a Merchant*, cap. 2.

Persia, and took for wife a daughter of the lord of San Mutra, who was of a lascivious disposition, and being enamoured of one of the principal lords of the court, sought wickedly to put her husband to death, that after his decease this lord might succeed to the throne. Then, having arranged a plan with her paramour for murdering Jacob, she prepared poison. The adulteress prepared a bath, as usual, with perfumes, knowing her husband's habits, who, with his son of eight or nine years of age, entered the bath and remained from the twenty-second hour of the day, till sunset. When Jacob Sultan came out and entered the ladies' seraglio, his wife, who had prepared a poisoned cup, knowing that Jacob was always accustomed to drink on coming out of the bath, came to meet him with a gold cup in which she had put the poison, appearing more friendly than usual. But he, seeing her face rather pale, became suspicious, as he had already seen some evil symptoms in her that day; but the wicked woman had dissimulated and excused herself so well, that he partly believed her, although his suspicions were not altogether cleared up. Therefore, when the lady came to meet him with such a pallid countenance holding the cup, Jacob commanded her to taste it first. The terrified woman could not refuse, and after she had drunk, her husband drank also, giving some to the little boy. This happened at the twenty-fourth hour of the day, and so noxious was the beverage, that by midnight they were all dead. The death of these three personages being announced the following day, all the great lords were thrown into consternation, and also the whole of Persia. Many of Jacob's relatives seized different places, as you shall hear. After the death of Jacob Patissa, there being no other son of Assambei, the throne was seized by a lord, a relation of Jacob, named Julauer, who, although he reigned three years, did nothing of importance. To him succeeded a Baysingir,[1] who reigned two years. Rustan, a youth about twenty years of age, succeeded him and reigned seven years; in his time the father of the Sophi was killed, as the king himself was afterwards by the hands of a lord with the connivance of his own mother, with whom this lord, named Agmat,[2] was in love, who, after the death of Rustan, made himself king, and reigned five months. After Rustan's murder his troops joined one of his captains, named Carabes, who lived at Van, and who, hearing of the king's death and the succession, after biding his time, marched to Tauris, met this Agmat, and cut him to pieces. The kingdom now came to a youth named Aluan,[3] a relation of Ussun Cassano, who lived at Amit, whence he was summoned by the popular voice, and made king, but reigned only a short time, being expelled by the Sophi.

CHAP. XII.—Secchaidar, the father of the Sophi, marches against Rustan King of Persia, but is defeated and slain; Rustan sends to take his wife and three sons, and gives them in custody, but the latter escape.

During the reign of Rustan in Tauris, Sechaidar,[4] the father of the Sophi, who had married a daughter of the King Assambei, through his wife, became rightful heir of the realm of Persia.[5] He resolved to raise an army and drive out Rustan, and for this purpose collected a number of Suffaveans, who all followed him as their chief and also because he was considered a saint; he was accustomed to reside in the city of Ardouil,[6] three days' journey distant from Tauris, towards the East, like an abbot with a number of

[1] Baisongor.   [2] Ahmed.
[3] Eluan-Alwung, or Alumut, son of Sultan Yakoob.
[4] Sheikh Hyder.
[5] There were sons of Shah Yakoob living. namely, Aluan Beg and Morad Khan, who were more direct descendants of Uzun Hassan.
[6] Ardebil.

disciples. Having assembled an army of twenty-two thousand men, he marched towards Tauris;[1] but the King Rustan having heard of the preparations of the enemy, had also raised an army of fifty thousand men, and as he himself was very young, he gave the command in this enterprise against Sechaidar to one of his captains, named Sulimanbec. Sechaidar, hearing that the hostile army was more powerful than his, retreated to a place named Van, near Coi,[2] expecting to be joined from the West by some other chiefs, hostile to Rustan. But such was the rapidity of Sulimanbec, Rustan's general, that Sechaidar was forced to join battle without waiting for further reinforcements, and a fierce contest began.[3] The Suffaveans fought like lions; nevertheless, at length after numbers of men had been killed on both sides, those of Tauris came off victorious, Sechaidar being killed with numbers of his men. After the rout they sought out the body of Sechaidar, which was found by an Armenian priest and taken to Ardouil to be buried. In Tauris the victory caused great rejoicings. Rustan, hearing the news of the defeat of the enemy, and the death of Sechaidar, sent immediately to Ardouil to seize his wife and three sons, and wished to put them to death; but to please some lords, they were liberated, keeping them, however, in charge in an island in the lake of Astumar,[4] inhabited by Armenian Christians. There are there more than six hundred houses, a church named after the Holy Cross, in which are more than a hundred priests governed by a patriarch. Here, then, were sent the three sons of Sechaidar, but the

[1] The other authors give a different account; they expressly state that Sheikh Hyder was not up in arms against the king, whatever his ulterior object may have been, but was engaged in an expedition into Circassia.

[2] Khoi.

[3] Zeno says the battle took place near Derbend—far enough, certainly, from Van.

[4] Ak Tammar, the Van Lake, so called by the Armenians. The island is, to this day, the seat of the Catholicos, and is fully described by Layard.

mother remained in Tauris, and was married for the second time to a lord who was an enemy of her former husband. The sons remained three years in the island; but Rustan, being apprehensive of their escape, and being persuaded by some of his friends to put them to death, sent to take them. The day that the messenger asked for them on behalf of Rustan, they were given up to him by the Armenians, although very reluctantly, as they were very much beloved, especially Ismael the second, for his beauty and pleasing manners. After they had given them up (notice well the influence of Providence to carry out what it has determined) one of the principal Armenians addressed the others, saying, "We have given up these boys to this messenger without having seen any command from the King Rustan; it may easily happen that we have been deceived, and that they may be taken away and escape somewhere, so that we would receive great blame, and our sovereign might well say, ' Where is my order'. Thus it is my opinion that we ought not to deliver them to him unless he brings credentials in writings, which we may keep for security." All the others agreed to this, more especially because they were very loth to give them up. Then they told the messenger to bring credentials from the king; and as it was some distance thence to Tauris, he was more than seven days before he returned. During this time the boys and their[1] mother were conducted in a boat from the island to the country of Carabas[2] on the east. This country borders on Sumacchia[3] and Ardouil, which belonged to the father of these boys, and its inhabitants are for the most part Suffaveans, and had great reverence for the father. Here they were hidden without anyone hearing anything of them for

---

[1] See above, where it is stated that their mother was married a second time; and page 105, where it is said Ismail put her to death. It is more probable that another of their father's wives is denoted in these other cases.   [2] Kara Bagh.   [3] Schamachi.

the space of five years. Ismael at this time was nine years old, and when he attacked Sumacchia was not quite fourteen.[1]

CHAP. XIII.—How Ismael, the son of Haidar, was born and brought up; he becomes a captain, attacks and defeats Sermangoli, possessing himself of his realm; he marches against, and takes Tauris.

During these five years these boys were incited by many of their father's friends, who came to visit them, to assemble troops to recover his possessions; having collected five hundred brave and faithful men, and the whole country being friendly disposed towards them, they elected Ismael their captain, as he was a fiery, brave, and courteous youth. This Ismael, when he was born, issued from his mother's womb with fists clenched and covered with blood: a remarkable fact, and when his father saw him, he said, "Surely he will grow up a bad man"; and agreed with his mother that he should not be reared; but God disposed otherwise, as when they sent him away to be put to death, those who were charged with the deed, touched by his beauty, had pity on him and brought him up. After three years the boy giving great promise, they determined to show him to his father, and when an opportunity occurred they placed him before him, and when, he being taken with him, asked who he was, they told him he was his son, at which he was delighted, and received him with great show of affection.

Then, having assembled five hundred horse and foot soldiers, they crossed a large river called the Cur,[2] flowing in the direction of Sumacchia,[3] into the Caspian Sea; then marching towards Sumacchi they received intelligence that the lord of that place, named Sermangoli, was assembling

[1] Vide *Travels of a Merchant*, cap. 13.
[2] Kur, or Cyrus.   [3] Schamachi.

his chiefs to collect an army against them. One of these chiefs said, "Sire, leave the business to me, and I will engage to bring you this fellow's head"; and, then collecting seven thousand men, marched against him. The Suffaveans, seeing the Sumacchians coming against them in great force in a plain, retreated to the top of a hill. The Sumacchians surrounded it to besiege the enemy, but fortune was propitious to the Sophi, who attacked them in the weakest quarter, and intending to fall sword in hand, their assault was so impetuous that fifteen hundred of the enemy surrendered at once, the others being cut to pieces. The Suffaveans provided themselves with arms and horses from the booty, and followed up their victory, by marching towards Sumacchia. The king, hearing of this defeat, issued into the plain with the rest of his men; but, being without discipline, they were routed, and the King Sermangoli taken prisoner. Ismael spared his life, and having captured the city, made great presents to his soldiers; he also took the other numerous fortresses in the country of Sermangoli. Ismael having made himself lord of this country, besieged a castle called Pucosco on the way to Tauris, a very rich place, which he took by assault (his younger brother, Bassingur, being killed in the fight), and gave all the wealth they found in the place to his soldiers. Hence, the fame was spread abroad, that Ismael, the son of Sechaidar, had recovered his dominions, and that his liberality to his men made them devoted to him; and an almost incredible number of people joined him; thus, having about forty thousand men[1] under him, he determined to march on Tauris. Before he set out he inquired what the Greeks did, when they held the empire of Persia; and hearing that they would not harm the country in anything, but were friendly to everyone, he then marched to Tauris, committing such severities that everyone was

[1] Zeno, p. 51, says he had only sixteen thousand men under him after being joined by the Georgians.

thrown into mortal terror and dared not take up arms against him. Aluan, who was then king, seeing that he could not defend himself from the fury of the enemy, resolved to fly. Taking with him his wife and treasure, he went to Amit, his former city.[1] Thus, in 1499, in the same year, and six months from the commencement of the war, the Sophi made himself master of Tauris. On his entry he used great cruelty towards the opposing faction, as he cut to pieces many people, doctors, women, and children; wherefore, all the surrounding places sent in their allegiance, and all the city wore his ensign, that is, the red caftan; in this war more than twenty thousand people were killed. He then caused the bones of several lords who were already dead to be disinterred and burnt; he put to death his own mother,[2] recollecting, as he had been told, that she had wished to kill him after his birth, and also because she was by birth of the opposing faction.

CHAP. XIV.—Ismael raises war against Moratcan, defeats him, and makes himself king. After his victory he is advised to marry, which he does, and then attacks Bagadet, is victorious, and thus becomes master of many countries.

Ismael having remained all the winter at Tauris, in 1500, early in the year, determined to go against a certain Moratcan,[3] who had seized the country of Erach[4] after the death of Jacob, which country comprises Spaan, Ies, and Syras,[5] with many other cities, which used to be under the dominion of the kings of Persia. He therefore assembled an army of twenty thousand men, all brave Suffaveans, and, marching towards the enemy's country, he heard that Moratcan was prepared to receive him with fifty thousand men. Never-

---

[1] Diarbekr, the hereditary city of the Ak Koinloos.
[2] Step-mother, according to Zeno, which is certainly more probable.
[3] Morad Khan, brother of Aluan Beg.   [4] Irak-el Ajim.
[5] Ispahan, Yezd, and Shiraz.

theless, he continued his route to Chizaron, having advanced a long way from Tauris, and from thence to Syras, bordering on the country of Carason[1] or Gon. Here they met in battle, and at length Moratcan was killed[2] and his men defeated and dispersed, when Ismael made himself master of all those realms. After this victory, before returning to Tauris, all his friends counselled him to marry; but while he was considering this step, they could find no lady worthy of such a match. At length, after many discussions, they said that a certain lord had a lady in his house, a granddaughter of Sultan Jacob, the son of Ussun Cassano, who was beautiful, and named Taslucanum; wherefore, he sent to the lord demanding her of him. The lord replied to the messengers that she was not there; but Ismael, insisting on her being sent, the lord had another dressed up instead of her, saying he had no other in the house. The messengers, seeing that she did not correspond to the description given of her, said that it was not this one that they wanted, and ordered all the girls to be brought, among whom was Taslucanum, but went away without recognising her. The Sophi ordered them to return and have the girls shown again, which they did, and recognised her this time, and had her dressed up and brought with them. Ismael, when he saw her, said "This is she I was told of"; and took her for wife. But, as the king was very young, only fifteen or sixteen years old, he gave her to a lord to take care of. After three years the king asked for her, and said to the lord, "You have been able to do just as you liked with her during three years." He replied, "Sire, do not believe it; I would sooner kill myself". The Sophi said, "You have been a great fool"; and took her as his wife. After the Sophi had conquered the country of Erach, he returned to Tauris in 1501, and caused

---

[1] Khorassan.

[2] The other authors agree in stating that he escaped to Alla-ed Doulch's country: at any rate, he was no further trouble to Ismail Sofi.

great rejoicings to be made on account of his victory. The following year he determined to invade the country of Bagadet, three hundred miles distant from Tauris towards the south and south-west, a large district, and having assembled an army, he set out. The lord[1] of the country held himself in readiness with many troops, not in the field, but in the city of Baldac,[2] anciently called Babylon the Great, through the midst of which flows the river Euphrates. The king, arriving two miles distant from it, one night a great part of the wall fell down, and caused so great a panic in the city, that everyone fled. The lord also was forced to fly across the sandy plains of Arabia Deserta, sixteen days' journey in extent, from Baldac to Damascus, and thence to Aleppo, where, after residing some time, the Prince Aladuli gave him his daughter in marriage, and settled him there. The Sophi remained in Baldac and took the land of Bagadet, and afterwards Mosul and Gresire,[3] a large city, through which the river Tigris flows. This is also called the country of Mesopotamia. The Sophi having made these conquests in 1503, returned to Tauris and made great feasts and rejoicings in honour of his victory. While he was in Tauris, after his return in 1504, he heard that while he was away at Mosul and Bagadet the King of Gilan had rebelled, and, determining to be revenged, he prepared an army and marched against him. Hearing this the King of Gilan sent ambassadors to him immediately, asking pardon. With great reluctance, after many entreaties, the Sophi pardoned him, but doubled the tribute. He then returned, and remained in peace and quiet till the year 1507.

[1] Morad Khan.
[2] Bagdad is situated on the Tigris, not the Euphrates, but the modern city of Hillah is supposed to represent the site of the ancient Babylon.
[3] Jezireh ebn Omar on the Tigris. See *Travels of a Merchant*, cap. 4.

CHAP. XV.—Ismael goes against Alidoli; ruins his country and people. Aluan, who had escaped from Tauris, is taken prisoner. The son of Alidoli is killed at the capture of the city. Then, repulsing the Great Khan of Tartary when invading Persia, he returns to Tauris, and causes great feasts and rejoicings to be held.

The Sophi, having under his sway a part of the country of Diarbec, that is, Orfa, Moredin,[1] Arsunchief,[2] and other places, and hearing continually that Abnadulat[3] was ravaging that part of the country, and had taken the city of Cartibiert,[4] placing one of his sons in it, determined to make an expedition against this Abnadulat; since these places had always been under the sway of Persia, until this Alidoli,[5] after the death of Jacob, while Persia was in a state of anarchy, had seized them. Then, having assembled seventy thousand men, he marched towards Arsingan,[6] a fine city on the borders of Trebizond and Natolia. Having arrived here, he halted forty days, fearing lest the Ottoman and the Soldan should take into their heads to defend Alidoli, as his country was on the frontiers of both. While in this doubt, he sent two ambassadors, one named Culibech,[7] to the Ottoman Emperor of Constantinople; and the other named Zaccarabech,[8] to the Soldan of Cairo, swearing by his head and other oaths that he would do them no harm, but that he only wished to destroy his enemy Alidolit. After forty days Ismael left Arsingan, from which place it is four days' journey to the country of Alidoli. But he would not take

[1] Orfa and Mardin. See *Travels of a Merchant*, caps. 2 and 4.

[2] Hesn Keyf, Ciphas of Procopius. Baldwin de Bourg and Jocelyn de Courtenay were confined here after their capture by Sookman, the Ortokide lord of the place, and Dejekermish, lord of Mosul. See *Travels of a Merchant*, cap. 4.   [3] Alla-ed Douleh.

[4] Kharput. Jocelyn was again captured, together with his kinsman, by Balak, the Ortokide, and confined in this place. See *Travels of a Merchant*, cap. 3.

[5] Alla-ed Douleh, written "Abnadulat" above.

[6] Erzingan.   [7] Ko-li Beg.   [8] Zekkaria Beg.

the ordinary route, but went to Caisaria,[1] a city belonging to the Ottoman, where he supplied himself with provisions, paying for everything, and proclaiming abroad that everyone might bring supplies to the camp for sale, and that anyone taking anything without paying for it, would be put to death. In this city he remained four days, and then advanced to Albustan,[2] situated on a river[3] and in a beautiful plain, and belonging to Alidoli. From this to Maras[4] is a journey of two days, and after burning the country of Albustan, he advanced to Maras. But Alidoli had disappeared, and retired to some strongholds in the mountains. These mountains are called Carathas,[5] and have only one very difficult pass. Ismael ravaged the country, and cut to pieces many soldiers, who from time to time descended from the mountains to attack the Suffaveans, but who were discovered by his sentinels and by the people of the country. It was in the month of July 1507 that Ismael entered the country of Alidoli, and he remained there till the middle of November. Then, on account of the snow and cold, he determined to return to Persia, and on his way to Tauris arrived at Malacia,[6] where he met one of his adherents, named Amirbec,[7] who wore the seal of the Sophi, and was a man high in authority. He had taken Sultan Aluan, who had escaped from Tauris, prisoner, in the following manner: he set out from Mosul with four thousand fighting men to support the Sophi, and passing by Amit,[8] where Sultan Aluan was, he gave out that he had come to assist him against the Sophi, and was thus received in Amit. Having entered Amit, he threw Aluan into chains, took him prisoner in the name of Ismael, and conducted him to Malacia, where he was shortly afterwards put to death; and I myself saw him

---

[1] Kaisarieh.
[2] El Bostan, or Albistan. See Zeno, p. 54.
[3] The Jihoon.
[4] Marash. See Zeno, p. 54.
[5] Kara Dagh.
[6] Malatia.
[7] Amir Beg.
[8] Diarbekr.

in chains there. After this, Ismael proceeded and crossed the Euphrates, which river is ten miles distant from Malacia on the east, and advanced to Cartibiert,[1] which was governed by a son[2] of Alidoli. This place was well provided with men and provisions, but these were of no avail, as the place was taken, and the governor put to death. They then advanced towards Tauris, but were overtaken by snow six days' journey distant from Coi,[3] so that many men, horses, and camels died of the cold, and a great portion of the booty they had taken in the country of Alidoli was lost. At last they arrived at Coi, where was a magnificent palace built by Ismael, and there they remained till the spring. He then returned to Tauris, where he rested that summer, and in the following year was forced into another war, as Jesilbas,[4] the ruler of Samarcand, called the Grand Tartar, whose people are named after the green caftans, had assembled an immense army, and entered the country of Corasan and Strave,[5] places belonging to Persia, and then seized the lands of some neighbouring chieftains to be able to advance against the Sophi. But Ismael was in readiness, and went with an immense camp to Spàan,[6] fourteen days' journey distant from Tauris towards the east, and there halted. The Tartar, hearing this, advanced no further, but thought to outwit Ismael by demanding a free passage to Mecca through his territory; but the latter perceived the stratagem, refused him a passage, and while the Tartar was in Corasan, Ismael remained in Spàan, watching the movements of the enemy. At the close of the year 1508 the Tartars returned to their country, and Ismael likewise to Tauris. In honour of his return they arranged and ornamented the bazaars and palaces, causing great feasts and games to be held, as you will hear. The Sophi had a high pole or mast erected in

---

[1] Kharput.   [2] Named Becarbec.   [3] Khoi.
[4] Sheibani Khan. See Zeno, p. 55.
[5] Khorassan and Astrabad.   [6] Ispahan.

the maidan, that is, in the piazza, on which was placed a golden apple, and whoever running past could knock it down with their arrows or other missiles, took it for their own. After the golden one they set up a silver one, and so on, twenty in number, ten gold and ten silver; between the knocking down of each apple, Ismael rested a short time, drinking several confections and delicate wines; and while he was amusing himself, there stood before him two beautiful boys: one of whom held a vase of gold with a cup; and the other, two jugs of refreshing drinks. At his sport he has a guard of a thousand soldiers, besides whom, a crowd of perhaps thirty thousand soldiers and citizens stand by to see the game. After his recreation he goes with his lords to sup in a palace[1] in the country built by Sultan Assambei, but the lords sup apart. This Sophi is fair, handsome, and very pleasing; not very tall, but of a light and well-framed figure; rather stout than slight, with broad shoulders. His hair is reddish; he only wears moustachios, and uses his left hand instead of his right. He is as brave as a game cock, and stronger than any of his lords; in the archery contests, out of the ten apples that are knocked down, he knocks down seven: while he is at his sport they play on various instruments and sing his praises.

CHAP. XVI.—Ismael being with his army in the country of Carabas,[2] sends two captains to invade Sumacchia, while he himself went towards the Caspian Sea, taking many places, and among others the castle of the city of Derbant, an important place.

Ismail having remained fifteen days in Tauris, set out in 1510 with his camp to Coi, where he remained two months, and whence in the year 1509 he determined to attack Sermangoli, to whom, besides his life, he had presented for the

[1] Called Astibisti in the *Travels of a Merchant*, cap. 8.
[2] Kara Bagh.

second time the realm of Servan and Sumachia;[1] but who, when he was engaged in the war with the Tartars, had broken the conditions of peace. Therefore, having assembled his army, he marched towards the country of Carabas, where there is a plain of immense extent, in which is situated a fortress named Canar, with many villages belonging to it. Here they manufacture the silk which is called Canarian, after the name of the place. As this region was very rich, he halted here eight days, and having nominated two captains, one named Dalabec and the other Bairabac,[2] he gave them charge of the expedition against Sumacchia, making them a present of the city. When they arrived there, according to their instructions, they found the city deserted, the king having fled to Culustan, a large and well fortified castle, situated on a mountain, but whose governor had orders to surrender it if Ismael appeared in person. The two captains, with ten thousand valiant men, encamped round this place, which is half a mile distant from the city, but were not able to assault on any side, as there were no engineers or artillery with them. About this time Ismael left Canar and went to the castle of Maumutaga, a port on the shores of the Caspian Sea, eight days' journey distant from Tauris, which he took, and with it much booty. He then marched along the coast to take possession of all the other fortresses of the country of Servan. From Maumutaga to Derbent is seven days' journey along the coast, on which are many towns and castles, Sumacchia being one day's journey distant. On our march we reached a place named Baccara, four days' journey from Maumutaga, and two from Sumacchia. It is also called Baccuc,[3] and is one of the ports of Tauris, with an excellent harbour; it was anciently the principal place on the sea, which

---

[1] Shirvan and Schamachi.
[2] Bairambec, the conqueror of Van and Ismael's brother-in-law. See *Travels of a Merchant*, cap. 6.   [3] Baku.

is called the Sea of Baccuc after it, although others call it the Caspian, from the Caspian mountains; others, the Hyrcanian Sea from Hyrcania, now called the country of Strava,[1] from whence comes the silk of Strava. One day's journey further from Baccara is a fortress named Sirech, situated on a mountain. The inhabitants held out three days before coming to terms with Ismael, who, at length agreeing to their conditions, sent in sixty men, leaving the former governor; but these sixty Suffaveans, behaving outrageously, were cut to pieces by the former occupants, who, from fear of the consequences, fled by night to the heights of the mountains; the castle was in consequence demolished. A little further was an unwalled city, named Sebran, which we found deserted, as everyone had fled: some in order to lay waste the country, and others from fear. Leaving this, we arrived at Derbant[2] in four days, and found all the people fled: some to the country of the Tartars; some to the head of the Caspian Sea; and some to the heights of the mountains: so that only the castle, which is large, well-built, and strong, held out; the towers were all newly erected, and on their summits were men with lances, slings, bows, etc. This castle has two gates, which are walled round with immense stones, like flint; and while about this city, I will give a description of it before going on to anything else. The city of Derbant, called by some Tenicarpi,[3] is situated on the Caspian Sea, near a high chain of mountains, called the Caspian Mountains, the only pass into Tartary or Circassia being in this place. Near this mountain there is an open bit of sea-beach of about a mile in extent, from the sea to the mountain, enclosed by two walls, commencing at the sea and going as far as the mountain, half a mile distant one from the other. These walls project into the sea up to six feet depth of water, so that no one either on foot or

---

[1] Astrabad.   [2] Derbend. See Zeno, p. 44.
[3] Demir Kapoo, or the Iron Gate.

horseback can pass except by the gates. Between these walls there are numerous houses, as this place is a port with many ships, which trade to Citrachan[1] and other places. They used to have large ships of eight hundred tons burden, but now only those of two hundred can enter. On the mountain is an almost impregnable castle, before which the Sufi monarch encamped. Passing this city towards the west, one has the sea on the east for a space of sixty miles, and when it bends round to the left the mountains recede from the sea, near which place, on the summit of a mountain, is the Church of Saint Mary of the Caspian Mountains. But I will not relate anything more about this, as it is not the proper place for it. The Sophi remained besieging the castle for twenty days, having dug three mines without any effect. They then excavated under the foundations of a tower, and filled the hollow up with wood; having set fire to this, a great smoke rose in the air, which, being seen by the governor, he sent to Ismael at midnight and proposed to capitulate on condition of safety for their lives and property; Ismael, seeing that very little was gained by the fire, was satisfied and agreed to their request. The following morning he took possession of the castle, in which was a great quantity of provisions, ammunition, and arms; and I myself saw many of the suits of armour which were brought into the presence of the sovereign.

CHAP. XVII.—Many chiefs give in their allegiance to Ismael, who, after his return in great triumph to Tauris, makes a second expedition against the Lord of Sammarcant, defeats, and puts him to death; he makes his sons swear fealty to him, but, having released them, they revolt.

Having made himself master of the castle he remained there eight or nine days to rest his men, and during this

[1] Astrakhan.

time many of the neighbouring chiefs came to give in their submission to him, putting on the red caftan, and swearing obedience to the Sophi. After that he returned to Tauris, where, on his arrival, the bazaars were richly decked out, a triumphal procession taking place in the city and rich banquets being held, according to custom. This monarch is almost, so to speak, worshipped, more especially by his soldiers, many of whom fight without armour, being willing to die for their master. They go into battle with naked breasts, crying out " Schiac, Schiac",[1] which, in the Persian language, signifies " God, God". Others consider him a prophet; but it is certain that all are of opinion that he will never die. While I was in Tauris I heard that the king is displeased with this adoration, and being called God. Their custom is to wear a red caftan, coming half a cubit over the head, which widens at the part which covers the head; it gets narrower towards the top, and is made with twelve fringes, a finger in thickness, symbolising the twelve Sacraments[2] of their religion; neither do they ever shave their beards or moustachios. They have made no change in their dress; their armour consists of cuirasses of gilt plates made of the finest steel of Syras. Their horse-armour is of copper: not like ours, but in pieces like those of Soria;[3] they also have helmets or head-pieces of a great weight of metal. Everyone of them rides on horseback: some with a lance, sword, and shield; others with bow and arrows, and a mace. While Ismael was in Tauris in the winter, there came three Negro ambassadors, who were received with great honour by the Sophi monarch, and having fulfilled their mission, returned to their master with many presents. Ismael, while resting, as we have related, received news that Jesilbas,[4] the Lord of Sammarcant, with an Usbec chief, with an immense army,

---

[1] " Sheikh, Sheikh." In this sense it means simply a holy man, not God. [2] Rather the twelve Imaums.

[3] Syria. [4] Sheibani Khan, the Usbeg. See Zeno, p 55.

was ravaging the country of Hirac,[1] that is, Iespatan[2] and other places. He determined to take vengeance, and taking the field, ordered all his troops to assemble at Cassan,[3] a place twenty days' journey to the east of Tauris; he chose this city for the muster, as it abounded in provisions. This city is walled with stone, and is three miles in circumference; there are great manufacturers of silk and cotton. After he had collected a hundred thousand men, learning from an Armenian Bishop of his adversary's immense army, he set out to meet him, having a deep grudge against these Tartars; as, on the previous occasion when peace was made with them, they broke the treaty before the year was out. Thus Ismael marched against the hostile army, which was at Strava,[4] on the confines of Hirach, in the year 1501. Leaving Cassan with his army, he went to Spaàn, four days' journey from Cassan, then hurried eagerly forward in pursuit of the enemy, who, hearing that Ismael was coming, retired to a river named Efra, anciently called Iarit,[5] rising in a lake called the lake of Corassan. In the middle of the river is a town named Chiraer, in which the Tartars took up a position, making head against the Suffaveans, who, on their arrival, encamped close to them, and prepared for battle; Ismael exhorting his troops and making such great promises, that all were eager for the fight. Then the Suffaveans were arrayed in three columns, the first being given to Busambet,[6] Lord of Sumacchia; the second to Gustagielit;[7] while the king commanded the third in person; the Tartars doing likewise. The following morning the Sophi ordered all his martial instruments to be sounded, while everyone shouted, "Long live Ismael our king". In this manner, at the first hour of the day the two armies en-

[1] Irak Ajemi.   [2] Ispahan.   [3] Kashan.
[4] Astrabad.   [5] Jarood.
[6] Most probably Bairambec, the king's brother-in-law, mentioned before.   [7] Custagialu, another brother-in-law of the king.

gaged, and, at the first assault, the Tartars repulsed the Sophi's division, and cut numbers to pieces. The Tartars still gaining, the Sophi seeing his destruction imminent, threw himself into the front rank of the battle, fighting bravely and giving new courage to his soldiers, who were confused by the rout of the first division; so that they, seeing their monarch in danger, made head and fought bravely against the Tartars for four hours. At length they put to flight the division commanded by Usbec, the others following the example; so that the Sophi gained great honour by his victory over the Tartars, and by showing in this, as in his previous enterprises, his great valour and generalship. Usbec and Jesilbas were taken prisoners with their sons; the heads of the two former were immediately cut off and sent, one to the Soldan, and the other to the Turk. In this battle there was greater slaughter on both sides than has ever taken place in Persia. He did not put the princes to death, but threw them into prison, and took away their realm: Strava,[1] Rassan, Heri, and other neighbouring places coming under his sway. When the Sophi was about to set out on his return journey, he caused the sons of Jesilbas to be brought before him, and said to them: "You are the sons of a great monarch, who, having broken his faith, and ravaged my territories, forced me to attack him; I have conquered him, and put him to death; but I will spare your lives, and allow you to return to your country on condition that you wear the red caftan, and that this river be your boundary." The young men replied, "Sire, we are content with what pleases your majesty, and will give in our submission." Thus they were released, and went to Sammarcant, while we returned to Cassan[2] and remained there all the winter of 1510.[3] When the young men returned to

[1] Astrabad, Khorassan, Herat.   [2] Kashan.
[3] The battle of Merv Shah Jehan, in which Sheibani Khan was killed, took place in 1514.

Sammarcant, the report reached their maternal uncle that they had promised allegiance to the Sophi. This uncle was one of the seven Soldans of Tartary, and came to them, and said: "Oh, fools, you have disgraced our name by wearing the ensign of a dog, who is neither Christian nor Mahometan," being exceedingly enraged with them. The young men answered: "We did all in our power, seeing our father dead, ourselves captives, our realm seized, and the troops dispersed." They then recanted, and put on the green caftan, while their uncle promised to assist them with troops against the Sophi. The year 1512 these princes, with their uncle, collected an immense army and entered the country of Corassan, belonging to the Sophi, and took the city of Chirazzo, cutting to pieces the Suffaveans, and, following up their victory, took several other places. The news coming to the Sophi, who was with his army at Coraldava, he set out immediately against the wearers of the green caftans, and chased them out of the country of Corassan, beyond the river Efra[1] into some mountains near the Caspian Sea, where he did not think it prudent to follow them, and so returned to Chirazzo, leaving one of his sons, four years of age, with a wise and brave general. He then went on to Tauris, leaving his whole army behind him from apprehension of the return of the Tartars.

CHAP. XVIII.—Some Persian noblemen invite the Ottoman to attack the Sophi in Persia, which he does with a great number of men, and having joined battle gains the victory, and thereupon returns to Amasia.

While the Sophi was in Tauris, some of his tributary chiefs in the territory bordering on the Turks seeing that the army was away in Corassan, came to an understanding with the Ottoman, and invited him to attack Persia; but for

[1] Jarood.

which invitation the Turk would never have mustered courage to do so. Being summoned by such great chiefs and principally by the Curds, who were enemies of the Sophi monarch, who inhabited the mountains of Bitlis,[1] knowing the power of the Tartars, and thinking that the Sophi would be in difficulties, he determined in 1514 to form an army and invade Persia, apprehensive that if the Sophi were victorious against the Tartars, he would make an alliance with the Soldan for his destruction. Hence he set out from Constantinople, and made his way with a great number of men to Amasia. Having provided all that was necessary in this place, he marched towards Toccat in the month of May. Here it will be convenient to recount the distance in miles of some places one from the other. First, then, from Constantinople to Amasia there are five hundred miles. Thence to the river Lais,[2] that is, Sivas, passing through the country of Toccat, are a hundred and fifty miles. From Lais, the frontier of the Sophi's dominions, to the Euphrates,[3] are a hundred miles; thence to Carpiert[4] eighty miles; to Amit fifty miles; thence to Bitlis two hundred and forty miles; from Bitlis to the lake[5] fifty miles; the lake is a hundred miles long; from thence to Coi[6] are fifty miles; and from Coi to Tauris seventy-five miles. Through the Sophi's dominions seven hundred and forty-five miles to Tauris, to Constantinople, in all 1395 miles. Having crossed the Toccat, he reached Sivas, and then the country of Arsingan,[7] making great booty, and sending many people to Amasia and Constantinople, principally artizans and skilled workmen, and also men of rank. The Sophi, who was in Tauris, hearing this, as his army was still in Corassan, determined

[1] Bitlis. See Zeno, p. 8.   [2] Iris.
[3] At Gumish Knaneh.   [4] Kharput.
[5] The Van lake, *at its nearest point*, is scarcely twenty English miles from Bitlis.   [6] Khoi is nearly a hundred miles from the Van lake.
[7] This is the shortest and most direct route from Tocat to Persia and quite different from the one just mentioned.

to collect as many men as he could. Therefore he hastily sent two great generals, one called Stugiali Mametbei, the other Carbec Sampira, into the country of Diarbec, who collected about twenty thousand men and marched with them to the fords of the Euphrates. But hearing that Selim was coming in great force, they did not feel strong enough to oppose him, but returned to Coi, where there is a wide valley or plain named Calderan. Here they halted, and the Sophi joined them in person. While they were here the Turk kept on advancing, so that he arrived not far from that place, ravaging and burning all the country he passed through. The Sophi monarch having left for Tauris in order to assemble more troops, the two generals seeing the enemy approaching so near determined to attack them. On the other hand, the Turks fought with desperation, as their provisions were failing, and if they had been defeated all would have perished. On the 23rd[1] of August, therefore, in the year 1514, the first division of the Suffaveans under Stugiali Mametbei, with half the troops, began the fight by routing those opposed to them, who were all inhabitants of Natolia, dispersing and cutting them to pieces. But Sinan Bassà, with his troops, who came from Roumania, coming up, many on both sides were killed, and at length the squadron of Stugiali was defeated, he himself being taken prisoner and his head cut off, which was afterwards sent to the Sophi. At this moment the second division of the Persians came up, and fought so valiantly, that they put the enemy to flight, so that the Turk was compelled to retire with his whole force to where the janissaries and the artillery were, his troops being in confusion; but the genius of Sinan Bassà rallied them, and the Suffaveans were routed and all the camp taken, together with one of the Sophi's wives. The whole army being lost, both generals were killed; but one of them named Carbec, before he died, was taken before the Turk, who said to him:

[1] Zeno. p. 60.

"O, dog, who art thou, who hast had the courage to oppose our majesty; knowest thou not that my father and I are vicars of the prophet Mahomet, and that God is with us?" The captain Carbec replied: "If God had been with you, you would not have come to fight against my master the Sophi; but I believe that God has taken away his hand from you." Then Selim said: "Kill this dog;" and the captain replied: "I know it is my hour now, but you, Selim, prepare yourself for another occasion, when my master will slay you as you now are slaying me;" upon which he was immediately put to death. The Turk, after his victory, rested at Coi, as many of his troops had been killed; the news of the defeat came to the Sophi in Tauris, who immediately set out with his men who had escaped, his wife named Tasluchanum, and his treasures, to Casibi,[1] in order to collect another army to oppose the Turk. This place is seven days' journey to the east of Tauris. The people of Tauris, seeing their king escaping, were in dread of the Turk, and sent two ambassadors to him with presents. The Turk then came to Tauris, and immediately seeking out seven hundred families of skilled workmen, sent them to Constantinople. He remained in Tauris three days when, being in want of provisions and fearing lest the Persians should attack him in great force, he departed; on his journey he was greatly distressed for want of supplies and harassed by the Iberians, but at length arrived at Amasia.

CHAP. XIX.—The Sophi sends ambassadors to the Soldan, to Alidolat, and the Iberians, making a league with them against the Turk; to whom he also sends ambassadors, ironically making rich presents to him, and threatening him. The Turk, having attacked Alidolat, defeats him, and puts him to death, with two of his sons.

On the return of the Sophi to Tauris he determined to send ambassadors to Cairo, to Alidolat, and to the Iberians,

[1] Casveen.

this happening in the month of October. Those sent to the Soldan[1] arrived in December, and made known to him the object of their mission, to which the Soldan replied that he would be well satisfied to assist the Sophi and make an alliance with him against the Turk, sending him aid in troops and trying their fortune together. The Sophi, however, made it a condition, that if the Turk sent any ambassadors to him he should not receive them, either publicly or secretly, or else the peace would be broken between them; and thus was the alliance concluded between the Soldan and the Sophi. The other ambassadors who went on the same mission to Alidolat, had the same success, and equally so with the Iberians, who besides agreed to assist Ismael with the largest force they could raise everytime he went against Selim. After this the Sophi sent legates to the Turk in Amasia, with a sceptre of gold ornamented with jewels, a saddle and a sword likewise covered with jewels,[2] and a letter, saying: "We, Ismael, Lord of Persia, herewith send you these regal presents, equal in value to your realm; if you are a man, keep them well, as I shall come and take them back, and not them only, but also your throne and life." Selim hearing this wished to put the ambassadors to death, but his Pashas dissuaded him, and so contenting himself with cutting off their noses and ears he let them go, saying: "Tell your master that I treat him as a dog, and that he may do his worst." [The countries I am about to mention are under the sway of the Turk, kept in subjection by his janissaries. They rule over the country of Arsingan and Baibiert,[3] where there are many towns and castles; these countries are the Turkish frontiers towards Trebizond,[4] and are both in Lesser Armenia. Thence from the

---

[1] Khafour el Ghouri, called Campson Gauri later on.
[2] We have an instance of this sort in our own annals, viz., the presents sent by the Dauphin to Henry V.   [3] Baiburt.
[4] These were the latest conquests made by Selim from Persia.

Euphrates, the country of Diarbec, the metropolis of which is Amit, in Greater Armenia; also, the land of Mosul and the great plain as far as the borders of Bagadet, being part of Mesopotamia.] Matters being at this crisis, the Turk came to the Toccat and to Amasia in 1515, with a few of his troops, as he had divided his forces into two parts. One he had given the command of to Scander, sending him to attack a city belonging to Ismael called Tania,[1] of a hundred and fifty thousand inhabitants. With the other division he set out on an enterprise against Alidolat, who had taken up a position in the strongholds of the mountains. The latter prince hearing of the intention of the Turk, sent ambassadors to him, saying that he had always been his friend, and that he did not know his reasons for seizing his dominion; but, nevertheless, he resolved to die like a brave man. The Turk replied that he wished to give him a lesson as to what business he had to receive ambassadors from the Sophi, and promise him aid against himself. The general Scander took Tania by assault with great slaughter. The Ottoman marching towards Cassaria,[2] near Alidolat, the Alidolians attacked him, but were repulsed and roughly handled, Alidolat[3] being taken prisoner with two of his sons, and their heads cut off; the others fled to the mountains. Thus the Turk gained a great victory, and the captain, Scander, an equal one, as he caused a great massacre among the people of Tania. Having achieved these successes, the Turk determined to leave his sons in Amasia, while he himself returned to Constantinople.

[1] Euxaghly, near Malatia, called Ciamassum by Knolles, who says it was situated near the confluence of the Melas (Kara Su) with the Euphrates. [2] Kaisarieh.
[3] Knolles says that Aladeules was betrayed by his nephew, Alis Beg, who became the Turkish governor of the country.

CHAP. XX.—The Turk makes an expedition against the Soldan, and meeting him in battle, defeats him, the Soldan being slain.

In the year 1516, the Turk hearing of the agreement between the Soldan and the Sophi, and seeing that Ismael was hard pressed by those of the green caftans, determined to set out with a large army against the Soldan. In the same year, in the month of May, he sent his troops across the strait into Natolia under his general Sinan Bassa, with a number of arquebusiers and artillerymen, commanding him to march towards Caramania. Traversing the country of the Turcomans he arrived at a place named Albustan, and remained there several days to refresh his troops. The Sophi hearing this sent envoys to the Sultan of the Mamelukes, Campson, named the Gauri, to tell him that he would advance from one quarter and that the Gauri should do the same from the other, and together crush Sinan Pasha. The Soldan agreed to all, and, having assembled a great number of soldiers, leaving Cairo, went to Aleppo; the Turk hearing this, set out from Constantinople on the 5th June, 1516, to join Sinan Bassa, and while on the journey sent forward as his envoys the Cadi Lascher,[1] and Zachaia Bassa to enquire of the Soldan his reasons for coming in this unexpected way to Aleppo. But he received no satisfactory answer, which plainly shewed an understanding with the Sophi. Therefore the Turk summoned all the Doctors and learned men, and enquired of them the will of God. They answered that it was his duty first to root-out that obnoxious thorn, and then to follow the path in which God would guide him. Hearing the reply he marched toward Aleppo with an immense army, and great rejoicings, and on his arrival there encamped in a beautiful plain near the venerated tomb of the prophet David, sending

[1] Kazi Asker.

the vanguard in advance in four divisions; so that the troops were under arms both night and day. The Mamelukes, arriving the following day, arrayed themselves in order of battle.[1] The Turk having information of this, rose to his feet in his tent, making supplication to God, beseeching him for his great name's sake and the reverence they bore him, that he would give the victory that day to the army of good Mussulmans. Having ended his prayer, he mounted his horse and went to exhort the Bassas to put their troops in array, which was done; the different pieces of artillery, both large and small, being put in order, they began to march; all his pages, about twelve hundred in number, mounted on horses and clad with rich vests, while attentive to their rank and order, made prayer to God for the success of their Sovereign. The monarch also arrayed himself, having in attendance a noble youth named Mergis, and three thousand men clad in dresses embroidered with gold, and armed with bows, who were his slaves. On the left were three thousand five hundred of the men of his court, then seventeen hundred Solacchi and the white roses of the garden of the camp, and thirteen thousand janissaries with arquebuses and pieces of artillery. On the left of these were the troops of Natolia, armed with lances, at the head of whom was their Sangiacco[2] named Sachinalogier, chief of the Turcomans. On the right were the fighting men of Greece with their captain Sinan Bassa, and the Begliarbei of the newly acquired territory of Azimia, named Buichimehemet, with all the warriors of Amasia sword in hand. Arrayed in this manner on the 24th[3] of August, at the third hour of the day they joined in a fierce and sanguinary contest which lasted till mid day. Opposed to the Greeks was the ruler of Damascus, a great chief named Sibes,[4] and opposed to the

---

[1] This was contrary to the advice of Algazeli, who advised Campson to protract the war and not to risk all on one battle.
[2] Sanjak.   [3] Knolles says the 7th.   [4] Sybeius Baluan.

Natolians was Caierbec[1] the ruler of Aleppo; Sinan Bassa fighting bravely drove back those opposed to him as far as their standards, and the other troops seeing the valour of the Bassa followed up their success, both parties bearing themselves bravely, and repulsing the enemy in turn five or six times. At last the ruler of Aleppo turned his back, and fled with all his troops, when the Bassa turned his arms against the ruler of Damascus, who was not able to resist any longer and fled to the great Soldan. He was pursued by one of the Grecian warriors, who cut off his head, and shortly afterwards the Soldan[2] Campson the Gauri was slain. Their army being routed, abandoning their tents, arms, and treasures, a great number of the Mamelukes fled to Aleppo, and having remained there a short time went on to Damascus and Cairo. The Turkish monarch coming to Aleppo, remained there some time in order to make himself master of several castles in which he placed garrisons of janissaries, and then sent Janus Bassa,[3] with some of the Greek troops to pursue the enemy. Having overtaken them near a city called Caman, Caierbec, the lord of Aleppo, and another chief named Algazeli approached. The lord of Aleppo advanced to meet the Bassa, promising allegiance to the great Turkish monarch; Algazeli fled to Cairo, and Caierbec came to the presence of the Sultan, by whom he was well received and presented with rich gifts of gold, silk, wool

---

[1] Knolles says that the Mamelukes lost the battle through the treachery of Caierbec, who had a secret understanding with Selim. The Turks were almost put to rout by Sibes and Algazeli, when the desertion of the Governor of Aleppo and the opportune arrival of Sinan Pasha turned the fortune of the fight. Sibes and Campson Gauri were both killed in the battle, which took place, according to Knolles, on the 7th of August, 1516, the same day that the battle of Schalderan took place two years before.

[2] Kafoor el Ghouri, the last Soldan of Egypt but one, died 1516, and was succeeded by Tomant Bey.

[3] Jonnses Pasha put to death soon afterwards by Selim.

and cotton, and made to sit down with the great lords. The monarch rode towards Damascus, and, before entering it, had his tent erected near the city, and held a court with great splendour and magnificence, as there were people speaking seventy-two different languages in the city. This court was one of the most splendid ever seen. Having rested several days in the city he ordered two of the Greek captains named Mametbei and Scanderbei, to advance with their troops to Gazzara[1] on the frontiers of the district, and to halt there. Setting out with this command, they were on the journey greatly harassed by Moors and Arabs, but nevertheless arrived at Gazzara and entered the place, expecting to enjoy themselves.

CHAP. XXI.—Tomombei, the new Soldan, hearing of the victory of the Turk, sends Algazeli against the Turks in Gazzara; but Sinan Bassà going to their assistance, confronts and defeats him. The Turk leaves Damascus and goes to Jerusalem, where he gives alms and offers sacrifices.

The new Soldan of Cairo, the great Diodar[2] surnamed Tomombei,[3] was quickly informed of this victory; and Algazeli who was a brave General, on his arrival at Cairo asked permission to go and attack this force. The Turks who had arrived at Gazzara stood firm, and this Algazeli, setting out from Cairo with five thousand well armed Mamelukes, hurried through the country raising troops. The Turks at Gazzara became apprehensive, but nevertheless determined to perish sword in hand; the Grand Turk, on receiving the news, determined to reinforce the troops at Gazzara, and for this purpose send Sinan[4] Bassà with fifteen thousand

[1] Gaza.   [2] Devetdar.
[3] Tomant Bey, last Soldan of Egypt.
[4] Sinan Pasha, Selim's best general—his valour and generalship had saved him upon more than one occasion; for instance, at the battle of Schalderan, and again in the conflict with the Mamelukes.

men. Algazeli having left Cairo arrived at Catia, and after crossing the sandy desert and coming to a caravanserai or villa where he halted, received intelligence of Sinan's arrival at Gazzara; though this was to his great disgust, as it prevented him accomplishing his object, he nevertheless plucked up spirits, and exhorted his men to fight valiantly, promising them the victory. Having arranged an assault on the Turks during the night, news of this determination came to the ears of the enemy, and Sinan Bassà arrayed his troops for the battle, and resolved to conquer or die; there being no other alternative left them, as they were surrounded by such a number of Moors. That night they held great rejoicings with salutes and bonfires, praying to Allah for victory, and set out on their march; hence the people of Gazzara imagined that they were retreating to join their sovereign, the Grand Turk, and therefore they put to death all the wounded in Gazzara, and informed Algazeli that our troops had fled. This caused him great satisfaction, but at the third hour of the day, seeing the dust made by the army which he thought had fled, coming to meet him in battle, his satisfaction was turned to disgust, and he seemed struck with astonishment. Our men drawing near, dismounted, tightened the girths of their horses, and then asking forgiveness one of another, they shook hands, embraced, and commenced praying to God for the sake of his prophet Mahomet, and his four vicars, Abu Beker, Omar, Osman, and Ali, and all the other prophets, his predecessors, that he would give the victory to the army of the true Mussulmans. Then Sinan Bassà, turning to the army, exhorted them all, saying that they had often before routed larger armies and gained more important battles than these;[1] tell-

---

[1] Knolles says, in his *History of the Turks*, p. 535:—"The Bassà had placed his harquebusiers in the wings of his battell, which were raunged of a great length in their rankes, thereby to use their peeces at more liberty and with more ease to enclose the enemie: in the middle

ing them that they should stand firm, as he who was destined to die would perish even if he fled, and he who was not destined to fall would not do so even if he fought on; and that as male wethers are proper for sacrifices, so ought they to fight for their sovereign. "Let us avenge our friends, whom these dogs have slain at the first outset, whose corpses, if they could speak, would cry, 'Slay, slay'; if you conquer you will receive great rewards from our ruler, and obtain great fame, as many of you who are now of low rank will be promoted." They all replied, saying: "God give long life to

were placed the horsemen to receive the first charge of the Mamalukes. Gazelles approaching the enemy, sent before the troupes of the Arabian light horsemen to trouble the wings of the enemies battell, and with a square battell of his Mamalukes charged the middle battell of the Turks. The battell was a great while most terrible, and the victorie doubtfull; for, although the Turkes in number farre exceeded, yet were they not able to endure the armed and courageous Mamalukes, but were glad to give ground; and, quite disordered by the breaking-in of the Mamalukes, as men discouraged, began to look about them which way they might flie; when, by the commaundement of Sinan, the harquebusiers, who, with the first volley of their shot, had repulsed the Arabians, wheeling about enclosed all the enemies battell. By which means both men and horse were a farre off slaine, with the multitude of the deadly shot, where true valour helped not them, so on every side enclosed. For where any troupe of the Mamalukes pressed forward upon the Turkes, they quickly retired, and in all places of the battell, as much as they could, shunned to encounter their enemies with their horsemen, labouring onely to gaule them with shot. Gazelles seeing his horses spent with extreame wearinesse, and that he was not to expect any further helpe, his Arabians now beginning to fall from him; and also, considering that many of his most valiant souldiours were either slaine or wounded, and having also himselfe received a great wound in his necke, he, with the rest of his armie, made way through the middest of his enemies, and having lost divers of his ensignes, fled back againe to Caire, through the same sandie deserts whereby he came. In this battell was lost the Governor of Alexandria and Orchamus, Governor of Caire (both men of great account among the Mamalukes), and beside them a great number of Arabians, with a thousand or more of the Mamaluke horseman. Neither got Sinan a joyfull or unbloudie victorie, having lost above two thousand of his best horsemen, and amongst them certaine commaunders, men of great marke."

our sovereign; may the whole earth be subjected to him; and let him who does not submit be put to death. Forward! forward!" Having marched, therefore, and the two armies having met, the Circassians resisted our attack with great courage and daring, each side repulsing the other in turn several times from the third hour till noon, numbers being slain. At last the Circassians were routed, while our troops were highly elated with the victory and immense booty; the Mamelukes fled to Cairo, pursued by some of our men. The others returned to Gazzara with Sinan Bassà, stuffing with straw the heads of the dead chiefs, while the others they fixed to the palm trees in memory of the battle. The great monarch sent two hundred Solacchi to meet Sinan Bassà, and request him to ride forward and meet him in a certain place. But not finding the Bassà, they set out on their return. On the march, numbers of them died, and being again attacked by the Arabs, all but six were killed. These rejoined the great monarch and reported that they had heard nothing of Sinan or of his army. The Sultan hearing this rose up in a great fury to march to the rescue of the valiant Greeks; but just then there arrived some Moors with the news of the rout of Algazeli by the Turkish troops, who had returned in triumph to Gazzara. The Moors were rewarded for their tidings, and the emperor was in the highest spirits; marching from Damascus he came to Peneti, where the two hundred Solacchi were slain, which place he sacked and burnt. He then went to Jerusalem, but had a great deal of rain and bad weather on the road, which caused much suffering and the death of many. In Jerusalem the monarch bestowed much money on the poor of the city, and also made offerings of good rams; so that the sacrificing priests were satisfied with his bounty. Proceeding on the route to Gazzara they arrived at a fearful gorge,[1] where only two horses could advance abreast. The

---

[1] Petra?

Arabs had seized the defile and had collected huge stones above to roll down when the Sultan was passing; they had also numerous archers. The monarch having heard this, ordered the artillery and the arquebuses to be prepared; but when the need came they could not be discharged, owing to the wind and rain. Nevertheless, the valiant janissaries managed to make use of the arquebuses and put to flight the Moors with great slaughter. When we approached Gazzara the valiant Greek troops, fully armed and sumptuously clad in the spoils of the enemy, came a bowshot out of the city to meet their sovereign. The Moors seeing this great array were filled with astonishment, while the Sanzacchi dismounted to kiss the hand of the Sultan, and the whole army separated into two parts, having the monarch in the centre, and saluted him. Then he met Sinan Bassà, and thanked him, the army, and the Spachi, which means noblemen, and made them many presents. Having remained four days at Gazzara, they advanced to Casali, where they had not been able to go previously from want of water. But the desert being full of water from the rains, they proceeded at their ease, and immediately on arriving Casali was given up to pillage, in retaliation for the attack on the Sultan in the valley above mentioned.

CHAP. XXII.—The Turk marches on Cairo, and the Soldan, with Algazeli, confronts him; but in the battle is defeated and flies in disguise; while the Turk enters the capital of the Soldan.

We then set out on the straight route to Cairo, where the newly created Soldan Tomombei[1] was making preparations by digging moats and raising embankments of earth[2] with a great number of labourers. He also posted pieces of artillery with the design when our army appeared of sweeping it all

---

[1] Tomant Bey.   [2] At Maharra, six miles from Cairo.

away, and by a sally of fourteen thousand Mamelukes and twenty thousand auxiliaries to rout it utterly. When we arrived in the country six thousand Mamelukes deserted, and informed the Grand Turk of everything. Therefore he turned suddenly into another road, which was unguarded, and in which he could not be molested by the enemy's artillery. The Circassians and the Soldan seeing that the Sultan was advancing by another route, attacked us with great shouts and yells: Algazeli against the Greek troops, a vizier named Allem[1] against those of Natolia, and the Soldan against the Grand Turk himself; so that, from the morning till mid-day, there was a fierce fight. And in the battle, unfortunately, Sinan Bassà was killed,[2] and with him a great number of his retainers who had partaken of his bread and salt, and who, clad in garments he had given them, devoted themselves to death with their master. They bathed him with their tears, and having enveloped him in a fine cloth, and having sprinkled him in some water called Abzenzom found at Mecca,[3] they buried him in a grave they dug for him. Mustafà Bassà, seeing that all depended on him, with loud shouts and great valour began the combat, which being seen by the men of Natolia, at the head of whom he was, they got so enraged that they cut down the Circassians like grass in the most marvellous manner. The troops of the monarch and of Greece also fought bravely, but at the hour of evening prayers each retired from fatigue, and the Circassians, wearied out, were put to flight, part into Cairo and part to the open country.[4] The Greeks pursued them till night, plundering and slaughtering them;

---

[1] Allem, called Heylims the Devetdar, by Knolles.

[2] By a Mamaluke captain named Bidon, frequently mentioned by Knolles.   [3] The well of Zemzem.

[4] Knolles says, Tomant Bey, after showing great personal courage, was forced to order a retreat, which soon became a flight. The battle was fought on the 24th January, 1517.

the monarch remained that night on the field of battle, and ordered all the prisoners to be put to death, which was done. They remained here three days, and on the fourth reached the river Nile at a place called Bichieri, where they halted two days. The Mamelukes who had advanced joined the Soldan to the number of nine thousand, planning a night attack; but the Sultan, hearing this, ordered the troops to remain under arms all night. But the enemy, hearing this, changed their plan and determined to attack us by day, and thus came on with fearful yells. The janizzaries fought bravely, and the troops of Greece mounted and fought on horseback. Still, not being able to conquer the enemies that day, both armies retreated. The following morning the great monarch rose with the dawn, and, having returned thanks to God, ordered all the army to be put in array, all mounting, moving with great solemnity and display against the Circassians, who, with their usual cries, began the battle, one side being soon hidden from the other by the dust. The Mamelukes[1] were desperate, and wished for nothing better than to die sword in hand, it appearing to them a disgrace to escape and leave all their possessions in the hands of the enemy, a calamity from which God preserve every one, and more especially all good Mahometans. The monarch, seeing that he could not destroy the Circassians, ordered the city to be set on fire, which the janizzaries did in several places. The Mamelukes, seeing this, cried out for quarter with loud and terrible yells; and the Sultan, having pity on them, ordered the fire to be extinguished, it being almost by a miracle that the whole city was not burnt down. The Circassians renewed the contest with such vigour that the arrows fell like rain; and so many fell on both sides, that the streets of Cairo ran blood, the fight continuing the entire day. At night, the

[1] The Mamelukes were repulsed, and were then attacked in Cairo by Selim.

Circassians, being faint and exhausted, retired into a mosque, in which as a citadel they kept up a gallant defence for three days and three nights. But at length, a grand attack being made, the mosque was taken by storm. The Soldan Tomombei escaped in disguise, when the great monarch went to rest and his followers to get booty and prisoners; the heads of these prisoners were afterwards cut off by the banks of the Nile. Algazeli, who had been away from Cairo in order to collect forces of Arabs, was already approaching the city when he was informed that the Turk had proclaimed a free pardon to all the Circassians who came in in the course of three days. Hence many Circassians who had been concealed presented themselves and received gifts; Algazeli also did the same, and gave in his submission to the king. And to him also were presents made. After this the Grand Turk, with the great white standard, with drums, fifes, and naccare, went to the residence of the Soldan; while on the way, they discovered a conspiracy of some Mamelukes who wished to escape, for which some were put to death, and others confined in certain prisons till some days afterwards, when they were drowned in the Nile. In this manner did this monarch Sultan Selim revenge himself on his enemies; also, when at Cairo, hearing that the people of a town named Catia had insulted our soldiers who had been sent there, he commissioned Algazeli and a Beglerbei to go and chastise the Moors and to plunder the city. This being done and the Moors being all put to death, the other places in the vicinity became quite submissive.

CHAP. XXIII.—The Turk sends Ambassadors to the Soldan, who had fled, advising him to submit; but, these men being killed by the Circassians, he sends Mustafà with an army to revenge them. The Soldan is defeated; and, being pursued by Mustafà, is taken prisoner, and brought to the Grand Turk, who causes him to be impaled by one of the gates of Cairo.

We remained at Cairo alert to all the movements of the Soldan, who had crossed the Nile and taken flight into the country of the Saettò.[1] As he wished to be informed of what the Turks were doing, he sent secret emissaries to Cairo to stir up the citizens to molest our troops. While things were in this train, Omar,[2] a lord of the Moors, came secretly to kiss the hand of the Sultan, told him all, and was rewarded by a good Sangiacato in the regions of the Saettò. Sentinels were posted everywhere, and artillery to command the river, so that not even a bird could have crossed. They then determined to send two chiefs with the Cadis of Cairo to the Soldan to advise him to submit himself to the Grand Turk, who promised to give him the government of Cairo. But the Circassians, when they got the ambassadors into their power, put them to death. The monarch, hearing of this cruelty, caused bridges to be erected over the river, and commanded Mustafà to cross with the entire army, which was reported to the Soldan, who, with five thousand Circassians and ten thousand Arabs, advanced to meet them by forced marches in one day and one night. At this juncture part of the Greek troops had crossed and others were crossing, not having any intelligence of this; but God so willed it that those who were seeking a good spot to pitch the Sultan's tent, saw the dust raised by the approaching squadrons, and, being utterly amazed, rode off to tell the news. The monarch ordered Mustafà to mount and set the army in array. The

---

[1] Delta?   [2] Called Albuchomar by Knolles.

Circassians charged and drove back our troops as far as the standard, but, being reinforced, we repulsed them; the Circassians, seeing this, again closed and drove us back with such slaughter that the blood ran in rivers. The Moors fought only to give the Circassians time to rest, so that our men were at a great disadvantage, fighting on bravely still, but with immense loss. The Bassa, who was in attendance on the Sultan, seeing this, and that the day was in a way to be lost, seized his scimitar and bosdocan furiously, and rushed towards the Soldan, intending to cut the life out of his body before dying himself. The Greeks, seeing this act of valour, struggled on to assist their chief. And it is certain that if their courage had failed them then, they would have lost their lives, as they would all have been cut to pieces. But their bravery showed the Soldan that they would gain the victory, and, seeing that from a great and rich monarch he would become a poor and solitary outcast, looking up to heaven he bewailed his sad lot with such bitter words as to make all who heard him pity him. After many words, accompanied with tears, he took to flight, riding night and day till he reached a bridge, where he rested a short time. Mustafà[1] and the Greeks pursued him, but he managed to keep in advance of them. The Turk set out from Cairo, and halted half a day's journey distant from Mustafà, who had pursued the Soldan for four days and as many nights, till he forced him from fatigue to take refuge in a Casal of the Moors. Our men, also being very much fatigued, could not get possession of him; so they determined to write to the people of the Casal ordering them under pain of fire and sword to prevent the Soldan proceeding any further. Thence the chief of the fortress, named Sheikh Assaim, told all his men, and Tomombei and the Circassians were surrounded by the Moors, so that they could not escape till the arrival of our men, who soon got

---

[1] Mustafà, Algazeli, and Caierbec were sent in pursuit.

them into their power. The Circassians threw themselves into a neighbouring lake, while our soldiers cut some of them to pieces and made prisoners of the others. Tomombei was taken standing up to his knees in water, and conducted to the Bassà, who despatched a troop to the monarch with intelligence of all that had occurred. The messenger on his arrival was received with great rejoicings, and all the Sangiacchi and the lords kissed the Grand Turk's hand. The Soldan was not brought to his presence, but kept in good custody in a tent near his. After this there was another battle with the Moors in another fortress near the Nile; the inhabitants and some Mamelukes were continually killing and robbing our men. Mustafà set out and destroyed the fortress, and, after remaining four days, returned to the Turk, who was holding a court, and had commanded that Tomombei Soldan[1] should be led through the country of Cairo on a mule, with a chain round his neck, and that at a gate of the city called Bebzomele he should be impaled, which was immediately done. This was the termination of the kingdom of the Mamelukes and the commencement of the greater power of Selim Sultan. The history of this last expedition of Selim against the Soldan and the Mamelukes was carefully written by a *Cadi Lascher*,[2] who was with the army, to a Cadi in Constantinople, and translated from the Turkish into Tuscan on the 22nd October, 1517.

In 1524, in the month of August, news came that the celebrated Sophi monarch was dead, and that his younger son had seized the power, but was opposed by the elder with a great number of soldiers. Ismael had left four sons, the eldest named Schiacthecmes,[3] the second Alcas el Mirza,[4]

---

[1] He was first tortured to make him reveal where he was supposed to have hidden the great treasures of Campson Gauri.
[2] Cazi Asker.   [3] Shah Tamasp.
[4] Elias Mirza, King of Shirvan. *Vide* Alessandri.

the third Päerham[1] el Mirza, the fourth Sam el Mirza; Mirza being a title meaning prince. The eldest was then fourteen years old, and his father had left him as a governor a man, named Chiocha Sultan, to govern the kingdom till the boy came of age to rule. This regent was wise, and of a great influence. But it came to pass that some of the other nobles, from envy of the regent, began to make war on one another, and having taken the field, came as far as the tent of Schiacthecmes,[2] wishing to slay the regent; but the matter was compromised.

[1] Bahram Mirza.   [2] Shah Tamasp.

THE TRAVELS

OF A

MERCHANT IN PERSIA.

THE

TRAVELS OF A MERCHANT IN PERSIA.

Chap. I.—The apology the Author makes for this his Narrative.

It is well-known that naturally all men, and especially students, love knowledge, and, therefore, always go out of their way to investigate new things. On this account I have thought that by writing an account of my travels in Persia and narrating all that I have, with my slight genius, been able to learn in the east, in the space of eight years and eight months of my stay there, that these my writings might be interesting to my readers, both by the novelty of the subject and by the information respecting so many great cities, peoples, and foreign customs. And if in any passage I become confused and lengthy, I ask my kind readers' pardon, as it will not proceed from anything but my being unaccustomed to composition; but they may be assured for the rest that I will tell nothing but the truth of what I have seen and heard, not exaggerating anything, but simply narrating as becomes an honest merchant who does not know how to adorn his tale by his words.

And, to begin about the places and regions where I have been, I will say that when Shiec Ismael came against Aladuli[1] in Caramania, in 1507, I happened to be in his army at Arsingan,[2] where I remained forty days, and afterwards at Cimischasac,[3] when I crossed the river Euphrates,

---

[1] Alla ed Douleh. [2] Erzingan. See p. 7, Caterino Zeno.
[3] Tchimish Gazak, or birthplace of Zimisces; identified by the Armenians with the ancient Hierapolis, though called by its present name

entering the country of Aladuli. I was present also during his expedition against Sirmacchia[1] and the country of Sirvan,[2] and in Tauris, on Siech Ismael's return there with his army. I was absent, however, when there were districts and castles taken, and some battles fought and victories gained, by the same Siech Ismael near Dierbec. Nevertheless, I will recount them, having been enabled to learn the facts from different persons who were present. This I did easily, as I knew perfectly the languages of Ajemi,[3] Turkey, and Arabia.

Chap. II.—The cities one finds on leaving Aleppo to go to Persia; of the city of Bir, of Orfa, and of the fountain of Saint Abram; the water of which cures fever: and the fishes there are in it; of a well which cures lepers; and of the magnificence of the above-mentioned city of Orfa.

And to return to my journey, I say that on leaving Aleppo to go to Persia in general, and to Tauris in particular, at three days' journey distant is a place named Bir,[4] which is on the bank of the river Euphrates on the other side, and is of small extent. Sultan Cartibec[5] had it walled round, as it was not fortified before, but always had a strong fine castle, which has been besieged by many, and also by Diodar,[6] who rebelled against the Soldan, without anyone having been able to take it. All the country, the city, and castles which are across the river, have always after the birth of Zimisces. the Byzantine Emperor; it is now a town of about five thousand inhabitants, but without any relics of the Roman period.   [1] Schamachi.

[2] Shirvan.   [3] Irak-Ajemi.

[4] Bir, on the Euphrates; formerly a large town. It was taken and destroyed by Timour, the ancient Apamea.   [5] Kaiid Beg.

[6] Devetdar, an officer of Mamelukes. Tomant Bey, the last of the Soldans of Cairo, defeated and put to death by Selim I. in 1517, after a gallant resistance to the Turkish arms; he succeeded Campson Gauri.

been, and still are, under the sway of the King of Persia; on this side of the river, towards Aleppo, all is governed by the Soldan of Cairo. In all the countries, provinces, towns, and fortresses between Aleppo and Tauris, and from Tauris as far as Derbant, on the shores of the Caspian Sea, I have remained some time and traded, as you will learn when I come to relate about them. Two days' journey from Bir there is a large town named Orfa,[1] which the inhabitants and their chronicles say was anciently founded and walled round by the great Nembroth;[2] and in truth they show very ancient walls extending ten miles in circuit without a ditch round them. There is within it a magnificent castle with walls of immense size and thickness, but also without any fosse, and in it there are two fine lofty columns, equal in size to those of Venice, in the Piazza of St. Mark, on which they say that Nembrot had his idols, and they are still as upright as when they were first erected. In this city is also the place where our father Abraham was about to sacrifice to God his son Isaac (?).

[1] Orfa, anciently called Edessa by the successors of Alexander, and more recently Rhoa. It became a Roman colony, and one of their chief strongholds against the Parthians. At the time of the Crusades it was the residence of the Courtneys, who were called Counts of Edessa, and was taken from them by Saladin. Timour sacked it in 1426; it is now subject to Turkey. Kinneir, in his *Geographical Memoir of Persia*, says:—" It is situated in a barren country, sixty-seven miles from Bir and two hundred and thirty-two from Diarbekr. The town is surrounded by a stone wall and defended by a citadel. The ditch, which is broad and deep, is hewn out of the rock, and, when necessary, can be filled with water from the river Scirtus. The houses are well built, and the inhabitants, who are composed of Turks, Arabs, Armenians, Jews, and Nestorians, are said to amount to about twenty thousand souls. The chief ornaments of the city are a magnificent mosque consecrated to Abraham, and the cathedral of the Armenians, now fallen to decay. On a mountain, which overlooks and commands the citadel, are the ruins of a building called by the Arabs the Palace of Nimrod, and several extraordinary subterraneous apartments apparently of great antiquity."

[2] Nimrod.

And it is said that in this very place at that time there sprang forth an excellent clear fountain, large enough to work seven mills in the city and to irrigate the country round. And where it sprang forth the Christians built a church dedicated to the holy Abraham,[1] which when they had lost power was changed by the Mahometans into a mosque, while to the present the fountain is called the fountain of Abraham (which in Turkish is "Ibrahim calil bonare"). It is even now much reverenced by both Christians and Mahometans for the virtue it possesses of curing anyone ill of fever who goes in with faith. In this fountain are many fish,[2] which are never caught, but are considered sacred.

Six miles outside the city is a wonderful well which heals lepers, provided they go there with devotion, keeping this order. First they must fast five days, and each day of the fast they drink frequently of the water, and every time they drink they must wash themselves with it, but after the five days they do not wash any more, but still drink up to the tenth or twelfth day; and so the virtue of the holy water frees them from this infirmity, or at least keeps it from going further. And I have seen this effect with my own eyes in Orfa, many who came infirm going away well. On my way back to Aleppo from Tauris, I came to Orfa, where was a Cypriote named Hector, who lived at Nicosia; this man, by going to the sacred well, came back freed from many complaints. This city used to be a regal one, as is seen by the ancient monuments and buildings. There are ten or twelve large churches built of marble, more imposing than I can describe in words. This city has as beautiful and pleasant a country about it as one could wish.[3] Towards

---

[1] Now the mosque of Ibrahim al Khaleel.

[2] The same tradition prevails now, and the fish alluded to seem as plentiful as ever, it being held sacrilege to catch them.

[3] The region is now very barren.

the west there is a fine hill covered with inhabited villas, and many ancient castles now deserted. There are vast and beautiful gardens close to the city, full of all kinds of fruit, with as great an abundance of provisions as one can desire. Besides, it is on the routes from Bagadet,[1] Persia, Turkey, and Soria;[2] and the inhabitants are honest and good. This city is the first in the dominions of Sultan Scicch Ismael, and is a metropolis and capital city of a province named Dierbec, in which are six large cities with five hundred fortresses, as shall be related.

CHAP. III.—Of the castle Jumilen; of the great city Caramit, founded by the Emperor Constantine; and of the fine buildings, churches, and streams there are in it, and which is inhabited more by Christians, Greeks, Armenians, and Jews, than by Mahometans; of the province of Dierbec, its cities, and by whom it is governed.

Two days' journey from Orfà is a castle named Jumilen,[3] which is on a mountain, with walls not very strong, and with a small fosse dug out of the rock. Round the castle is a town of houses dug into the mountain like grottoes, in which the peasants live: a low race like gipsies. This district is very arid, and has no water; but in the grottoes they have excavated they have made deep reservoirs, which they fill with water in the spring, and which serve them the whole year. Three days' journey from this castle is the great city of Caramit,[4] which, according to their chronicles, was built by the Emperor Constantine, and has a circuit of ten or twelve miles.[5] It is surrounded by walls of black stone, so placed, that it appears painted, and has in the whole circumference three hundred and sixty towers and

---

[1] Bagdad.   [2] Syria.   [3] Jemelcyn.
[4] Kara Amid, or Amid-Diarbekr. See Zeno.
[5] An error. The Emperor Constantine repaired the old Roman walls only.

turrets. I rode the whole circuit twice for my pleasure, looking at the towers and turrets of very different forms and sizes;[1] still no one who is not a geometrician would not be pleased to see them, so marvellous are the structures; and in several parts on them I saw the imperial arms carved with an eagle with two heads and two crowns.[2] In this city are many wonderful churches, palaces, and marble monuments, inscribed with Greek letters. The churches are about the size of that of SS. Giovanni and Paulo or the Frati Minori at Venice. And in many of them are relics of saints and particularly of Saint Quirinus, which, at the time the Christians had the upper hand, were shown openly; and in the church of St. George I saw the arm of a saint in a case of silver, which they say was the arm of St. Peter, and which they keep with great reverence. In this church is also the tomb of Despinacaton,[3] the daughter of the King of Trebizond, named Caloianni,[4] who is meanly buried under a portico near the door of the church in the earth, and above the tomb is a thing like a box one cubit high and one wide and about three in length, built of bricks and earth. There is also a church of St. John, beautifully built, and several others of great beauty and splendour; and while I remember, I must not pass over one of them named the church of St. Mary, the account of which will interest my readers. It is a large edifice,[5] with sixty altars, as one sees before chapels; the interior is built up with

---

[1] These towers were built at various periods by the chiefs of the different dynasties that reigned there. There are inscriptions from Valens down to Sultan Selim, that each successive possessor placed on the walls.

[2] This was the emblem of the Ortokide and Eioobite rulers, and not the Imperial arms.

[3] Despina Khatoon, the latter word meaning "lady" or "madam", and so "queen".

[4] Calo Johannes, or Black John. See p. 42, Zeno.

[5] Now the Ooloo Jami.

vaults, and the vaults are supported by more than three hundred columns. There are also vaults above vaults, equally supported by columns; and, as far as I could judge, this church was never covered in, in the middle, as taking into consideration the mode of its erection, and, above all, the sacred christening font, which I saw was in the open air. This baptismal font is situated in the middle of the church, and is of fine alabaster, made like an immense mastebe,[1] carved inside with various designs and most splendidly worked. It is covered by a magnificent block of the finest marble, supported by six columns of marble as clear as crystal, and these columns also are worked with fine and gorgeous carvings, while the whole church is inlaid with marble. Nowadays, the eastern part of this church has been made a mosque, while the other part is in the same state it always has been, as it was the convent where the priests lived; in it there is a wonderful fountain of water, as clear as crystal. This church is so nobly built that it appears like a paradise, so rich is it in fine and splendid marbles, having columns upon columns, like the palace of St. Mark at Venice. There is also a campanile with bells, and in many other churches there are steeples without bells.

This city abounds in water, as springs rise in many places; and it is partly on a plain and partly on a mountain—in the midst of a great plain, round which many fresh-water springs gush forth. It has six gates,[2] well guarded by corporals and soldiers; the corporal of every gate has ten, twelve, or twenty men under him, and by every gate there is a large clear fountain. There are here, also, people of many religious persuasions in greater numbers than Mahometans, namely, Christians, Greeks, Armenians, and Jews. Each religion has its separate church with its own service, without being molested by the Mahometans.

Among the other rivers flowing through this city is one

[1] A stone seat fastened to a wall.   [2] It has only four now.

from the East named the Set,[1] which, in the spring, rises wonderfully and flows rapidly towards Asanchif and Gizire,[2] in Bagadet, entering the river Euphrates, and the two then fall into the Persian Gulf. Custagialu Mahumutbec rules this city with the whole province of Dierbec, Sciech Ismael having given it to him as his relative, being his sister's husband, and most devoted to him. This province has six great cities and five large fortresses, as I have said; of which cities there were three, namely, the one we have been relating about, *i.e.*, Caramit,[3] the second Orfà, and the third Cartibiert, formerly ruled over by Aliduli,[4] who had subdued them. At the time that Jacob Sultan passed from this life, they were occupied by Aliduli; although it cost him dear, as, when Sciech Ismael gave the fine province of Dierbec to Custagialu Mahmutbec, he commanded him at all hazards to recover Orfà and Cartibiert, and this commission he, as a faithful vassal, prepared to execute. Therefore, he siezed Orfà, cutting all within it to pieces, but could not take Caramit,[5] since Sultan Custalumut had surrounded it with walls, neither could he take Cartibiert. Custagialu, seeing this, left Orfà, and came to Mardin,[6] which he took

[1] The Tigris, or Shat (Arabic for river). After the junction of the Euphrates and Tigris, the river, on its way to the Persian Gulf, goes by the name of the Shat ul Arab.
[2] Hisn Keyf and Jezireh.   [3] Kara Amid-Diarbekr.
[4] Kharput, called by Arabic historians Khutburt and Hisn Ziyad, now Mauooriet el Azeezeh in Turkish official documents. It was a chief seat of the Orlokides, and here it was that Balak, the son of Behram, the son of Ortog, confined the gallant crusaders, Jocelyn de Courtenay and Baldwin du Bourg, after they had been liberated by their conquerors, Dejekermish and Soukman Ibn Ortok. Balak destroyed all his prisoners, with the exception of the royal captives, by throwing them over the battlements. It is now fast falling into decay, the fine old castle in the lower part of the town being now in ruins.
[5] Diarbekr.
[6] Mardin, the ancient Roman colony of Marde, still a prosperous town. Kinneir says, "Although in so elevated a situation, it has within itself a plentiful supply of the finest water; and, as the vine is cultivated

without bloodshed or resistance, as they surrendered voluntarily. While Custagialu remained at Mirdin, Aliduli advanced and endeavoured to recover Orfà, ravaging the country, plundering and slaying the inhabitants, and threatening to do great things against Sciech Ismael, who then came to subdue Aliduli, as shall be related at the proper time and place, to the satisfaction of those who desire to hear of the origin of Sultan Sciech Ismael.

CHAP. IV.—Of the castle of Dedu; of the magnificent city of Mirdin, built on a high mountain near a vast plain; of the city of Gizire, situated on an island, and very wealthy; of the royal city of Asanchif, filled with innumerable inhabitants and different religions; the two castles which Custagialu, the relative of Sciech Ismael, is now besieging; and of the wonderful bridge in this city.

Now, continuing my journey one day from Caramit, one arrives at a fine castle named Dedu; which is on an eminence, near a high mountain, and has many villages below it, and is a very rich place. Proceeding a day's journey further, one sees the magnificent city of Mirdin, which is

with success in the recesses of the mountains, wine and brandy (arrack) are made by the Armenians in considerable quantities. The houses are all built of fine hewn stone, and appear to be very old. The windows are small, grated with iron, and, from the position of the town on a declivity, added to the narrowness of the streets, the buildings seem, progressively, to rise one on the top of the other. The population of Merdin amounts to nearly 11,000 souls, of which fifteen hundred are Armenians and two hundred Jews; the remainder are Turks, Arabs, and Kurds. The Armenians have here several churches, and a patriarch who was educated at Rome; he is a well-informed man, highly respected even by the Turks. The walls of the city are kept in tolerable repair, and a few old pieces of cannon are mounted on the towers of the castle, which is now in a very dilapidated state, and has never been completely repaired since the place was taken by Timour. Merdin is forty-six furlongs from Mosul and eighteen from Diarbekr. It is the frontier town of the Pashalik of Bagdad, towards Constantinople, and under the government of a Mussaleem appointed by the Pasha."

about four or five miles in circumference, on a high mountain, with a castle a long crossbow shot above the city, and one mile in circumference, which, if one looks at from below, is terrifying, as, when one is on the mountain at its foot, one sees numerous huge rocks as large as houses, and which always seem about to fall. At the foot of this castle the city is surrounded by high walls, and, as I have said, is situated on a high mountain, and has within it beautiful palaces and mosques. It is true there is a want of water,[1] since the water of this region is salt and scarce; otherwise, this would be the finest city of Diarbec, being in a most beautiful and pleasant climate. This city is so high, that from within, looking down towards the east, it appears hanging over, like the battlement of a fortress. It is also appalling, looking from the foot of the walls of the city up to the height of the castle; which is so far off, that the colour becomes softened off into that of the sky, and this is seen principally from the plain on the east below the city. This plain commences at Orfa, goes as far as Bagadet, and thence extends to Gizire, wonderfully wide and grand. This city is inhabited far more by Armenian Christians and Jews than by Mahometans, and each sect officiates in its separate church, according to their custom.

Travelling from this city for two days towards the East, one finds another city named Gizire,[2] inhabited by the same people, by Curds, and very many other races, and is situated on an island. The river Set spreads itself out in that region, flowing by another mountain, where they are building a fine castle. This city is governed by a Curd, although in subjection to Custagialu Mahumutbec, and abounding in

---

[1] According to Kinneir this is not the case now. See preceding note.

[2] Jezireh, on the Tigris, representing the old fortress of Bezabde, was an important town till the invasion of Timour, by whom it was taken and destroyed. It was a chief seat of the Atabegs, the ruins of whose castle still exist.

everything that one can ask. I have thought fit to make mention of this city although it is not on the direct road to Tauris, but on one's right hand on the route to the East. But following the direct road to Tauris in the ordinary manner, I say that in four days from the above-named city of Mirdin, one comes to another city named Asanchif,[1] which is a royal city, and a metropolis of the province of Diarbec, and is ruled over by a lord named Sultan Calil,[2] who is a Curd, has married a sister of Sultan Sciech Ismael, and is chief of several Curdish lords of those territories. This city is four or five miles in circuit, and is fortified at the foot of a high mountain, while by the opposite side of the mountain flows the large river Set,[3] the city being built

---

[1] Hesn Keyf.

[2] Sultan Khalil, the Eioobite. His tomb exists there yet. Hesn el Kahef or Hesn Keyf, three hours and a half from Redhwanis, mentioned by Procopius as Ciphas, while an Armenian author, writing about the first crusade, speaks of it under the name of Harsenko, and says that after the defeat of Baldwin de Bourg, Count of Edessa, and Jocelyn de Courtenay by Dejekermish and Soukman, which resulted in the capture of those two chiefs, Jocelyn was sent a prisoner to Hesn Keyf, while Baldwin was incarcerated at Mosul. They were ransomed for a considerable sum, but fell into the hands of Balak the son of Behram, the son of Ortok, who confined them at Kharput. The modern town is perched on the top of a steep and nearly inaccessible rock, having at the eastern end the old castle built by the Ortokides on the ruins of a more ancient edifice. In a small plain at the foot of the mountains that here press down upon the Tigris, are the ruins of the old town of the same name, the seat of the Ortokides and Eioobites. A noble bridge of three large and three smaller pointed arches, but now in ruins, spanned the river close under the town. But by far the most interesting relics of the place are the myriads of grots that stretch for three miles in one direction, and occupy the sides of six other separate ravines, scooped out of the hills to the east of, and round the town. They exist, tier above tier, in parallel lines all up to the top, communicating with each other by stairs and by a narrow zigzag path, that passing each cell reaches from the highest cave to the plain. In the same manner the water of some springs on the top of the hill was conducted by a narrow channel past each of them and within easy reach of their inhabitants.

[3] Tigris.

between the mountain and the river, and in it there is a countless population of Christians, Mahometans, and Jews—a very rich and trading community.[1] I remained there two months, kept in by the deep snow on the road to Tauris, where I was sent by my correspondents. Custagialu Mahumutbec was there with an army of ten thousand men, since Sultan Calil, the relative[2] of Sciech Ismael, as we have said, ruled that country, but not in his allegiance, since he was a Curd, and the Curds are disobedient and insubordinate; and although they wear the red caftans[3] they are not Suffaveans at heart, but only outwardly. Sciech Ismael, therefore, who is of a masterly and sagacious character, easily understood the need of his realm; and as he wished Asanchif and the whole of Diarbec, of which Asanchif is one of the principal territories, to be ruled by Custagialu, who is a Natolian and a true Suffavean of the sect of Sciech Ismael, very devoted, and as nearly related to him, took the measure of sending him in person to take possession of this territory from Sultan Calil. Having thus entered Asanchif, as I have said, with ten thousand men, this Sultan Calil, seeing his enemy upon him by order of Sciech Ismael, having hastily furnished himself with provisions, shut himself up in two castles, upon two mountains commanding the city, one being a mile in circuit, and the other about half a mile. In the larger one there are no rooms nor any habitations, only a very steep mountain about a mile round, rising as perpendicularly as a wall, and inaccessible, except in one quarter, where high walls are built, with many towers for the defence of the pass, and the soldiers who lodge in the fortress have their apartments in the towers. The other, which is smaller, is well built, and inhabited, and here it was that Sultan

[1] It is now a miserable village of one hundred and fifty houses only.
[2] Brother-in-law.
[3] Kizzilbashes, or red-heads. The seven Turkish tribes who bore this name were the "Oostkajalu," "Shamlu," "Nikallu," "Baharlu," "Zulkudder," "Kajar," and "Affshar."

Calil, with Calconchatun,[1] his wife, the sister of Sieche Ismael, with the rest of his family, lived. In this city all the lords of Diarbech came together by command of Custagialu Mahumutbec, bringing with them all the men they could, to the number, before mentioned, of ten thousand; and they kept up fighting night and day, but they gained but little, as the two castles were impregnable, and their horses, lances, arrows, crossbows, and guns availed nothing. Similarly, a mortar of bronze, of four spans, which they brought from Mirdin, where it used always to stand before the door of the fort of that city, was useless. This mortar was cast in that country at the time of Jacob Sultan, and by his orders. And while I was at Asanchif I went several times to see the fighting and the firing of this same mortar; and Custagialu also had another larger one cast by a young Armenian, who cast it in the Turkish manner—all in one piece. The breech was half the length of the whole piece, and the mortar was five spans in bore at the muzzle. They had only these two pieces to bombard the castles, in which there was no artillery, except three or four muskets of the shape of Azemi,[2] with a small barrel, which, with a contrivance locked on to the stock about the size of a good arquebuse, carry very far. They also had a certain kind of crossbow, made like bows of horn, but made on purpose stronger than those which are drawn by hand, and have a handle, with a contrivance like ours for bending them, and are without nuts, but instead of them they have a bit of iron. Their bolts are long, about half the length of an arrow, and slender; they are feathered, and have points like the Turkish arrows, and go a great distance. Of these crossbows there were about twenty in one of these castles; I think it was in the smaller one.

In this city there is a hill, on which they have built a rampart of planks and beams, behind which are a number

[1] Khatun "lady" or "princess."   [2] Irak Ajemi.

of men with slings, who fire into the castle, as also those in the castle do into the town. They have made this rampart on the highest point of the city, and from thence they cast down many stones. The two cannons were directed on the castle to sweep away some outposts, which did a great deal of harm, and had caused the death of a great many of the citizens. They also made a rampart of a number of great beams, which could be raised and lowered like a drawbridge. This was all completed in one night; and when they wished to fire one of the cannons they raised and then lowered the door; and many perished on both sides. Since before dawn they began to sound their warlike instruments, continuing till the setting of the sun. For two months while I remained there was continual fighting, so that the unfortunate city was half besieged by the number of soldiers and people who came to the fighting, causing great disturbances. All this was tolerated by Custagialu Mahumutbec in order to have money to pay his soldiers

This city was always considered a separate realm, but subject to the King of Persia. And really the inhabitants appear to me to be very worthy, good people. There are many traders and prettier women than in any other part of Diarbec. Outside the city there are four suburbs, as I will relate to you. On the east, in the mountain under the castle, there are a number of grottoes enough to form a city; below this is another borough with very large houses. On the other side of the river are heights far above the stream full of excavated grottoes, with rooms, palaces, with many staircases[1] (by which they descend to the river to

---

[1] From the courtyard of the old castle at the eastern end of the modern town, a curious covered way, containing a winding stair of two hundred steps, is scooped out of the solid rock, leading down to the river. A little further on are the remains of a similar stair, which, like the former, was evidently used by the townspeople to supply themselves with water from the Tigris. Where the stairs are at all exposed to the attack of an

draw water), finer than any of the houses. Near this place is another suburb of houses, with a magnificent bazaar and a chan for the accommodation of merchants. Going to the city from this bazaar, one crosses the river by a magnificent stone bridge,[1] which is wonderfully built, and in my opinion has no superior. It has five lofty, wide, solid arches; the one in the middle is built on a firm foundation of stones, two and three paces long and more than one pace broad. This foundation is so large that it is about twenty paces in circumference, made in the form of a column, and sustains the centre arch, being fixed in the middle of the river. The arch is so wide and lofty that a vessel of three hundred tons, with all its sails set, can pass under it; and, in truth, many a time when I have been standing on it and looking down into the river, the great height has made me shudder. But while I recollect it I will say that I consider three things in Persia great marvels—this bridge of Asanchif, the palace of Assambei Sultan, and the castle of Cimischasac.[2]

CHAP. V.—Of the castle of Cafondur; of the town of Bitlis; of the Kurdish tribes; and of the Curd, Sarasbec, the lord of that city, who has but little respect for Sciech Ismael.

As I think I have now said quite enough about this city and its state, it seems to me I ought to continue the journey I have begun. Therefore, at the end of two months I set out towards Bitlis, and at the end of five days' journey arrived at a castle called Cafondur,[3] inhabited by a Curdish enemy from the opposite side, they are pitted with innumerable small holes, probably caused by flights of arrows that had been shot against these exposed parts to prevent any communication with the river.

[1] The foundations are Parthian. The only remaining arch fell in last year—1869.
[2] Tchimishgazak. In ruins now.
[3] Now Keffendo. The ruins are situated in the narrow gorge of the Bitlis valley.

chief who governs it in the allegiance of the ruler of Bitlis. It is a small castle built on a peaked mountain, the whole country being mountainous and arid, as from Asanchif to Bitlis the whole road is hilly with some narrow and dangerous passes.

And, although I had promised to describe my journey straight on, nevertheless, for my own satisfaction, and to please my readers, I will make mention of a city a little out of the road named Sert,[1] where nuts and chesnuts grow in large quantities, and also gall for tanning. There are also three fine castles under the kingdom of Asanchif, called Aixu, Sanson,[2] Arcem;[3] this Arcem is governed by a tall Saracen negro, a slave of Sciech Ismael, named Gambarbec, of gigantic height and strength. Sciech Ismael made him a Sultan, and placed him under Custagialu.

I now recollect that I mentioned before that there were six great cities and five castles in the province of Diarbec; but I did not name them at the time; but now I will give the name of each. The cities are Orfà, Caramit, Mirdin, Gizire, Asanchif, and Sert;[4] the castles are Jumilen,[5] Dedu, Arcem, Aixu, Sanson, all of which have their particular rulers subject to Custagialu Mahumutbec. But to return to the castle of Cafondur[6] we have mentioned, near which, in a deep valley, is a stream,[7] and a fine large chan built, for

[1] Saert, on the Bohtan Su or Eastern Tigris, also called Asaerd and Mobaelra, has been identified by d'Anville and Kinneir as the ancient Tigranocerta, though Mr. Ainsworth more recently has combated that idea, as no ruins are to be seen above ground. Tacitus and Strabo both place Tigranocerta near Nisibin; but coins of Tigranes are to be found here.   [2] Sassone.

[3] Arzen, on the Huzu Arzen, near the village of Giri Hassan, has fallen into ruins, which are still very extensive. Numerous coins have been found here.

[4] Orfà, Kara Amid (Diarbekr), Mardin, Jezireh, Hesn Keyf, and Saert.
[5] Jemeleyn.   [6] Keffendo.

[7] The Bitlis Tchai, rising near the Van Lake, flows into the Bohtan Su or Eastern Tigris.

the accommodation of people travelling during the deep snow, as it snows in an extraordinary manner in that country. I myself was compelled to remain a month in this chan, not being able to continue my journey to Bitlis, on account of the deep snow which covered all the country. In this place one gets dear bread, victuals, barley, and fodder, from some Curdish peasants, who inhabit certain villages on the mountains.[1] This country is perfectly free from robbers, as the whole time I remained in that chan I was molested by no one, although I went about a great deal with the servant of our Carimbassi;[2] and, although he had some of the goods of this same Carimbassi with other merchandise left at Asanchif, to the value of ten thousand ducats, and I had three thousand ducats in my possession, we never had any hindrance. Setting out at the beginning of the month, I arrived at Bitlis as best I could, and remained there about fifteen days expecting Comminit of Casvem, with whom I had been sent by my employers to Tauris to recover some money.

This city of Bitlis[3] is neither very large nor walled round, but has a fine castle on a hill in its midst, which is large and well built, and, according to their chronicles and traditions, was founded by Alexander the Great; it is surrounded by high walls, with many turrets and lofty towers. This city, together with the castle, is governed by a Curd named Sarasbec, half a rebel against Sultan Sciech Ismael, and who is considered in Persia as the master of this fine fortress. All the Curds are truer Mahometans than the other inhabitants of Persia, since the Persians have embraced the Suffavean doctrine, while the Curds would not be converted to it: and, though they wear the red caftans, yet in their hearts they bear a deadly hatred to them. This same city is situated among high mountains in a valley; so that it is,

---

[1] Modern travellers give a very different account of this region.
[2] Caravan Bashi.
[3] Bitlis. See Zeno, p. 8.

as it were, hidden, and one does not perceive it till one is close upon it. And all that region is a kind of receptacle or reservoir of snow, and so much falls that they are only three or four months of the year without it, and they cannot sow their corn before the 15th or 20th of April. Many merchants leave this city to trade in Aleppo, Tauris, and Bursa, as there is nothing to buy in it, nor any merchandise to be retailed, as the inhabitants are all Curds and a vile race. There are also many Armenian Christians: a people far worse than the Mahometans, though not so much so in this place as throughout the rest of Persia, wherever one finds them. A stream[1] passes through the centre of this city, so that it is well supplied with water. There is also a spring in the castle, which, though it supplies but little water, is sufficient for their wants. In the winter every one collects a quantity of snow, putting it in cisterns, and then makes use of it in summer. This Curd, Sarasbec, who rules this city, has but little respect for Sultan Sciech Ismael, who, while I was at Tauris, I remember, sent several times to summon him to his court; but he would never trust himself to go there. On this account, Sciech Ismael sent one of his captains, named Sophi Zimammitbec, with about six thousand horsemen, who, when they arrived at a distance of two days' journey from Bitlis, were overtaken by a courier with orders from the sovereign to the captain to return at once to Tauris. He, turning about with his men, went back to Sciech Ismael, whom he found in great perturbation because the Usbec, named Casilbas,[2] had invaded his country, ravaging the territory of Jesel.[3] Ismael determining to avenge himself, assembled all his horse and foot soldiers, and marched against this same Casilbas, who was a kinsman of the great Tamberlane, and ruler of Tar-

---

[1] The Bitlis Tchai. See p. 156.
[2] Sheibani Khan, Yeshilbash. See Zeno, p. 55.
[3] Yezd.

tary, Curidin,[1] and the borders, as far as Sammarcant. What followed, I shall keep for a more convenient place, and narrate the whole of it in detail. I will now return to my first undertaking.

CHAP. VI.—Of a sea or salt lake, and of the castles round it; of the city of Arminig, situated on an island of this sea, inhabited solely by Armenian Christians; of the fortresses of Vastan and Van, where the ruler is named Zidibec, a rebel against Sciech Ismael; Bairdunbec was sent against him, and besieged him three months; when the castle capitulated, Zidibec having escaped by night.

Then, setting out from Bitlis, on the second day I arrived at Totouan,[2] a small fort on a mountain stretching out into the sea, as you shall hear. In this country there is a sea or lake, the water of which is salt; but not so much so as the Adriatic sea. It is three hundred miles long, and a hundred and fifty broad in the widest part, and has round it many inlets, with a fertile region full of villages, the greater number of the villagers being Armenians. Round this sea are seven splendid castles, inhabited by Curds and Armenians, in all of which I have traded; as on my way to Tauris I went on one side, and came back on the other, as this sea was in the middle of the route. There are four of the castles on the east, namely, Totouan, already mentioned, Vastan, Van,[3]

---

[1] Sheibani Khan was a descendant of Gengis Khan, and an enemy of the house of Timour.

[2] Tadvan, on the Van Lake.

[3] Van, the ancient Artemita, according to Kinneir, is situated two miles from the lake. "It is surrounded with a good wall and deep ditch, and has four gates: one, corresponding with the palace of the governor; another, to the east, called the Gate of Tauris; the third, to the south, called the Middle Gate; and the fourth, fronting the lake, known by the appellation of the Gate *Sinla*. On the north is a castle built on a high and perpendicular hill, which rises abruptly from the plain. This fortress can only be approached by one passage, so narrow as to admit only two persons abreast; it is always supplied with corn and military

and Belgari;[1] on the west are Argis,[2] Abalgiris, and Calata.[3] This Calata was anciently a large city, as can be seen by the buildings,[4] but is now reduced to a small fortress. Between Totouan and Vastan is a lofty island in the sea,[5] two miles from the mainland, all of hard rock, on which is a small city about two miles in circumference, the city being the same size as the island. This city is named Arminig, is very populous, and inhabited only by Armenian Christians, without one Mahometan; it has many churches, all for the services of Armenian Christians; of these, that of St. John is the largest, and has a steeple made like a tower, so high that it overlooks the whole city, and among the bells is one so large, that when it is struck, it resounds over all the mainland. Opposite the city or island is a large gulf, with a delightful plain with many villages inhabited by Armenian Christians, with much cultivated land, and beautiful gardens with trees that produce every sort of fruit. This region has a delightful and healthy atmosphere, and all round it are mountains so high, that they appear to touch the sky; and, not only in the circuit of this gulf, but also round the whole sea there are bleak mountains covered with eternal snow.

stores, and in the centre of the works stands the palace of the Aga of the Janissaries. This city is abundantly supplied with water and provisions; the houses are built of stone and tile; the streets are spacious and well paved; and the population is said to amount to fifty thousand souls, two thirds of which number are Turks, and the remainder Kurds and Armenians. The air is pure, and the environs of the city delightful."

[1] Peygri, now Beygir Kellah, hardly on the lake, but a short distance from it, on a small stream falling into the same.

[2] Arjish, Ardh-el Jivaz.

[3] Iklat, a very ancient Armenian town. Subsequently it became the seat of the Eioobites, and then of the Ak-koinloo.

[4] Arjish (the ancient Arzes) is a town containing six thousand inhabitants, situated on the north-west side of the lake, three days' journey from Van.

[5] Island of Ak-Tamar, the seat of the Catholicos of the Armenians, described by Layard.

At two days' journey from this place, one finds the castle of Vastan,[1] which was demolished by Sciech Ismael, and only a town with a bazaar remains. It is on a large gulf of this sea, with numbers of villages, all inhabited by Curds. There is a greater abundance of provisions here than in any other place, and a good deal of white honey is made here, which from time to time is sent by caravans to Tauris to be sold, together with fine ointment and cheese.

Proceeding a day's journey further is the fortress of Van, which is built on a mountain or hill of hard rock, from which fresh water springs forth everywhere; it is more than a mile in circumference, but narrow and long, like the rock on which it is built; also on the summit of this rock, in one part which is as steep as a wall, is a fountain the water of which is used by all in the fortress.[2] This citadel is ruled over by a Curdish chief named Zidibec, who is a great lord, and very proud, from having in his possession this fine fortress with many other castles in these mountains. He had money coined with his own stamp of gold, silver, and copper. Below the castle is a large town, and the greater part of the inhabitants are Armenians, but within the castle they are all Curds. This place is a good mile from the sea, and is well supplied with provisions. This chief has many sons, who govern the castles round; and, as I have said, he is very arrogant from his power, and is a rebel against Sciech Ismael, who at another time sent one of his captains named Bairambec with ten thousand picked troops against him. While I was in Tauris, I learnt all the events from soldiers who had returned, but in particular from a chief of bombardiers, a good man, and a great friend of mine, named Camusabec of Trebizond. I heard that when Bairambec arrived beneath

---

[1] Vastan in ruins to the south of the lake, nearly opposite the island of Aktamar.

[2] There are numerous cuneiform inscriptions on the castle walls, of which it is curious he should make no mention.

M

the castle with his army, Zidibec, full of treachery, sent one of his men to Bairambec to ask a safe conduct for him to come and kiss his hand. Having obtained his demand, Zidibec came down from the castle with a few companions all unarmed; and, having arrived in the presence of Bairambec, saluted him in the Persian or Suffavean manner, saying that he wondered that his Excellency had come to that place with that army, there being no necessity for it, as although in the past he had been disobedient, yet for the future he wished to be a faithful vassal of Sultan Sciech Ismael—inclining his head to the ground, as he did whenever he named Sciech Ismael, as if out of reverence for that great name, showing much humble respect in his discourse, as it was his duty to do. And at length he warmly entreated Bairambec that, when he returned to the noble presence of Sciech Ismael his sovereign, he would deign to defend him, and help him to make his apologies; this the commander Bairambec promised to do. And, besides the promise, he made him a banquet, magnificent enough for any king. After they had dined together in the plain, Zidibec began to make excuses, asking pardon of Bairambec for the trouble and difficulty he had had on his account, coming to that place with so large an army; and, rising to his feet, said: "My lord, send with me whomsoever you please, and I will surrender the castle into his hands; and I beg of you to give me two days' time, that I may make ready to go with you to the presence of Sultan Sciech Ismael." The general conceded his request; and, having called a nobleman named Mansorbec, ordered him to go with Zidibec to the castle, and to take it in charge until orders came from Sciech Ismael, and also promised Zidibec to use his influence with Sciech Ismael, that he might remain master of the castle and of the fine territory.

Having made this agreement and these conditions, Zidibec took leave, and with him went this same Baron Mansorbec, with perhaps a hundred men, intending to take possession of the castle in the name of Sciech Ismael. When they arrived at the gate, Zidibec entered first, and after him Mansorbec and his men, when suddenly the gate was shut, and fifteen hundred armed men appeared, who had been standing prepared for this, and cut to pieces Mansorbec with all his men. Zidibec then went with the same soldiers towards the camp, where, as he had given his word of honour to Bairambec, he found him with all his soldiers without suspicion, and unarmed. Then he began boldly to fight against the whole army, of which a great number of men were killed, and of his own men about three hundred were killed, and a good many others wounded; and Bairambec, the general, received three wounds. Zidibec retreated as well as he could into the castle, and, closing the gates, fortified himself in it, considering himself secure against assault. After this success, Bairambec, having two moderate-sized cannons in his camp, began to batter the castle; but they were able to do no harm, as the walls were too strong and the gunners too little skilled. And after besieging the castle for three months, the artillerymen at last found a place where a fountain sprang forth inside the fortress, whence the besieged got their water. Near this spot they planted the two cannons, and fired so much that the spout by which the water issued broke into several pieces, and the water which used to rise all went downwards. Thus at once the castle was at their mercy; and Zidibec, now seeing himself insecure, determined when night came to escape from that place; so descending from the walls with about fifty of his court, without saying a word to anyone else, he took his treasures, his wife, and two daughters, and, after disguising himself, fled across the mountains to some of his other strongholds. The following morning the tidings were known everywhere that Zidibec had fled; therefore the people sent at once to Bairambec, offering to surrender the castle if he would ensure to them their lives and property. Bairambec being wearied by the siege, which had already lasted three months, promised it on his honour, and conceded their request. Then they opened the gates to him, and when he had entered they told him of the flight of Zidibec with his court during the night. Let every one judge for himself of the indignation and grief he felt in not getting him into his hands. And, having appointed a governor with sufficient troops to keep the place, he returned to Tauris, where Sciech Ismael caused great festivities and games to be held in sign of rejoicing, as they are accustomed to do on receipt of like news. He then left Tauris with many of his lords, and went to Coi,[1] where he remained some time, occupying himself with the chase and other amusements.

CHAP. VII.—Of the castle of Elatamedia; of the city of Merent and of Coi; of the city of Tauris, where the kings of Persia have their residence; of the castle, the palaces, fountains, and baths there are in it; of the wonderful mosque in the midst of the city; of the quality of the men and women; and of the customs and trade of this city.

Now after having abandoned my first proposition in order to give some information about this interesting affair, I must return to the abovementioned castle of Van, from which, after three days' journey distant, one arrives at another castle called Elatamedia, inhabited and ruled over only by Turcomans, a fine race. Proceeding three days from this place, one arrives at Merent,[2] which in old times was a large city, as is seen by the ancient buildings; it is situated in a

---

[1] Khoi.

[2] Marand, a town about halfway between Tabreez and Khoi, seems, by the name, to denote the town mentioned; but the traveller here expressly states that it is between Van and Khoi; so we must look for it somewhere on the blank space of Kiepert's map to the east of Lake Van.

beautiful plain with many streams and gardens, but within there is only a small town and a bazaar. Three days' journey further on, lies a fine large plain, surrounded by high mountains, in the midst of which is a large place named Coi, which in ancient times was a large city, as can be seen by the great space occupied by the ruins. In this place, it was anciently the custom (which is still observed) for the troops to assemble when the King of Persia was about to take the field with his army. This city, a short time ago, was in ruins; but when Sciech Ismael succeeded to the throne he began to rebuild it, and has now restored the greater part. And, among other things, a large palace has been built, which in the Persian tongue is called Douler Chana,[1] signifying "pleasant abode." This palace is all walled round with bricks, and is of great extent, with an Arim[2] all together; within there are many halls and chambers, and it is built in one vault—that is to say, with one flooring; and it has a large and magnificent garden. It has two gates, with two fine courts, beautifully decorated, and these entrances are like two cloisters of a convent of friars. Before the gate which looks west are three round turrets, each of them eight yards in circumference, and about fifteen or sixteen high. These turrets are built of the horns of Namphroni stags, and it is considered that there are none like them in the world. The Persians also consider these things very magnificent. Therefore for show they have built these three turrets of the horns of these animals, as the mountains are rocky and full of game. And Sultan Sciech Ismael boasts that he and his lords have killed all these animals. And truly Sciech Ismael takes the greatest pleasure in the chase; and to show that he is a skilful hunter he has had those three turrets built, and takes more delight in living in this place than in Tauris, as this country is well adapted for hunting. In this city, they also make much crimson dye,

---

[1] Doulet Khaneh.   [2] Harem.

by using some red roots, which they dig out of the ground with spades and hoes, and then take to Ormus, and they are employed as red dyes in many parts of India.

One day's journey from this place is a small town named Merent,[1] from which a day's journey further is another small place named Sophian,[2] situated in the plain of Tauris, at the foot of a mountain; it is a beautiful country, and has many rivulets and gardens.

From this, one arrives at the great and noble city of Tauris, where was the abode of Darius, King of Persia, who was afterwards defeated and slain by Alexander the Great, and which has always been the seat of the kings of Persia. Here lived Sultan Assambei,[3] and, after him, Jacob Sultan, his son. This great city[4] is about twenty-four miles in cir-

---

[1] Marand. See p. 164.

[2] Sofian, on the Ak Tchai, a tributary of the Aras, on the direct route to Tabreez. [3] Hassan Beg.

[4] Tauris, or Tabreez, as it is now called, is supposed by most to be the ancient Ecbatana. Kinneir says:—

"The Persians conceive Zobeida, the celebrated wife of Haroun-ul-Rashid to be its founder; but, as they are in general very ignorant regarding the history of their cities, little reliance can be placed on any information obtained from them. That Tauris was a favourite residence of Haroun-ul-Rashid cannot be denied, and, although he might not actually have founded the city, he may yet have improved and embellished it to a considerable degree. It was, in the days of Chardin, one of the largest and most populous cities in the East, and contained, according to that traveller, five hundred thousand inhabitants. But no town has experienced to a greater degree the ravages of war. Situated towards the frontiers of contending empires, it has alternately been in the hands of the Turks, Tartars, and Persians, and has been taken and sacked eight different times; but its ruin has been chiefly owing to the number of earthquakes, which have at different times levelled its proudest edifices with the dust.

"Tabreez does not now contain more than thirty thousand inhabitants, and is, upon the whole, one of the most wretched cities I have seen in Persia. It is seated in an immense plain at the foot of a mountain, on the banks of a small river, whose waters are consumed in the cultivation of the land. It is surrounded with a decayed wall, and the only decent house in the place is a new barrack, erected by the Prince for the accom-

cumference in my judgment, and is without walls, like Venice. In it there are immense palaces, as memorials of the kings who have ruled over Persia. There are many splendid houses.

Two streams flow through it; and half a mile outside the city, towards the west, there is a large river of salt water, which is crossed by a stone bridge. In all the neighbouring region there are fountains, the water of which is brought by underground aqueducts. The numerous palaces of former kings are wonderfully decorated within, and covered with gold on the outside, and of different colours; and each palace has its own mosque and bath, which are equally overlaid, and worked with minute and beautiful designs. Every citizen of Tauris has his room all overlaid in the inside, and decorated with ultramarine blue, in various patterns; many mosques, also, are so worked as to cause admiration in all who behold them; among these, there is one in the middle of the city so well built that I do not know how I am to describe it; but at any rate I will attempt to do so in a way. This mosque is called "Imareth alegeat", and is very large, but has never been covered in in the centre. On the side towards which the Mahometans worship, there is a choir that is a vault of such a size that a good bowshot would not reach the top; but the place has never been finished, and all round it is vaulted in with fine stones, which are sustained by marble columns, which are so fine and transparent that they resemble fine crystal, and are all equal in height and thickness, the height being about five or six paces. This mosque has three doors, of which two only are used, and are

modation of his troops. The ruins of the ancient city are very extensive and very mean, being nothing but a confused mass of old mud walls.

"The observations of the gentlemen of the Mission give the latitude of Tabreez in 38 deg. 10 min. N., and 46 deg. 37 min. E."

The population and trade of Tabreez have greatly increased since Kinneir's time, partly owing to the intercourse with Russia; it has now nearly eighty thousand inhabitants.

arched; they are about four paces wide and about twenty high, and have a pillar, made not of marble, but of stone of different colours, while the rest of the vault is all of layers of decorated plaster. In each doorway there is a tablet of transparent marble, so clear and fine that one might see one's face in it. And the mosque can be seen from the whole country round about; and even at the distance of a mile, one can clearly see these tablets, which are three yards each way, the door which opens and shuts being three yards broad and five high, of huge beams cut into planks, covered with large cast bronze plates, smoothed down and gilt. Before the principal door of the mosque is a stream flowing under stone arches. In the midst of the edifice is a large fountain, not springing there naturally, but brought artificially, as the water comes in by one pipe and is emptied by a second, as they please. This fountain is a hundred paces in length and as many in breadth, and is six feet deep in the middle, where is built a beautiful platform or pedestal on six pilasters of the purest marble, all overlaid, and carved inside and out. The building is very ancient, but the platform has been recently put up, and there is a bridge leading from the side of the fountain on to the platform. There is a beautiful boat like a bucentaur, which Sultan Sciech Ismael used often when a boy (as he still does now) to get into, with four or five of his lords, and row about the fountain.

I will say no more about this, but will go on to mention two enormous elm-trees, beneath each of which more than a hundred and fifty men can stand; and here they preach,[1]

---

[1] The followers of what is called the "Shiah sect", curse the memories of Abu Bekr, Omar, and Othman, whom they look upon as usurpers of Ali's rights; and they despise all the "Soonee", or body of traditions collected during their reigns, which are venerated by all orthodox Mahometans. They believe that Ali, the beloved son-in-law of Mohammed, is almost equal to the Prophet himself; and that if Mohammed is the Apostle, Ali and his descendants, the twelve Imaums, were the Vicars

declaring and setting forth the new faith or Suffavean doctrine. The preachers are two doctors of this sect; and one of them, as many people say, taught Sultan Sciech Ismael, and the other is required to attend with care to preaching and converting people to their sect.

This city has also a fine castle on the east at the foot of a hill, but which is uninhabited, and has no other rooms in it but a magnificent palace, which is built partly into the hill; it is most wonderful, as you will learn from what I am about to tell you. This palace is very lofty, and seems solid half way through. Outside there is a flight of steps eight or ten paces long, and three broad, which mounts to the royal gate of the palace; the entrance is in a very large hall, on one side of which is a solid cube, intended to be a hiding place, sustained by four large columns, five paces and about twice the grasp of my arms in girth. The capitals of these columns are wonderfully carved; the cement is of a certain mixture or stone like fine jasper, as I really believed it to be; but trying it with my knife, I found it was not hard. They were placed here not so much for use as for show, as the cube (dome) is sustained by strong thick walls. Then, further in, there is another long narrow hall, with many little

---

of God. These Imaums all suffered martyrdom, except Mahadi, the last, and he is said to have mysteriously disappeared, and is believed to be still alive. The twelve Imaums are—
1. Ali, the son-in-law of Mohammed.
2. Hassan } his sons.
3. Hossein }
4. Zein al Abudeen. Put to death by Caliph Walid I.
5. Mohammed al Badkir. Put to death by Caliph Hashem.
6. Jaffier al Sadick.
7. Moôssâh Kazim, from whom the Suffavean family is descended.
8. Ali Riza; buried at Meshed.
9. Mohammed al Takee.
10. Ali al Nukee.
11. Hassan Askeri.

All put to death, generally by order of the Caliphs.

12. Mohammed al Mahadi. Mysteriously disappeared.

chambers like rooms; and entering further, one finds a vast hall with many windows looking on to the city, since the palace is above it, as I have said, standing on a hill overlooking the city and the country round for a long way. All these rooms are beautifully decorated with layers of cement of various colours. All the ceilings of the rooms are decorated and coloured with gilding and ultramarine blue. The large hall looking on to the city has many columns round it, which seem to support the roof; still it is kept up by strong walls, and they are placed there for the sake of appearance, as they are of the most beautiful marbles, not white, but in colour like silver, so that in each one of them are reflected the city, the hall, all the columns and people there. And at each window of this hall, there are pilasters of fine marble of the same kind and appearance as the columns, which reflect in the same way but in a greater degree, as they are flat, so that one can see not only the city, but also the surrounding country, the mountains and hills more than twenty miles distant, all the gardens and the great plain.

This city has, besides, some other great advantages. The principal one is its being situated in a marvellous position at the head of a fine large plain towards the east, in a place like a small inlet at the foot of a high mountain, though this belongs to the chain ten miles further to the east. On the west there is another, but not very extensive, plain, stretching three miles from the city.

The air here is so fine and salubrious as to induce people to remain willingly and with great enjoyment; nor did I ever see anyone in bad health there. They almost all eat mutton there, which has a very delicate taste. The beef there is most vile; so that but little is eaten by the inhabitants. Their bread is of flour as white as milk; they have little wine, but still there are some red wines, and some wines white in colour, and tasting like malmsey. There are also a good many fish, which are caught in a lake,[1] a day's journey distant from the city, which is salt like those of Vastan and Van. The fish have not a natural taste, but have a strange smell and taste of sulphur. To this place there are also brought many sturgeon,[2] smaller than those of the Mediterranean, but still excellent. There is delicious caviar also, which, as well as the sturgeon, is brought from the Caspian Sea, nine days' journey distant from this place, from a castle named Manmutaga. There also come from this sea fresh   , as large as men, and so good that they are better than the flesh of pheasants; but they only come during the spring, as their season only lasts two months.

There are also the common fruits, as over all the world, few nuts, most delicious olives, and Adam's apples; but no oil, oranges, or lemons. These fruits, which fail in spring-time, are brought from Chilan,[3] a little province on the southern shore of the Caspian Sea, extending twenty-five miles from the sea. This city is also ornamented with numerous gardens, in which there are the common herbs like cabbages, lettuces, greens, and other small vegetables, like those at Venice; rape and carrots, small radishes, marjoram, parsley, and rosemary. There is also much rice, and great abundance of corn and barley.

Besides all this, the city is thickly inhabited by Persians, Turkomans, and gipsies, who are treated as people of the Suffavean sect, and wear the red caftans like the rest of the people. There are a good number of Armenian Christians; but beyond Tauris there are no Christians of any kind to be found. There are also Jews, but not permanent inhabitants, as they are all foreigners from Bagadet, Cassan, and Jesede,[4] and come to Tauris, are Suffavean subjects, and live in

---

[1] The Lake of Urumea, into which the Adschy Tchai, the river close to Tabreez, flows.   [2] From the Caspian.
[3] Ghilan.   [4] Bagdad, Kashan, and Yezd.

alcharan saradi[1] like all foreign merchants. Of the inhabitants you will learn wonderful things. The men are ordinarily taller than in our country, are very bold, robust in appearance, and of high spirit. The women are short in proportion to the men, and as white as snow. Their dress is the same as always has been—the Persian costume—wearing it open at the breast, showing their bosoms and even their bodies, the whiteness of which resembles ivory. All the Persian women, and particularly in Tauris, are wanton, and wear men's robes, and put them on over their heads, covering them altogether. These are robes of silk, some of crimson cloth, woollen cloth, velvet, and cloth of gold, according to the condition of the wearer. A quantity of velvet and cloth of gold is brought from Bursa and Cafà. In this city there is an order, as throughout the whole of Persia, that a revenue farmer levies all the excise and tolls as taxes and customs. There is also a vile usage, which has always existed, that every merchant who has a shop in the bazaar pays each day either two or six aspri, or even a ducat, according to their business; likewise, a payment is fixed for the masters of every art according to their condition. Also the harlots, who frequent the public places, are bound to pay according to their beauty, as the prettier they are the more they have to pay; and far worse than the others I have mentioned is this cursed, horrible, disgraceful custom, the evil odour of which ascends to heaven; and from the following instance you may learn their iniquities, as in this city there is a public place and school of Sodomy, where likewise they pay tribute according to their beauty.

All the money they collect is for the private advantage of the revenue-farmers, and no difference is made between Christians and Mussulmans in going to the prostitutes. Besides these taxes, they have the tariff, of which the Christians pay ten per cent. on every kind of merchandise from

[1] Caravan serai.

whatever quarter it may come. The Mussulmans only pay five per cent. on everything; and if they do not sell in Tauris, and the goods are in transit, they do not pay per cent., but weigh the whole quantity and pay a certain proportion on it. In a load worth forty or forty-five ducats, or one of fine or heavy goods, the payment is limited. Of everything one buys in this city, what one has to pay is also fixed according to the class of merchandise, and all is collected by the revenue-farmer. At the time I was in Tauris, a certain man named Capirali held this office and received an income of sixty thousand ducats from these taxes. There is much traffic in this city, and there are silks of every quality, raw and manufactured. There are rhubarb, musk, ultramarine blue, pearls of Orimes[1] of every water, coin of all sorts, lake dye of great beauty, fine indigo, woollen and other cloths from Aleppo, Bursa, and Constantinople, since crimson silks are exported from Tauris to Aleppo and Turkey, and are paid for in cloth and silver.

Chap. VIII.—Description of the royal palace built by Assambei outside the city of Tauris.

Having given full enough particulars of the different matters of this city, I do not think I ought to omit to mention a beautiful palace which the great Sultan Assambei had built; and though there are many large and beautiful palaces in the city built by the kings, his predecessors, yet this, without comparison, far excels them all; so great was the magnificence of Assambei that, up to the present time, he has never had an equal in Persia. The palace is built in the centre of a large and beautiful garden, close to the city, with only a stream dividing them to the north, and in the same circumference a fine mosque is built with a rich and useful hospital attached. The palace in the Persian language is

[1] Ormuz.

called Astibisti,[1] which, in our tongue, signifies "eight parts", as it has eight divisions. It is thirty paces high, and is about seventy or eighty yards round, divided into eight parts, which are subdivided into four rooms and four anterooms, each room having the anteroom towards the entrance, and the rest of the palace is a fine circular dome. This palace is under one roof, or, as one should say, with one storey, and has only one flight of steps to ascend to the dome, the rooms and anterooms, since the staircase leads to the dome, and from the dome one enters the rooms and anterooms. This building, on the ground floor, has four entrances, with many more apartments, all enamelled and gilt in various ways, and so beautiful that I can hardly find words to express it. This palace, as I have already said, is situated in the centre of the garden, and is built on a terrace, or rather the mastabé has been raised round for appearance, being a yard and a half high and five yards wide, like a piazza. By every door of the palace there is a way paved with marble leading to the mastabé. By the door of the chief palace there is a small flight of steps of the finest marble by which one mounts to the mastabé, which is all made of fine marble, while in the centre of the mastabé there is a channel of a streamlet paved and skilfully worked out in marble. This streamlet is four fingers broad and four deep, and flows all round in the form of a vine or a snake. It rises at one part, flows round, and at the same place again the water is conducted away elsewhere. For three yards above the mastabé is all of fine marble. All below is plastered in different colours, and is conspicuous far off like a mirror.

The terrace of the palace has for each angle a gutter or spout, which spurts out water, and the spout is immensely large, and made in the form of a dragon; they are of bronze, and so large that they would do for a cannon, and so well

[1] Hesht Behesht. eight heavens.

made as to be taken for live dragons. Within the palace, on the ceiling of the great hall, are represented in gold, silver, and ultramarine blue, all the battles which took place in Persia a long time since; and some embassies are to be seen which came from the Ottoman to Tauris presenting themselves before Assambei, with their demands and the answer he gave them written in the Persian character. There are also represented his hunting expeditions, on which he was accompanied by many lords, all on horseback, with dogs and falcons. There are also seen many animals like elephants and rhinoceroses, all signifying adventures which had happened to him. The ceiling of the great hall is all decorated with beautiful gilding and ultramarine. The figures are so well drawn that they appear like real living human beings.

On the floor of the hall is spread a magnificent carpet, apparently of silk, worked in the Persian manner with beautiful patterns, which is round, and of the exact measurement the place requires; likewise in the other rooms the floor is all covered. This hall has no light except what it gets from the anterooms and chambers. Still there are entrances from the centre hall to the apartments and anterooms where there are many windows all giving light, each anteroom having only one window, but that one as large as the whole side of a room, and beautifully fitted. Thus when these doors are open, the palace, or rather the hall, is so brilliant with these beautiful figures, that it is a wonder to see. This is the palace where Assambei used to give audience. About a bowshot from the palace there is a harem of one storey, so large that a thousand women might conveniently live there in different rooms. Among the rooms is a large one like a hall, with the walls all adorned with gold and plaster, looking like emerald and many other colours. The ceiling of this harem is ornamented with gold and ultramarine. From this hall there are many chambers on every side, with all the doors superbly decorated with gold and blue, and many signs and letters made of mother of pearl, in beautiful patterns; and through the centre of this hall flows a stream of pure water, a cubit in breadth and as much deep. On one side of this harem is a summer-house four yards square, beautifully decorated with enamel, gold, and ultramarine blue, in patterns really a wonder to see. Here the queen stays with her maidens to do needlework, according to their custom.

And in truth it would be too long and too tedious for me to recount everything about the palace and the harem, which is in the same garden, and has three entrances, one to the south, another to the north, and the third to the east. That to the south is arched with bricks, but not very large, and leads to the garden, the palace being a bowshot distant; passing through the gate, fifteen paces off on the left is a gallery, a bowshot in length and six paces broad, which from one end to the other has seats of the finest marble, with a kind of railing with a design, as an ornament in relief of plaster, of various colours, quite a wonder to behold from the excellence of the workmanship. The roof is all ornamented with gold and plaster. This gallery is supported from one end to the other by columns of fine marble; in front of it there is a fountain, as long as the gallery, of fine marble likewise, which is always full of water, and is twenty-five paces broad. In it there are always four or five couple of swans; round it there are rose trees and jessamines, and a smooth road leading direct to the royal palace.

On the north side, one must enter a certain place like a cloister, paved with bricks, with seats of marble round it. This place is so large that it will hold three hundred horses, as the lords who came to the court used to dismount here when Assambei was reigning. In this place there is a door entering the garden on the way to the king's palace, which is an arch fifteen yards high and four yards wide, beautifully worked in plaster from top to bottom. The door is made of marble, in one square carved piece about four yards each way; its height about a yard and a half; its breadth about the same. The rest of the marble is cut into designs, and when it is exposed to the rays of the sun it shines so brilliantly on both sides, that it appears like crystal, since the marbles found in Persia do not resemble ours, but are much finer; they are not opaque, but are more a species of crystal. Beyond this lordly door there is a fine paved road leading to the royal palace.

The other door, towards the east, is on an immense maidan or piazza, and leads into the garden. This door has a wall of bricks, in the form of an arch, three yards high and two broad, without any decorations, but simply whitened with plaster, and through it there is a fine large fountain. Over this there is a large edifice with many rooms, and a covered hall looking over the garden. On the side towards the maidan there is an arched gallery, so white as to exceed in whiteness anything I think I have ever seen. Into this building Assambei used to retire with many lords whenever a feast was made on this maidan, and frequently when ambassadors came they used to put them up here, as it was a fine place and had many apartments. This door is further than the others from the royal palace, with a splendid view of the maidan, on which are the mosque and the hospital I have already mentioned. This mosque was built by Sultan Assambei, is very large, and has within many rooms all decorated with plaster, gold, and blue.

Also the hospital or moristan, is large, having many buildings, and within it is even more beautifully ornamented than the mosque, having many large wards about ten yards long and four broad, each of these being fitted with a carpet to its measurement. Between the hospital and the mosque there is a wall only, and outside the hospital, from one side to the other, is a mastebe one cubit high and two yards broad, and there used to be an iron chain drawn from one side to the other round the border of the mastebe; so that no horse might approach either the mosque, hospital, or mastebe. At the time that Assambei and Jacob Sultan reigned, more than a thousand poor people lived in the hospital, and the chain was kept until the death of Jacob Sultan, and was then taken away by the Turkomans. All these edifices were raised by the great Assambei, who was so excellent and worthy a man that there has never been his equal in Persia, as he conquered by force of arms many Persian lords who rebelled against him. And in the contest with the Ottoman Sultan he gained glory by defeating and routing his army, though another time he came off worst, as you will learn from what I am now about to relate to you.

Chap. IX.—Caloianni, King of Trebizond, sends an ambassador to Assambei, King of Persia, entreating his assistance against the Ottoman Grand Turk; the latter promises every aid if he would give him his daughter as his wife; he gives her on the condition that she may observe the Christian faith, and sends her to Tauris.

At this time there reigned in Trebizond a Christian king named Caloianni[1], who had a daughter named Despinacaton,[2] who was very beautiful, being considered the most beautiful woman of that time, and throughout Persia was spread the fame of her loveliness and grace. As this king was already much molested and troubled in his peaceful dominions by the Ottoman Grand Turk, and finding himself in a bad way and in danger of losing his kingdom, considering the great power of his enemy, he resolved to send an ambassador to Tauris, where Sultan Assambei[3] lived, to ask

[1] Calo Johannes. See Zeno, p. 9.   [2] "Queen Despina."
[3] Uzun Hassan, at the time of his marriage with Despina, was not King of Persia but only Prince of Diarbekr. Trebizond was taken by Mahomet II, Grand Turk, in 1461.

his assistance, knowing him to be a magnanimous monarch. The ambassador, who was most desirous to obtain the request of his sovereign and to return with full satisfaction, entreated Assambei not to refuse to give aid to his master, showing him many reasons why the destruction of the Christian king would cause harm to his dominions. Assambei being young and unmarried, and already in love with the above-mentioned lady from having heard so much talk of her beauty and talents, replied to the ambassador that if his master would give him his daughter as his wife, he would aid him against the Ottoman not only with his army, but also with his purse, and in person. The ambassador departed with this answer, and when he came to his sovereign expressed to him what Assambei demanded. Seeing that he had not sufficient power to resist the enemy who just then was attacking him, he was induced to agree to the request of Assambei, giving him his daughter as his wife, on the condition that she might observe the Christian faith and keep a chaplain to perform the sacred offices as ordered by our true religion.

Having made this compact Despinacaton arrived in Tauris accompanied by many lords: some sent by Assambei and many others coming from Trebizond. There also came with her many young maidens, daughters of noblemen of high condition, who were always to remain with her. She had also a greatly venerated chaplain, a worthy person, who always celebrated the eucharist according to the Christian custom while she lived with Ussuncassano, which she did a long time, and always in observance of our faith. She had her chapel in a separate place, saying her prayers there whenever it pleased her. This lady had four children: the eldest was Assambei;[1] the others were daughters, two of whom are still alive, and Christians.

[1] He was strangled by his half-brothers after Uzun Hassan's death.

CHAP. X.—The Ottoman makes preparations against Assambei and Caloianni, who send ambassadors to the Venetians, requesting their alliance, and asking for artillery; in the meantime, the Ottoman sends a Bassà, with his troops, to invade Persia. Assambei having marched against him, defeats him in a battle. The Grand Turk, collecting another army, sends against him and defeats him. He then retreats to Tauris. Afterwards, marching against the Soldan who had taken from him the city of Orfa, he defeats him near that place.

The Ottoman, in the year 1472, having heard fully of the compact and treaty that Assambei had made with the King of Trebizond, and being very angry and indignant with it, determined to prove the power and valour of these two monarchs, and therefore made great levies of men to go against Persia. Assambei receiving intelligence of it, not less full of anger and indignation than his enemy, ordered all his lords to assemble their troops with the greatest possible speed, since the King of Trebizond had informed him of the great preparations of the Turk against them both. It seems that Caloianni had relatives at Venice, or else a close friendship with some noblemen. Therefore Assambei, in accordance with his father-in-law, determined to do his utmost, and therefore sent two ambassadors to Venice, requesting their alliance to be able to subdue their Ottoman foe, giving him the chastisement his audacity deserved. And, as I hear, the ambassadors asked for artillery and gunners, and the Most Illustrious Government, for the defence of the King of Trebizond, gave as much as was demanded by the ambassadors, who were greatly honoured. A ship being equipped with the pieces of artillery on board, the ambassadors embarked to go to Giazza, as was their master's command. While the ambassadors were treating in Venice, Sultan Assambei assembled his army with great celerity, about thirty thousand fighting men, and marched, full of rage and fury, against the Ottoman foe, who had already sent a large force to ravage the Persian territory in the vicinity of Arsingan. Assambei, on arriving in the beautiful plain of Arsingan, remained there some days to refresh his troops, who, having been levied near Tauris, had had a long march. The Ottoman army, from fear of such a force of Persians, retreated towards Tocat; and Assambei, having rested his troops, who, in the meantime, had been largely reinforced from Persia, determined to attack the Turks. There being a distance of two days' journey on a good road between the two armies, he advanced to within a mile of the Turkish camp, and having pitched their tents in the morning Assambei sent notice to the Bassà in command of the Ottoman army that on the following day early he would join battle with them. Matters being in this case, at the hour fixed both armies were set in array, the first, second, and third columns being all in order by the break of day. Sultan Assambei was the first to attack, and the combat lasted till the hour of nine; at this point, a Bassà, with a large force of Turks, charged fiercely into the *mêlée*, and put the Persians to rout. Assambei, perceiving the disaster, and having a reserve of eight thousand picked men at hand to carry succour wherever it was needed, boldly charged the centre of the hostile army, encouraging his own soldiers and carrying death everywhere before him, so that the Turks were signally defeated in that engagement. Assambei having conquered the enemy in this battle, immediately occupied in triumph Tocat, Malacia, and Sivas,[1] three large cities. The Ottoman was greatly displeased and troubled on hearing the news of the rout and destruction of the greater part of his army, but more especially by that of the loss of the three cities; but, by collecting troops throughout his dominions, he assembled an immense army and directed it against Assambei, who had established himself in safety in Malacia. The latter having also suffered

---

[1] Tocat, Malatia, and Sivas. See Zeno.

severe loss in the battle, sent some of the chiefs back to Persia to levy all the troops they could to reinforce his army. Besides, he awaited with impatience the cannon and bombardiers sent by our Most Illustrious Government, but neither succour came with the speed the occasion required, while the Turkish forces arrived on the frontiers well provided with artillery. Assambei was disquieted about this; but being in necessity and in hourly expectation of the Persian reinforcements and the artillery, like a noble monarch he determined to face the enemy with the troops he had with him, about twenty-four or twenty-five thousand in number, while they had thirty-six thousand men. The enemy was stationed on one side of Malacia, while Assambei was on the other, as he had retreated half a day's journey between Malacia and Tocat, a place well suited for the operations of the armies. The Turks following him up, attacked him there with great bravery, each side proving their valour. After a great slaughter on either side Assambei was defeated and forced to retreat into his own country of Persia, abandoning the three cities. He arrived at Tauris, where he caused games and rejoicings to be held, not caring much for his reverse, as he had lost none of his dominions. After a certain time war broke out with the Soldan of Cairo, and he marched with a considerable force into the country of Diarbec. The Soldan of Cairo, with the Mamelukes and a large army of his subjects, crossed the Euphrates and took Orfà, which he pillaged at his leisure, Assambei not having yet come up. Assambei, who was already at Amit,[1] mustering his forces to attack the Mamelukes, hearing of the fall of Orfà,[2] quickly marched to the plain of Orfà, where he attacked the camp of the Mamelukes with such fury, that they were nearly all cut to pieces, the rest being forced to fly with the loss of all their baggage,

---

[1] Amida Diarbekr. See Zeno, p. 6.
[2] Orfa (Edessa). See Zeno, p. 98.

which afforded great spoil to Assambei and his chiefs. He then advanced to Bir, and took it, together with Besin,[1] Calat, and Efron, ravaging the whole country about there. After remaining six months at Bir, he returned in great triumph to Persia, holding feasts at Tauris in his palace of Astibisti.

CHAP. XI.—Assambei dying, is succeeded on the throne by his son Jacob, who takes for wife a licentious woman, an adulteress; she gives him poison, of which he dies as well as herself, and a little son. Whence the great lords of Persia make war among themselves for a long time, to prove who is to succeed to the throne, first one and then another.

Assambei had four children, one a son, Sultan Jacob, who succeeded his father; and three daughters, of whom two are still alive at Aleppo. I myself have often conversed with them in Trebizond Greek, which they had learnt from Queen Despinacaton, their mother. Assambei being at Tauris, and having already lived to a great age, died in the year 1478, and, as I mentioned above, was succeeded by his son, who was a great lord, and ruled Persia for some time. He took as wife a high-born lady, daughter of a Persian noble, but a most licentious woman: having fallen in love with a great lord of the court, this wicked woman sought means to kill Jacob Sultan her husband, designing to marry her paramour, and make him king, as, being closely related to Jacob, he would become so by right in default of children. Having arranged matters with him, she prepared an insidious poison for her husband, who having gone into a perfumed bath, as was his custom, with his young son, aged eight or nine years, remained there from the twenty-second hour till sunset. On coming out, he went into the harem, which was close to the bath, where he was met by his wicked wife with a cup and a gold vase containing the poison, which she

[1] Kalat en Nejm.

had got ready while he was in the bath, knowing that it was his custom to have something to drink on coming out of the bath. She caressed him more than usual, to effect her wicked purpose; but not having sufficient command over her countenance, became very pale, which excited the suspicion of Jacob, who had already begun to distrust her from some of her proceedings. He then commanded her to taste it first, which, although she knew it was certain death, she could not escape, and drank some; she then handed the gold cup to her husband Jacob, who, with his son, drank the rest. The poison was so powerful that by midnight they were all dead. The next morning the news was circulated of the sudden death of Jacob Sultan, his son and wife. The great lords hearing of their king's decease, had quarrels among themselves, so that for five or six years all Persia was in a state of civil war, first one and then another of the nobles becoming sultan. At last, a youth named Alumut,[1] aged fourteen years, was raised to the throne, which he held till the succession of Sheikh Ismael Sultan.

CHAP. XII.—Secaidar, chief of the Suffaveans, engages in battle with the general of the forces of Alumut, is defeated, taken prisoner, and his head being cut off, is taken to the king at Tauris, who causes it to be thrown to the dogs.

During the reign of Alumut, in a city four days' east from Tauris, lived a lord about the rank of a count, named Secaidar,[2] of a religion or sect named Sophi, reverenced by his co-religionists as a saint, and obeyed as a chief. There are numbers of them in different parts of Persia, as in Natolia and Caramania, all of whom bore great respect to this Secaidar, who was a native of this city of Ardouil,[3]

[1] A son of Yakoob Sultan; his brother, Murad Khan, disputed the throne with him, and seized Fars and Babylonia.
[2] Sheikh Hyder. See Zeno, p. 42.   [3] Ardebil.

where he had converted many to the Suffavean doctrine. Indeed, he was like the abbot of a nation of monks; he had six children, three boys and three girls, by a daughter of Assambei;[1] he also bore an intense hatred to the Christians. He frequently made incursions with his followers into Circassia, ravaging the country, and so brought away many slaves and much booty with him on his return, with great rejoicings, to Ardouil. Alumut Sultan having succeeded to the throne, Secaidar, wishing to return to his wonted expeditions into Circassia against the Christians, assembled his troops, and set out towards Sumacchia,[2] which he reached in eight days; from thence he took the road to Derbant,[3] where is the pass by which one enters Circassia, and was five days en route. Sultan Alumut and his lords hearing that Secaidar, with an army of four or five thousand Suffaveans, was marching into Circassia, joined by numbers of volunteers in hopes of plunder, quickly sent messengers to the king of the country, who was himself afraid of the number of troops Secaidar had with him, to tell him to use every means in his power to stop him. Secaidar and his Suffaveans had the previous year, with half the number of men, done great damage near that fortress, and so they feared he might do the same; therefore they wished to bar his passage, lest he should go on increasing his power, as he did every day on his march into Circassia, by being joined by such multitudes of volunteers for the sake of booty, by which means he would soon have become a great lord. Secaidar therefore, on his arrival at Derbant, found the pass closed by the order of Alumut Sultan. Derbant is a large city, and, according to their chronicles and traditions, was built by Alexander the Great; it is one mile wide and three in length, having on one side the Caspian Sea, and on the other a high mountain; no one can pass except through the gates of the city, as on the east is the sea, and on the west

[1] Martha.   [2] Schamachi.   [3] Derbend.

a mountain, so steep that not even a cat could climb it. Derbant, the name of this city, in Persian signifies " closed gate";[1] and any one wishing to go into Circassia, must pass through the city which borders on that country, and the greater part of whose inhabitants speak Circassian, or rather Turkish. Secaidar finding his passage barred as I have said, was very indignant, and began to attack the fortress and pass; there being few soldiers in the place, and insufficient numbers to resist the Suffaveans, news of their necessity was sent in great haste to the king of the country, who reported it to Alumut in Tauris. The latter ordered his lords to levy troops, and when they had assembled about ten thousand men, set out against Secaidar, who was besieging the fortress of Derbant, where they arrived in a few days. Secaidar perceiving the troops of Alumut, retired to a hill on one side, where he exhorted his soldiers to fight bravely, saying that he felt confident of victory, and promising them great things. This was in the evening, and every one swore to fight valiantly. The following morning, the Suffaveans were all admirably posted for the battle, while opposite them the general of Alumut had marshalled his troops. Secaidar seeing that an engagement was inevitable, was the first to attack the enemy, his Suffaveans fighting like lions, and cutting to pieces a third of Alumut's troops; but he was at length defeated, and his men massacred. He himself was taken prisoner; and his head being cut off, was presented to Alumut Sultan, who commanded it to be carried on a lance all through Tauris, with martial instruments sounding in honour of the victory, and afterwards taken to a maidan, where executions took place, and there thrown to be eaten by dogs. For this reason, the Suffaveans hate dogs, and kill all they come across.

[1] Demir Kapoo, or "iron gate", it is sometimes called.

CHAP. XIII.—Three sons of Secaidar, hearing of their father's death, escape in different directions; one of them, named Ismael, flies to an island inhabited by Armenian Christians, where he was instructed in the Holy Scriptures by an Armenian priest. Hence he goes to Chilan, and, determining to avenge his father's death, manages to take the castle of Maumutaga, which he sacks, and bestows all the booty on his followers. For this reason, many flocked to his banner, being voluntarily converted to Suffaveism.

Immediately on the news reaching Ardouil, where Secaidar's wife and six children were, the three sons fled, one going to Natolia, another to Aleppo, and the third to an island which, as I have mentioned before, is in the lake of Van or Vastan,[1] and contains a town of Armenian Christians. Here this son, named Ismael, who was a noble youth about thirteen or fourteen years old, remained four years in the house of a Papà or priest, who was slightly acquainted with astrology, by which he learnt that Ismael would one day become a great lord. For this reason he was particularly kind and attentive to him, also instructed him in our holy faith and in the Scriptures, showing him also the vanity and emptiness of the Mahometan religion. After four years Ismael determined to leave Arminy,[2] and went to Chilan,[3] where he lived a year with a goldsmith,[4] a great friend of his father's, who kept him in secret with great care and respect. During this period the youth frequently wrote secret letters to some of the chief personages in Ardouil, who had been friends of his father's, to arrange matters with them; in the spring of the year he determined to avenge his father's defeat, and collected, with the goldsmith, ten or twenty Suffaveans to make a sudden attack upon the castle of Maumutaga, having arranged that two hundred of his friends in Ardouil should come armed to the castle and conceal themselves near it in a glen filled with canes. Everything being

---

[1] The island of Ak Tamar, the seat of the Armenian Catholicos.
[2] Arminig.   [3] Ghilan.   [4] Pyrcall.

settled, Ismael set out from Chilan with his troop, and on arriving at Maumutaga[1] attacked the gate of the castle with great fury, killing the guards; as there were but few defenders in the castle they were all cut to pieces with the exception of the women and children. Ismael then mounted a tower, and having signalled to his two hundred allies, who joined him in great haste, together with them sallied out into the town below the castle, killing the inhabitants, and carrying with them great booty back into the castle where they had left the goldsmith and ten companions as a garrison. This fortress of Maumutaga is very rich, from being a port on the Caspian sea. All the ships coming from Strevi, Sara,[2] and Masanderan, loaded with merchandise for Tauris and Sumacchia, disembark at this place. Ismael found immense treasures in the town, which he divided among his men, keeping nothing for himself; thus the fame went abroad that Ismael, the son of Secaidar, had taken this fine fortress and had bestowed all he found there on his companions. Thus he was joined by numbers, even those who were not Suffaveans flocking to his standard, in hopes of receiving gifts of this nature from the valiant Ismael; in this way arrived at Maumutaga in the course of a few days more than four thousand Suffaveans. Alumut on hearing this news was much amazed, and wished to send a force against Maumutaga, but was dissuaded as the fortress was considered impregnable against assault, while with the sea open to it it could not be reduced by a regular siege or famine. Alumut then was compelled to send an army to keep Ismael in check, hoping to destroy him by some act of rashness, not knowing what was decreed by fate.

[1] See Zeno, pp. 48, 49.   [2] Astrabad, Sari.

CHAP. XIV.—Ismael marches against the King Sermangoli, takes and pillages his city of Sumacchia, giving everything to the soldiery; Alumut being alarmed, assembles his forces; whereupon, Ismael having sought and obtained the aid of the Iberians, surprises the camp of Alumut; the latter flies to Tauris, and thence to Amit; Ismael, following up his victory, takes Tauris, and, after many other acts of cruelty, causes the head of his own mother to be cut off.

Ismael was reinforced from day to day, making rich presents to all who joined him; when he found himself sufficiently powerful he resolved to take Sumacchia, and assembled his troops for that purpose. Sermangoli on the attack of the Suffaveans abandoned the city and retired to an almost impregnable castle, named Culistan,[1] situated on a high mountain and cut out of the solid rock, where he considered himself secure. Ismael soon performed the two days' march from Maumutaga to Sumacchia,[2] where he slaughtered many of the wretched inhabitants. This city is large and rich, a port, and the headquarters of a great trade, wherefore Ismael and his army enriched themselves with its spoils. The fame of the victories and generosity of Ismael spread throughout Persia and Natolia, so that every one became a Suffavean in hopes of advancement. Alumut beholding with no slight apprehension the rapid advances of Ismael and the increase of his partizans, hastily summoned his lords and commanded them to levy troops. Ismael also being alarmed on hearing this, sent messengers to Iberia, which is three, or rather four days' journey from Sumacchia. This Iberia is a large province inhabited by Christians, and governed by seven great chiefs, two or three of whom are on the frontiers of Persia or Tauris, and whose names are Alexander Bec, Gorgurambec, and Mirzambec. Ismael sent to them for assistance, promising wealth to all who joined him, and agreeing, in case he took Tauris, to free

[1] See Zeno, pp. 50, 56. [2] Schamachi. See Zeno, p. 56.

them from the tribute they paid to the King of Persia. Each of these Christian chiefs sent three thousand horse, being nine thousand in all. These Iberians are famous horsemen, and valiant in war; on their arrival at Sumacchia, Ismael bestowed rich presents on them, all from the plunder of the town. Alumut Sultan, who was a younger man than Ismael (Ismael[1] being nineteen years old, as I have been informed by many people, and Alumut only sixteen), hearing of Ismael's proceedings through his spies, set out from Tauris against him, while the latter also advanced with all his troops, fifteen or sixteen thousand in number. The rivals met in this way between Tauris and Sumacchia, near a river, over which there were two stone bridges half a mile apart. Alumut, with an army of thirty thousand men, having arrived first, caused the bridges to be broken so as to obstruct the passage, and then encamped there. On the following day, Ismael arrived on the opposite bank; but having by good fortune discovered a ford, he crossed with his whole army on the following night, and took the army of Alumut by surprise as they were sleeping in their tents overcome with wine and food, so that they were unable to defend themselves. Then began a great slaughter of these poor wretches, so much so that at the hour of three they were all cut to pieces, except Alumut, who escaped with a few companions to Tauris, where he kept his treasures and his harem, and thence to Amit. Ismael took an immense booty in tents, horses, arms, etc., while all his soldiers enriched themselves with spoil. He remained in that place four days to refresh his troops, who were wearied with the fighting, and then advanced on the city of Tauris, where they met with no resistance, but massacred many of the inhabitants. All the kinsman of Jacob Sultan were put to the edge of the sword, and even pregnant women were slaughtered with their unborn offspring. The tomb of

[1] See Zeno. p. 46.

Jacob Sultan, and those of many lords who had been present at the battle of Derbant where Ismael's father was killed, were opened, and their bones burnt. Three hundred public courtezans were then arranged in line, and their bodies divided in two. Then eight hundred avaricious Blasi who had been brought up under Alumut were beheaded. They even slaughtered all the dogs in Tauris, and committed many other atrocities. After this, Ismael sent for his own mother,[1] who was in some way related to Jacob Sultan (in what manner I have not been able to discover), and finding that she had married one of the lords who had been present at the battle of Derbant, after reviling her, caused her head to be cut off before him. From the time of Nero to the present, I doubt whether so bloodthirsty a tyrant has ever existed.

CHAP. XV.—Many cities and chiefs give in their submission to Ismael, with the exception of a fortress of Christians, which held out for five years; but, hearing of the death of Alumut, they surrender. In the villages near this fortress are found books written with Latin characters, in the Italian tongue.

At this time many districts, cities, and castles gave in their submission to Ismael. Many nobles also sought his presence, and paid him homage, putting on the red caftan, kissing his hands, and taking oaths of allegiance. There was one exception of the governor of a fortress named Alangiachana,[2] two days' distant from Tauris. This castle has twelve neighbouring villages inhabited by orthodox Christains, whose patriarch sends two men every year to the Pope with an offering of incense. They perform their worship in Armenian, having lost the use of the Italian

[1] Stepmother, according to others.

[2] Perhaps Alanja, near Maragha, on a small stream falling into Lake Urumia; but Zeno says it was to the north of Tauris.

language. In these villages there are many manuscripts and books in Italian; while I was in Tauris two were brought to me, one relating to astronomy and the other to the rules of grammar. They also produce a great quantity of rich crimson dye. As I have mentioned, this was one of the last castles belonging to the Christians, who have for some time forgotten their original language, the Italian. This governor, after Ismael had taken Tauris, still held out for four or five years, being a devoted adherent of Alumut Sultan, while Assambei Sultan and Jacob Sultan had also deposited immense treasures in the fortress for security. The news of Alumut's death at length reaching him, he no longer wished to hold out, and surrendered the castle and treasures to Ismael. Ismael having obtained the regal power was nominated Sultan by the whole nation, who admired his wonderful victories; and he reigned, honoured, loved, and respected by all.[1]

CHAP. XVI.—Muratcan, the son of Jacob Sultan, marches against Ismael to fight for the throne; but, his army being defeated and cut to pieces, he flies to Bagadet.

While Ismael Sultan was in Tauris, Muratcan[2] Sultan of Bagadet, with an army of 30,000 men, moved against him to seize the throne which was his by right. Ismael upon hearing this was moved with great indignation, and assembling his vassals and troops issued from Tauris to a wide plain, where he heard that Muratcan was hastily advancing, thinking to obtain great booty. This Muratcan was the son of Jacob Sultan. Then Ismael exhorted all his vassals and soldiers to bear themselves manfully, and also desired the Iberian Chieftains to encourage their men to deeds like those

[1] This is rather a contrast to his previous assertion, that he was one of the most bloodthirsty tyrants that ever existed. See p. 191.
[2] Murad Khan, brother of Alumut.

when they routed the army of Alumud; everyone promised this and waited with great impatience for the contest. Muratcan having advanced with his army to a spot not far distant from the camp of Ismael, in the plain of Tauris, halted on the banks of a rivulet to refresh his men; Ismael marched to the other bank, and took up his station there. In this position both armies challenged each other to the fight and reviled each other. At noon, Muratcan exhorted his followers to fight bravely against their Suffavean foes (Ismael doing the same on the other side), and then divided his army into three columns. Ismael Sultan, seeing the proceedings of the enemy, made two divisions of his army, one of Iberians 9,000 strong and the other of Suffaveans, separated from each other, and appointed captains as customary in battle, and the whole of the day and the following night both armies remained under arms. On the appearance of dawn they began to sound the numerous instruments the Persians use in battle, exhorting each other to fight valiantly. When day was fully broke, Muratcan was the first to throw himself with 10,000 men upon the Suffavean host, causing great slaughter, but in less than an hour all his soldiers were cut to pieces, so that he was forced to bring up his other two columns together into the contest, Ismael being compelled to do the same. Such a slaughter took place and more blood was shed than ever happened in one battle in Persia since the days of Darius,[1] the battle lasting from morning till noon, ending with the total rout of Muratcan, who fled with a few adherents to Babylon or rather Bagadet to his utter disgrace. On the opposite hand Ismael returned with great reputation, having made an immense booty of tents, pavilions, and horses, with but slight loss on his side; so he entered Tauris with a grand triumph, and spent some time in the great palace of Astibisti in sports

[1] This by no means equals the slaughter caused by Timour at Ispahan.

and rejoicings. But the Babylonians, with the exception of 50 or 70 who fled with Muratcan, were cut to pieces, about 30,000 in number, and mountains of their bones were piled up on the site of the battle. At this time Ismael was only nineteen, so that in this one year, the year 1499, all these exploits and actions took place.[1] And during my stay in Tauris, men were continually flocking to his standard, from all parts of the country, but especially from Natolia, Turkey, and Caramania, Ismael presenting gifts to them all according to their rank and condition.

Chap. XVII.—Sultan Calil, Lord of Asanchif, and Ustagialu Maumutbec, a chieftain of Natolia, give in their submission to Ismael, who gives to each of them one of his three sisters in marriage. Later on Ustagialu makes war on Sultan Calil, in accordance with the commands of Ismael, who, with an immense army, marched in person against Aliduli, ravaging his country and killing some of his sons, with an immense number of his people.

The province of Diarbec had always been subject to Persia, and therefore, Sultan Sciech Ismael having gained the throne wished to bring the whole country under his sway. Thus Sultan Calil,[2] the lord of Asanchif,[3] came in person to Ismael, put on the red caftan, and promised to be an obedient vassal, for which Ismael made him munificent presents, confirmed him in his realm, and gave him one of his sisters in marriage, so that he returned with great rejoicings to Asanchif. Another Natolian chieftain, named Ustagialu Maumutbec, who had come to the aid of Ismael with seven brothers, all valiant men, was granted for his services the fine province of Diarbec with the exception of Asanchif. Then Ustagialu made a conquest of this province,

[1] See Zeno, pp. 53, 54.
[2] Sultan Khalil, the Eiobbite.
[3] Hesn Keyf. See p. 108.

excepting the cities of Amit and Asanchif; and because Sultan Calil (as was said) had transgressed the orders of Ismael, the latter resolved that the whole province should be under the orders of Ustagialu, and sent commands to Calil to surrender the city and fortresses to Ustagialu. In like manner he ordered the latter to take possession of the city notwithstanding his relationship to Calil; for on setting out to conquer the province he had been given the second sister of Ismael as his wife, so that these two Chieftains were connected. But Sultan Calil was a Curd, and this people, though subject to the Suffaveans, are ill-disposed towards them, so Calil refused to give up anything to Ustagialu. Ustagialu then being moved with indignation, marched against him with 10,000 horsemen and waged continual war against him until the year 1510, which was that of my arrival from Azemia,[1] without being able to subdue him. The Alidulians were in the habit of making frequent incursions into this province of Diarbec and laying waste the country round Orfa, Somilon,[2] and Dedu. Orfa is a large city, the other two are fortresses; they also had in their possession a city named Cartibert,[3] governed by a son of Aliduli,[4] which Ustagialu had never been able to take. This city with its independent castle was in the realm of Persia, but the Alidulians had seized it during the reign of Sultan Jacob, and during the government of Ustagialu caused great damage throughout the country. On this account Ismael determined to march in person to destroy the Alidulians, and having recruited his army advanced to Arsingan, a fortress on the confines of Trebizond, Natolia, and Persia. Here he collected an immense force and took the place, which was held by one of the sons of the Grand Turk who had subdued Trebizond at the time of Sultan Jacob's death; and rested forty days in the place, where he

[1] Ajem.   [2] Jemeleyn.   [3] Kharput.
[4] Alla-ed Douleh, named Becarbec.

assembled a force of 60,000 fighting men, more than were sufficient to subdue the Alidulians, but because he distrusted the Ottoman and the Soldan of Cairo, between the borders of whose respective dominions the country of Aliduli was situated. During Ismael's stay in Arsingan he sent two ambassadors,[1] one named Culibec to the Ottoman in Natolia, and the other named Zachariabec to the Soldan of Cairo, swearing solemn oaths to these monarchs, that he intended no harm to their dominions, but was only marching against his enemy Aliduli. After a halt of forty days, Ismael set out from Arsingan against the enemy, with his 60,000 men. It is only a four days' march from Arsingan to the country of Aliduli; but Ismael took another route, passing by the Turkish city of Cesaria[2] in order to obtain supplies which he intended to pay for honestly. On his arrival, he caused proclamation to be made that everyone who brought provisions for sale should be liberally paid, and forbade his men under pain of death to take even as much as a handful of straw without paying for it, as it was a friendly city; having remained there four days, Ismael continued his march to the beautiful district of Bastan, where there is a fine river and numerous villages, just one day's journey from Aliduli's capital, a city named Marras.[3] Ismael having first ravaged Basten,[4] moved upon Marras, from whence Aliduli had fled with numerous followers to the high mountain named Caradag,[5] to which there was access by only one narrow pass. Ismael devastated the country, killing numbers of people, among them some of the sons of Aliduli who from time to time used to descend from the mountain to fall upon the Suffaveans, but were easily cut to pieces by them, as their descent was betrayed by the numerous scouts

---

[1] See Angiolello, p. 108.
[2] Kaisarieh.
[3] Marash. See Zeno, p. 54.
[4] El Bostan or Albistan. See Zeno, p. 54.
[5] Kara Dagh, Black Mountain.

kept by Ismael, and also by some secret Suffaveans among the Alidulians themselves. It was the 29th July, 1507, when Ismael entered the country of Aliduli, where he remained till the middle of November, when he was forced to leave from want of provisions in the country, and from the snow and cold which prevented a winter campaign.

CHAP. XVIII.—Amirbec makes a prisoner of Sultan Alumut, who had admitted him with his soldiers into Amit, and leads him in chains before Ismael, who cuts off his head with his own hands. He then takes the city of Cartibirt, with the son of Aliduli, whom he puts to death; after the winter he returns to Tauris.

During my stay in Malacia,[1] a city belonging to the Soldan of Cairo, on my return journey from Cimiscasac[2] and Arsingan to Aleppo, I met Amirbec the governor of Mosulminiato, a great adherent of Ismael's, who wore two gold chains, covered with rubies and diamonds, round his neck, to which was attached the seal of Ismael, a mark of his greatest confidence. When the latter required to seal anything it was Amirbec's duty to do so with his own hands. To do a favour to Sultan Ismael, he had put a number of lords to death, and while I was in Malacia, I found that he had captured, in the following manner, the young Sultan Alumut, who had been defeated by Sciech Ismael; he set out from Mosul with 400[3] men to Amit where Sultan Alumut lived, pretending to be coming to his aid as he was doubtful about Ismael's return, wherefore Alumut received him courteously as usual, for Amirbec had been one of his chiefs. Thus confiding in him, and having allowed him to enter the city with his 400 men, Amirbec suddenly placed his hand on the shoulder of the unfortunate young man, saying—You are the prisoner of Ismael Sultan. Leaving a governor in the city,

[1] Malatia.   [2] Tchimish Gazak.
[3] Next page says 4000.

he put him in chains and took him with him to meet Ismael at Malacia (where I then was), being the nearest place on the road to the country of Aliduli where Ismael was engaged in war. He remained there a day and a half with the 4,000 Suffaveans he had with him. and I myself saw the young Alumut bound in chains in a tent. Amirbec leaving took him as a grateful gift to Ismael, who had him brought into his presence and cut off his head with his own hands; he then hurried back to his own country for fear of the snow, passing through Malacia, where he only rested one day to supply his troops with provisions; he then crossed the Euphrates, which is only ten miles distant from Malacia, and encamped before Cartibert; which was governed by a son of Aliduli named Becarbec, and well furnished with troops and provisions; but all was of no avail, as Ismael took the place, cut off the young man's head with his own hands and then proceeded in great haste on his way to Tauris. On the six days' march to that city, the snow and cold caused great loss in men, horses, and camels, and they had to abandon part of the booty they had made in the country of Aliduli. But nevertheless Ismael rode on to a beautiful palace he had built at Coi, where he remained until the Naurus,[2] that is the new year, when he determined to march against Muratcan Sultan of Bagadet. Returning to Tauris he found that his two brothers whom he had left in charge of the city had not thoroughly observed his commands, so he was very nearly putting them to death; but in accordance with the entreaties of many of his lords the young men escaped, but were banished to their native province of Ardouil which they were not allowed to leave, being granted a train of only 200 horsemen each.

[1] Kharput.
[2] Nevruz, New Year's day, at the vernal equinox.

CHAP. XIX.—Ismael sets out with his army against Muratcan, many of whose lords and soldiers desert to Ismael; Muratcan, offering to become his vasaal, sends an ambassador to him, whom Ismael causes to be cut to pieces with all his train; Muratcan then flies, and finding shelter nowhere, goes to Aliduli, who gives him one of his daughters in marriage.

At the new year Ismael collected thirty or forty thousand fighting men, with whom he set out on his march to his city of Casun;[1] remaining there a few days he proceeded to Spain,[2] a large and populous city belonging to Moratcan, who foreseeing the storm had on his side assembled an army of 30,000 fighting men. He came to Siras,[3] a larger and more beautiful city than Cairo in Egypt, so that both were prepared, Moratcan in Siras and Ismael in Spain. Ismael had a large army all of Suffaveans and brave men; on the contrary, Moratcan's army came to the field compulsorily and with reluctance; hearing of Ismael's force they knew it would be impossible to resist him in the fight, as with a fewer number of men he had routed and cut to pieces the host of Muratcan 30,000 strong in the plains of Tauris, in the former battle. On this account, many of the chiefs and soldiers doubtful as to the issue fled to Ismael's camp. Moratcan perceiving the desertion sent two ambassadors with a train of five hundred to Ismael, followed by spies to learn the result of the embassy, which was to declare himself Ismael's vassal and that he was willing to pay him tribute. Ismael caused the ambassadors and their suite to be cut in pieces, saying "if Moratcan were willing to become my subject, he would have come in person and not have sent an embassy." The spies seeing the result, reported the news at once to Moratcan, who took to flight with all his belongings, as the rumour had spread throughout his camp, many

[1] Kashan.
[2] Ispahan, which rose to its greatest prosperity under Shah Abbas.
[3] Shiraz.

of his chiefs donning the red caftan. Moratcan fearing to be made captive in the same manner as Alumut, chose a guard, three thousand in number, of the adherents he thought most faithful, and with them he fled towards Aleppo from the fury of Ismael, who hearing of his flight dispatched six thousand Suffaveans in pursuit. After crossing a river by a stone bridge he caused it to be broken down, so on the speedy arrival of the Suffaveans on the opposite bank all further action was useless; Moratcan pursuing his route came to a castle, governed by one of his slaves, who seeing his master in flight, or having some understanding with Ismael, refused to admit him, for which, enraged by the loss of his treasure in the castle, Moratcan caused the inhabitants of a small town beneath the castle to be slaughtered. Advancing towards Aleppo, in a few days he arrived within thirty miles of the city, and waited till he sent to Cairbec, the governor,[1] to ask for a safe conduct, which was courteously granted, and a grand reception accorded him. He further sent some of his lords to Cairo to demand a safe conduct from the Soldan, who for some reason or other would not grant it, but sent information as to where he would find Aliduli. On joining the latter, he was heartily welcomed, Aliduli condoling with him for his losses from the Suffaveans, and Moratcan doing likewise on his side. Aliduli also, notwithstanding his condition, gave him one of his daughters in marriage.

CHAP. XX.—Ismael takes Bagadet and then returns to Spani to oppose the Tartars; after one year he re-enters Tauris, where great rejoicings were held with archery sports for fifteen days. A description of his qualities is given.

Ismael having seen the total destruction of his enemy proceeded to Siras and then to Bagadet, making great

[1] Caierbec, notorious for his treachery against Khafoor el Ghouri, the Soldan of Egypt, in his war with Selim I. See Angiolello, p. 122.

slaughter among the wretched inhabitants. About this time the great Tartar Iesilbas[1] had invaded Persia with a vast army, had over-run Corasan,[2] and taken the city of Eri,[3] a populous and commercial place, also Stravi,[4] Amixandaran,[5] and Sari, towns on the shores of the Caspian towards the East, and bordering on the new conquests of Ismael, who being alarmed at the news returned with his army to Spaan. The Tartar endeavouring to outwit Ismael, asked leave to pass through his territories on his way to Mecca, as he pretended he wished to make a pilgrimage to his prophet Mahomet, but Ismael perceiving the snare not only refused a passage, but sent insulting messages in reply and remained one year in Spaan to meet the Tartars. The great Tamerlane once took this very country with the whole of Persia and Soria, and there still remain memorials of him in Soria. At the end of a year Ismael returned to Tauris, where on his arrival great rejoicings took place; I happened to be there myself, having gone to recover debts from the traitor Chamainit of Casvene. For a fortnight Ismael continued to join in archery every day with his lords in a maidan, in the midst of which was a pole, on which was placed a golden apple (twenty apples, ten of gold and ten of silver, being provided for the days' sport), at which, they shot from their bows while running, and whoever hit it took it for his own. Every time one was hit they rested for a time, drinking delicate wines and eating sweetmeats; during the sports two beautiful youths stood beside the monarch, one holding a gold vase, and the other two plates of sweetmeats; the lords having their wine and sweetmeats separately. When

[1] Sheibani Khan. See Zeno, p. 56.   [2] Khorassan.
[3] Herat. See Zeno, p. 56.
[4] Astrabad, a city of about fifty thousand inhabitants, is situated near the mouth of the river Ester, on a bay of the Caspian. It is the capital of a small province of the same name often included in Maganderan; it is also a treasure city of the reigning family, being the centre of their hereditary possessions.
[5] Probably one of the ports of Mazanderan; perhaps Balfrush. Zeno.

Ismael rests, the youths approach with the wine and sweetmeats; he does so sometimes, even when no apple has been hit. He always has a guard of a thousand soldiers to attend him at these sports; besides there is a crowd of about thirty thousand people, composed of citizens and soldiers, round the maidan. At the entrance of the garden nearest the palace there is a large saloon, where a supper is prepared for the lords who have joined in the sports, while Ismael retires to his repast in the palace Astibisti. Then all the lords sing in praise of their master Ismael, extolling his graciousness towards them. At present he is about thirty-one, very handsome, of a magnanimous countenance, and about middle height; he is fair, stout, and with broad shoulders, his beard is shaved and he only wears a moustache, not appearing to be a very hairy man. He is as amiable as a girl, left-handed by nature, is as lively as a fawn, and stronger than any of his lords. In the archery trials at the apple, he is so expert, that of every ten knocked down he hits six; during the sports, music is played and dancing girls perform after their manner, singing the praises of Ismael; after a stay of a fortnight at Tauris he went with his army to Coi where he abode for two months.

Chap. XXI.—Sermangoli breaks the treaty with Ismael, sets out to ravage the country a second time, sending two captains on this expedition, while he himself, leaving Canar, marches towards the Caspian. taking many places, and among them the great and famous fortress of Derbant.

During his stay at Coi, Sermangoli the king of Servan,[1] a tributary of Ismael's, broke the treaty between them. Then Ismael, filled with anger, assembled his troops and marched against the country for the second time, having on the former occasion taken the country from this Sermangoli who was

[1] Shirvan.

the ruler, but having restored it to him on his promising to be a faithful subject; for his deceit he now set out to take it away from him. He first marched to Carabacdac,[1] a district more than a thousand miles in extent, in which is a large fortress named Canar, subject to which are many villages famous for the culture of silk, which from this place is named Canareso; here he remained some days as it was a fertile district. Here he appointed two captains, one named Lambec, and the other Bairambec the conqueror of Van, as I have before related, and a brother-in-law of Ismael's as he had married one of the latter's three sisters, Custagialutbec another, and Sultan Calil of Asanchif the third. These two captains being appointed, they were despatched against Sumacchia, which town they found quite deserted on their arrival, as the inhabitants had fled to a large and impregnable fortress named Culustan, situated on the summit of a mountain. It was held by a brave officer, devoted adherent of the king of Servan, who had given orders to him on the approach of Ismael to retire to it from the city, which is only half a mile distant. Lembec and Bairambec seeing that every one had retired to the castle, sat down with ten thousand men to besiege it, but could make no impression upon it as it was inaccessible on every side, and they had no artillery or engines. While they were engaged in the siege, Ismael left Canar and came to Maumutaga, which was immediately surrendered to him as the inhabitants had on a previous occasion experienced his cruelty; all the wealth found in the place was given to the soldiers. He further set out on his march along the shore of the Caspian, to subdue the other fortresses of the province of Servan, which extends from Maumutaga to Derbant, a seven days' journey. There are three large cities and three fortresses along this shore : the first is Sumacchia, which is a day's journey from the sea, but the others, Maumutaga and Derbant, are close to

[1] Kara Bagh Dagh, or Mountain of Kara Bagh.

it. The first castle he came to was called Baccara,[1] which was immediately given up to him; a day's journey further was a fine castle named Sirec on the summit of a mountain, which detained him three days while treating for terms, which Ismael granted, reinstating the former governor, but sending sixty Suffaveans to hold it, who by their arrogant conduct towards the inhabitants were all massacred by the latter, who then fled to the mountains by night, from fear of Ismael, who finding no one on whom to wreak his vengeance, caused the place to be demolished. Advancing a little further they came to a castle and a large unwalled town named Sabran, which was deserted, as the king of the country caused it to be wasted that Ismael might not procure supplies; however, fresh provisions reached the latter every day from Carabacdac. After four days' march, Ismael arrived at Derbant[2] where he found the inhabitants fled, either to the mountains or to Circassia, while only the citadel held out, which was very strong as I have already described, and defended on every side by men with lances and banners. This castle has only two gates, well built with stone and mortar. Ismael, who had arrived in about fifteen or twenty days, remained eleven days with his whole army forty thousand strong before the castle; they made two mines, neither of which succeeded. At last they made a large mine under a tower, digging out all the foundations, and supporting it with beams of wood; then filling the hollow with dry wood they set fire to it hoping that when the beams were burnt the tower would fall. The dry wood soon burnt and flames soon poured out of the hollow, but had little effect as they were choked in the cavern. But the governor fearing greater damage and the loss of the place, sent a messenger at midnight to Ismael, offering to yield the castle if lives and property were spared. Ismael

[1] Baku, after which the Caspian is sometimes named.
[2] Derbend. See Zeno.

having seen the ill success of the fire gave the promise as required to the messenger, and on the following morning the gates were opened and the castle surrendered. They found in it great quantities of arms, stores, and provisions, which were brought before Ismael, who remained eight or nine days to refresh his troops, during which stay many chiefs gave in their submission, and put on the red caftan.

CHAP. XXII.—Ismael returns to Tauris; great sports and feasts are prepared for his arrival; of the affection his soldiers bear him, and how he is adored almost as a God; of their clothes and armour; of the disgraceful act committed by him, and how he sets out for the second time with his army against the Tartar.

During these latter events I was at Tauris, endeavouring to hasten the recovery of my debts, for which I had to summon Camaidit of Casvene, but could not get satisfaction from him, as he had gained the favour of a friend of his, an usher of the court. I was then advised to have recourse to Ismael, so having drawn up a memorial I set off on horseback to find him, which I did in the midst of his army beneath the ruined citadel of Zirec. Finding some lords whom I had known in Tauris, I acquainted them with my wants, asking them to procure me an audience of Ismael, but they advised me to wait till he had subdued Derbant, when in his joy for his victory he would be inclined to grant anything I might ask, which counsel I took and remained the whole time in the camp. When the fortress was taken and the conquest completed, I sought out those lords, and giving them the memorial with the papers proving the debt, the matter was shown to Ismael, who despatched me immediately to Tauris with orders to all the officers that right should be done me. The decree was written in Ismael's name in large letters, and sealed with his seal with a sign resembling a Z, by the hands of Mirbec, the ruler of

Mosul, who wears the seal of Ismael on a chain round his neck; it is made out of a diamond set in a beautifully worked ring of gold; it is about half the size of a nut, and is engraved in minute letters with the name of Ismael surrounding the twelve sacraments of their sect.[1] On my arrival in Tauris I found I could do nothing as my adversary had fled, so I determined to proceed to Aleppo, but before I left, Ismael returned with his army, for whose coming there were great preparations made, and all the shops decorated for the festival and triumphs. He came every day to the maidan to divert himself with archery with his lords who received many gifts from him. And there was dancing, music and songs in honour of the great Sultan Ismael when he was present in the maidan. This Sophy is loved and reverenced by his people as a god, and especially by his soldiers, many of whom enter into battle without armour, expecting their master Ismael to watch over them in the fight. There are also others to go into battle without armour, being willing to die for their monarch, rushing on with naked breasts, crying " Schiac, Schiac." The name of God is forgotten throughout Persia and only that of Ismael remembered; if any one fall when riding or dismounted he appeals to no other god but Schiac, using the name in two ways; first as god Schiac; secondly as prophet; as the Mussulmans say "Laylla, laylla Mahamet resuralla," the Persians say " Laylla yllala Ismael vellialla;[2] besides this, everyone, and particularly his soldiers, consider him immortal, but I have heard that Ismael is not pleased with being called a god or a prophet. They are accustomed to wear a red caftan and above that a high conical turban made with a dozen folds, representing the twelve sacraments of their sect, or the twelve descendants of Ali; besides this, they neither shave either their beard or

---

[1] Probably the names of the twelve Imaums.
[2] La Illaha illa Allah. Ismael Wely Allah.

whiskers. Their dress has never changed; their armour is of beautifully worked and carved steel cuirasses, besides coats of mail, helmets like those of the Mamelukes; their harness is very strong, bound with cotton; sometimes it is of the fine steel of Siras, and sometimes of copper, but not like ours, but all in pieces like that of Soria: they have other helmets or headpieces of heavy mail. Everyone rides, and so there are no foot soldiers; they use lances, swords, and slings, besides bows with many shafts.

On his second arrival in Tauris, Ismael committed a most disgraceful act, as he caused twelve of the most beautiful youths in the town to be taken to his palace of Astibisti for him to work his wicked will upon them, and gave them away one by one to his lords for the same purpose; a short time previously he had caused ten children of respectable men to be seized in like manner. When he returned from Sumacchia three Georgian ambassadors arrived and were well received, and a damsel given them as a present. While engaged in these rejoicings, news came that the Usbecs, that is the subjects of the Tartar, had over-run the country of Gesti,[1] whereupon he had to decide to march against him at once, so he took the field and mustered his troops, ordering all his lords to assemble their retainers which they had to maintain during the campaign. In this way forces came together from all sides in numbers sufficient to meet Jeselbas,[2] a great many being necessary as the Tartar was a mighty monarch. I left Tauris on the 1st of May, 1520,[3] during the levying of this army, taking the route to Aleppo, and in spite of some dangerous fellow travellers, and by the favour of God arrived at Albir[4] on the 2nd July, 1520.[5]

[1] Yezd.
[2] Sheibani Khan.
[3] The battle of Merv took place in 1514.
[4] Bir or Birajik.
[5] He does not mention the Turkish invasion of Persia, under Selim I, in 1514, which must have come under his notice, if, as he says, he remained in Tauris till 1520.

NARRATIVE

OF THE

MOST NOBLE VINCENTIO D'ALESSANDRI,

Ambassador to the King of Persia for the Most Illustrious Republic of Venice.

VINCENTIO D'ALESSANDRI.

I HAVE now undertaken to give an account to your most Illustrious Government of the regions and kingdoms which are in Persia, of the produce, of the character of the people, of the person of the king, and the qualities of his mind, the government of the Court, the manner and custom of determining the affairs of State, of things of importance in the administration of justice, of the revenue and expenditure, of the number and quality of the Sultans, who are nothing but commanders of the soldiery, and in fine of all that may appear to me worthy of your greatness.

This king, named Tamas,[1] is of the house of Scili, a family illustrious from an antiquity of 980 years, coming in a direct line from Ali,[2] who was the son-in-law of Mahomet their Prophet. He was the son of Ismail the First, the father of whom was named Serdiadar,[3] a man of great goodness and learning, and considered by his people a saint, saying that it had been predicted a thousand years before, that his son should yet be king. Thus, Ismail, after having promised the kingdom to the son of the daughter of the King Ussuncassano, with no fear of God seized it for himself, causing the head of the aforesaid son to be cut off. In this way, although much harassed by the Ottoman Emperors, fortune was favourable to him, as he was the first who began to reduce the greatness of that power, and to recover some of the principal fortresses from Sultan Selim, who was the

---

[1] Tamasp.   [2] See Zeno. p. 48.   [3] Sheikh Hyder.

father of Sultan Suliman. This prince took possession of Coninut[1] a populous city of the greatest importance, a centre of manufactures, in a most beautiful situation, which being strong by nature, is now made almost impregnable by the industry of the Ottomans, governed by a Pasha of high rank. Dependent on this place are plains and fortresses which are all called Dirabech[2] by this same Ismail. Ismail had three other sons besides the present king, who was the eldest,—Elias Mirisce,[3] Saine Mirisce, and Baiaram Mirisce. Elias was a man of great valour and daring, who during a peace with the king, Barcam, King of Sirvan,[4] took both his city and country, which is very large and of great importance on the shores of the Caspian Sea.[5] All

---

[1] Kara Amid Diarbekr. See Zeno, p. 6.   [2] Diarbekr.
[3] Mirza "prince".   [4] Shirvan.
[5] In 1549, Knolles says:—"Solyman had now almost three yeares taken his rest, when it fortuned that Ercaces Imirza, King of Sirvan, moved with the often injuries of Tamas, his brother, the great Persian king, fled to Solyman at Constantinople, to crave aid of him against his brother. Solyman, glad of such an occasion to worke upon, entertained him with all courtesie, and promised to take upon him his quarrell and to protect him against his unnaturall brother; and when he had made all things readie for so great an expedition, passed over into Asia; and after long and painfull travell entered at last with a puissant armie into Armenia, and there, in the borders of the Persian kingdome, first besieged the citie of Van, which, after ten daies' siege, was yeelded unto him upon condition that the Persian souldiors there in garrison might, with life and libertie, depart with their armes as souldiors; which was at the first by Solyman granted, and so the citie surrendered. From thence, Solyman sent his chiefe commanders, with a great part of his armie, to burne and spoile the enemie's countrey, which they for a time cheerfully performed, and running farre into the countrey strive, as it were, among themselves who should doe most harme; where Imirza, among the rest, for whose sake Solyman had undertaken this warre, was as forward as the best to wast and spoile his brother's kingdome, sparing nothing that came to hand. The best and richest things he got he presented to Solyman, to draw him on still in that warre. But that served not his turne to recover againe his kingdome of Sirvan; for Tamas, without shewing any power to withstand the Turks, had, after his wonted manner, caused his people to withdraw themselves far into the mountain-

this territory came into the hands of his brother, who failed to show his gratitude towards him for the acquisition of so vast a region, and so was the cause of his becoming his enemy, and joining the Ottomans. He excited Sultan Suliman to march with a great army against his brother, taking in his country the town of Vam, then the principal fortress of Persia, six days distant from Tauris. For this reason the king caused him to be killed, as he had already done to Saine Mirisce, his second brother, fearing lest he also should rise against him, and as their father had already died a natural death, there only remained one brother, who had a principality in India.

And the king, wishing to marry him to one of his daughters, sent to summon him, but the people would never consent to let him go to Casmen, fearing lest he should do him some harm. The sons of this king are eleven, born from different wives, eleven say sons and three daughters; the eldest,

ous countrey, leaving nothing behind them in that wast countrey to relieve them but bare ground; so that the farther the Turks went the more they wanted, without hope of better successe than such as they had before to their losse made proofe of, in their former expeditions into that great kingdome. The conceit whereof so much pierced not the common souldiors only, but even the captaines themselves: that to make an end of that long and unprofitable warre, taken in hand for another man's good, they consulted among themselves either to kill Imirza, or else to disgrace him with Solyman; which they so cunningly wrought: some suggesting false suspitions of his treacherous dealing in the proceeding of that warre; and others, with like craft, under cover of friendship, giving him warning in secret of the danger he was in: the one filling Solyman's head with distrust, and the other, Imirza's with fear. Briefly, to shut the matter up in their owne tearmes, *they persuaded the hare to flie and the hounds to follow.* Imirza, doubting some sudden mischiefe, fled for succour to an old acquaintance of his, one of the princes of Chaldea, who most treacherously sent him in bonds to Tamas, his brother, his most cruell enemie, who, glad to have the author of all his troubles with the Turks delivered into his hands, cast him in prison, and that Solyman nor any other should in his behalfe further prosecute the warre, or by his means hope for victorie, caused him to be in prison murthered. In this expedition against the Persian king Solyman was

named Cababinde[1] Mirisce, aged forty-three years, is a man of a quiet disposition, and does not trouble himself about the affairs of this world, contenting himself with a small domain given him by his father in the region of Carasam, called Cheri. This Cababinde has three sons, the eldest of whom[2] is fifteen years of age, of noble aspect and lofty spirit, and is tenderly loved by the king for his virtues, and also because none of his other sons have children.

Ismail, the second son, is forty-one years of age, of robust frame and daring spirit, of great courage, and loving war; he has proved his valour on many occasions against the Ottomans, and particularly against the Bassa of Esrom,[3] as, with a small force of cavalry, he broke the army of the Bassa, which was very numerous; and if the latter had not quickly retreated, would have made himself master of the city. On this account, Maesum Bech, the chief vizier of the king, perceived that this young man had ambitious views, and that he had assembled an army without leave from his father, and entered the country of the Ottomans in a time of peace; considering this a want of obedience, he showed the king some letters sent to the Sultans throughout the provinces, inciting them to rise for a war against the Ottomans. In this way he persuaded the king to place him in a fortress, with a guard of Sultans and many soldiers. It is now more than seventeen years ago since he was thrown into prison, and this very year they have taken away the guard, but not set him at liberty. The king, wishing to gratify him, has sent him many beautiful women to be companions to him, but he

occupied a yeare and nine months: all which time the Turks endured great troubles and were oftentimes hardly distressed by the Persians; untill, at last, Solyman himselfe, wearie of that tedious warre, wherein he had got neither honour nor profit, thought it best to make an end; and thereupon returned againe to Constantinople in the yeare 1549."

[1] Mahomet Khodabundah Mirza, Prince Mahomet, the slave of God.
[2] Afterwards Shah Abbas, the Great.
[3] The Pasha of Erzeroum.

never will have any intercourse with them,[1] saying that he will support with patience his imprisonment by his father, but that it would be too heavy a burden for him to see his children prisoners too; and that slaves are not worthy of ladies.

And this same Ismail is particularly beloved by his father, but his fear of him is great, seeing how ardently he is desired as ruler by all the people; and the Sultans are especially afraid of him from his too proud disposition; so that if he ever comes to succeed to the throne he may have to replace a great number of the chiefs of the soldiery, and to oppose all his brothers, who have taken possession of many portions of the kingdom.

Sultan Caidar Mirisce,[2] the third son and Lieutenant of his father, is eighteen years old, of small stature, most fascinating and handsome in appearance, and excelling in oratory, elegance and horsemanship, and most beloved by his father; he is very fond of hearing people discourse about war, although he does not show himself much fitted for that exercise, from his too delicate and almost feminine nature; he is of good intellect, for his age is grave enough, and shows that he understands the affairs of government, and knows how the other monarchs of the world rule.

Sultans Mustaffa, Umircan, and Ennit Mirisce, are all three between fourteen and fifteen years old, and show great talent; the others also, between eight and eleven years, are at Carassam for instruction, except a young one of five years, who is with his father, as at that age he is very cheerful and pleasing. The daughters are all married to relations, to whom great possessions are given with them as dowries. The king is in the sixty-fourth year of his age, and the fifty-first of his reign, is of middling stature, well formed in person and features, although dark, of thick

[1] When he came to the throne he gave way altogether to debauchery.
[2] Hyder Mirza.

lips, and a grisly beard; he is more of a melancholy disposition than anything else, which is known by many signs, but principally by his not having come out of his palace for the space of eleven years, nor having gone once to the chase nor any other kind of amusement, to the great dissatisfaction of his people, who according to the customs of that country, not seeing their king, can only with the greatest difficulty make their petitions, and cannot have a voice in the decisions of justice; so that day and night they cry aloud before the palace for justice, sometimes a thousand, more or less. And the king, hearing the voices, usually orders them to be sent away, saying that there are judges deputed in the country, with whom rests the administration of justice, not taking into consideration that these things are against the tyrannical Judges and Sultans, who usually wait in the street to assassinate the people, seen by me as well as by many other people. I have been told as a fact, that in the book of lawsuits there are written more than ten thousand persons who have been killed during the last eight years. This evil comes principally from the Cuzzi,[1] who, as they do not receive pay, are forced to take bribes, and do so the more, as they see that in the matter of law affairs the king takes no thought or care. Hence it arises that throughout the kingdom the roads are unsafe, and in the houses themselves one runs great dangers, and the Judges nearly all allow themselves to be corrupted by money.

In truth, one may say that this king never had any inclination for war, although he talks a great deal as if he did, being a man of very little courage. And if, indeed, in any case he has shown himself with an army in the field, he did not do so from freewill, but of necessity; never having dared to show his face to the enemy, so that, to his infinite disgrace, he has lost in his reign the important city of Babilonia, near the river Euphrates, which belonged to a lord

[1] Judges.

Scharafbech,[1] ruler of some people who are called Chinedi,[2] who as he was not afforded assistance against the Turks, was chased away by them. Besides, near this is a place called Bichillas,[3] a pass of great importance, and the key to the following cities and regions, namely, Chilach, Ergis, Vastan, Adalgeras, Berghieri, Cassan, and Van,[4] a city and fortress of much importance, and a great extent of country belonging to the above-mentioned places, which would be enough for a great Principality, all of which were lost. But what above all is his greatest enjoyment, are women and money, and these women have acquired such an influence over his mind, that he remains a long time with them deliberating and consulting about affairs of state; and although this king is miserly by nature, with them one may say that he is a spendthrift, giving them money, jewels, and things in great quantities. The women at times have permission from the king to come out of the palace; those, indeed, who have children, under the pretext of seeing them when they are ill. And I saw the mother of the Sultan Mustaffa Mirisce, who was slightly indisposed, come out with her face covered with a black veil, riding like a man, accompanied by four slaves and six men on foot.

This king uses many contrivances for promoting his pleasures, and for this keeps people on purpose; and those who do most for it are greatly rewarded. He also gives women slaves to the Sultans, that they may not be an expense to him, and when he orders them to be brought to him, they are ornamented with jewels and rich garments. Although, in the things mentioned, the great avarice of the king is plainly to be seen, I shall go on to give to your Excellencies

[1] Sherf Beg.
[2] Khunneydee Kurds in the Bohtan mountains, near Mosul, tribesmen of Sherf Beg. [3] Bitlis.
[4] Ikhlat, Arjeesh, Van, Ardel, Jiraz, Pergri, all on the Van Lake. Ikhlat was the summer seat of the Akkoniloos, and its burial ground is full of the tombs of their chiefs.

some particulars which will make it more evident. This king sent to the East for Boscasinian cloth, and to Carassam for close velvets and other silken fabrics, and to Aleppo for woollen cloths, and from these stuffs he had clothes given as payment to the soldiers, at ten times their value. He will accept any sort of present, however small, nor does he always make one in return. As another instance, a soldier, in time of war, captured the son of a certain Orbech, one of the king's greatest enemies, who has great power on the frontiers of Cinasari, and to whom the king is forced to give every year four hundred talleri, which in our coinage make eight thousand scudi, that he may not molest the caravans coming from India. Another soldier offered to give this soldier, for his prisoner, a village and a thousand scudi, but he would not give him up, and presented him instead to the king, hoping to obtain a greater reward; the king, however, only gave him a horse in exchange for a prisoner of such importance. He shows the greatest liberality in making provisions for people, by appointing them to places which are never paid, except by force of great obligations and presents. He gives up, as a favour, many kinds of tribute, and taxes, but for the most it is not so in reality, since after two or three years, he generally requires all the arrears at once, as he did at the time when I was at his Court, in the territory of Zutta, inhabited by Armenians, who were all exempted from tribute. He suddenly required all the arrears, which caused the ruin of these poor Christians. Sending the majordomo of Sultan Caiadar Mirisco,[1] lieutenant of the king, to collect these moneys, he required twenty-five loads of cloths and shawls in addition, as he is accustomed to change his garments fifty times a day, which are afterwards distributed to the people at ten times their value. And no one dares to show reluctance

[1] Hyder Mirza.

in taking these clothes, but rather to be grateful to be allowed to have them.

This king sells jewels and makes other bargains, buying and selling with the cunning of a small merchant. It is true that six years ago he did a magnanimous act, having taken away all the tolls in his kingdom, which were greater than any others in the world, since he takes a seventh part of the merchandise, besides what is taken by the officials. It has, however, been said, that he had a dream in which the Angels took him by the throat, and asked him whether it was becoming to a king, surnamed the Just, and descended from the house of Ali, to get such immense profits by the ruin of so many poor people; and then ordered him to free the people from them. The king on waking, and full of fear, commanded that in all parts of his empire the tolls should be taken off. By this deed it is evident that he repented; as in the time past, in order to accumulate money, he did thousands and thousands of actions unworthy not only of a king but of a man, which I will not particularize for fear of wearying you with their length; but will go on to speak of his court, which is divided into two departments, one the service of the king, and the other the council of state. The king's service is divided into three classes; first, the women, daughters of Sultans, bought by the king, or received as presents into his harem, which is thus called from them, the Seraglio, as the abode of the women. They are all Georgian and Circassian slaves, and he is attended by them when he sleeps in the palace. When he sleeps out, he is attended by slaves in the lower duties, as in dressing and undressing; these are of the number of forty or fifty, and keep in order the tents and the larder.

The third class of people who attend him are the noble sons of Sultans, who do not sleep in the royal palace, but come morning and evening from their houses to their attendance, and generally are about one hundred in number.

The king is served by them in turn, by handing water to him, by presenting to him his robes, and by following him when he walks in the gardens. Pay is given by the king to the servants who attend him, from fifteen years of age to twenty-five and even thirty, as long as they have no beard. In this manner, in proportion to their service, he lends some twenty, some twenty-five, and some fifty thousand scudi, at twenty per cent., to some for ten, and others for twenty years, receiving for himself the interest from year to year. They then lend it on good security, at sixty and eighty per cent. to nobles of the Court who are in expectation of receiving rank and appointments from the sovereign, and if it happens that those who have borrowed the money do not compound for the capital with him who has advanced the money, they sell their houses and possessions, nor is any compensation to be had afterwards.

The rewards of service of the nobles are the appointments of the Court as centurions and captains of the king's guard, also Sultanates, which mean governorships of the provinces; these all belong to the service of the person of the king.

The Council is really one body, in which the king is the sole President, with the intervention of twelve Sultans, men of long experience in affairs of State. It is remarkably well attended by those Sultans who from time to time come to the Court, and who all enter the Council, which is held every day except when the king goes to the bath, or has his nails cut; the time of this council in summer as well as winter is from the twenty-second hour of the day, and according to the matters in hand, continues till the third, fourth, and sixth hour of the night. The king sits upon a Masthean, not very high from the ground, and behind his shoulders his sons sit when they are at Court, especially Sultan Caidar Mirise,[1] who, as Lieutenant of his father,

[1] Hyder Mirza.

does not leave the king's sight. The Sultan Councillors, who are four in number, named viceroys, sit in front. The king introduces the subjects, and discourses about them, asking their opinions from the Sultans, and each one as he states his opinion, rises, and comes near the king, speaking aloud, that he may be heard by his colleagues. If, in the course of argument, the king hears anything which strikes him, he has it noted by the grand Councillors, and very often takes a note of it with his own hand; and thus in their order in which the king inquires of them, the Sultans give their opinions. When the king has no doubt about the matter in question, it is settled at the first Council; and if he has doubts, he hears the arguments of the full Council, and then settles it after private consideration. In the number of the consulting Sultans is included the Curzibassa, chief of the king's guard, although he may not be a Sultan. The grand Councillors have no vote, and can say nothing unless they are called upon by the king; they, although of great dignity, cannot rise to the rank of Sultan, nor to any other appointments belonging to the military service, even if they are nobly born.

<small>Council.</small>

Knighthood is really more for deserving than for noble persons. While the Council is sitting every night, there is also a guard of three hundred armed Curzi, who, when the Council is up, do not leave, but remain to guard the king.

<small>Knighthood.</small>

As it seems to me that I have at last discoursed enough about the king's court, I will go on to speak of the guard of the state, of the government and capitals of the provinces and the pursuits of the people.

The country possessed by the King of Persia is bordered on the east by the Indies, which are between the rivers Ganges and Ondo (Indus); on the west by the river Tigris, which divides Persia from Mesopotamia, now called Diarbech, and running towards the frontiers of Babilonia enters

<small>Boundaries of Persia.</small>

the Euphrates,[1] then flowing together in one bed through Bolsora,[2] into the Persian Gulf, towards the south; on the north by the Caspian Sea, called also the sea of Baccu,[3] and by Tartary of the great Cattai. In this country there are the following regions possessed by this king, namely, Sunan,[4] the ancient kingdom of the Medes, Aras, near Greater Armenia, Carassan, Chiessen,[5] Cheri,[6] Diargomet, and Gilari,[7] which is now in a disturbed state, owing to an insurrection of the people. There are fifty-two cities in this realm: the chief are Tauris, metropolis of the whole kingdom, Carbin, Curassam, Naesimen,[8] Samachi,[9] and others I will not name, but must mention that there is not one in the whole kingdom which is walled, but all are open; the buildings are wretched, and the houses all of mud and cut straw, mixed together; neither are there mosques nor anything else to adorn these cities, although their sites are generally beautiful. The roads are disagreeable, from the great quantity of dust and mud by turns, rendering them difficult for travelling.

There is a very great abundance of corn, and generally the plains are beautiful; in the country they are accustomed to conduct the water to irrigate the fields, one week in one place, and the other in another, and thus they give sufficient water to the grain and vines. In spite of the scarcity of rain, in the ascents and other places, where water cannot be brought, they grow grass. There is also a great quantity of live stock, and particularly of sheep, of such a size, that I had seen some in Tauris, whose tails weighed ten bisti, or rather ten battuarii, which in our weights make nine pounds. With all this the supply has to be immense, as no people in the world eat more than the Persians,

---

[1] Called then the Shat-ul-Arab. [2] Basrat or Bassora.
[3] Baku.   [4] Shirvan.
[5] Yezd.   [6] Herat.
[7] Ghilan.   [8] Nakshivan.   [9] Schamachi.

it being the custom for both old and young to eat four times a day, the excellence of the water helping the digestion.

In the cities and towns they do not use many ornaments; everyone sleeps on the ground, and those who are of some position use a mattress on the carpet, others a simple mat. The women are mostly ugly, though of fine features and noble dispositions, their customs not being so refined as those of the Turkish ladies. They wear robes of silk, veils on their heads, and show their faces openly. They have pearls and other jewels on their heads, and on this account pearls are in great demand in these regions, as it is not very long since they came into use. *Women and their habits.*

The reverence and love of the people for the king, notwithstanding the things mentioned above, which make one think he ought to be hated, are incredible, as they worship him not as a king, but as a god, on account of his descent from the line of Ali, the great object of their veneration. Those who are in sickness or hardships do not call to aid the name of God so much as that of the king, making vows to present him with some gift, and some go to kiss the doors of the palace, that house being considered fortunate which is able to get some cloth or shawl from the king, or else some water in which he has washed his hands, which they consider a preventive of fever. To pass over many other things I might say about this matter, I will only mention that not only the people, but his own sons and the sultans speak to him as if they could not find epithets worthy of such greatness, saying, " Thou art the living faith, and in thee we believe." And not only in the neighbouring cities can one observe these signs of reverence, but also in the distant towns and places many hold that besides having the prophetic spirit, he has the power of raising the dead and of working other like miracles, saying that, as Ali, their chief saint, had eleven male children, this king has received from the Majesty of God the same favour as Ali. It is true *Love and reverence of the people of Persia for the king.* *Superstition of the Persian people.*

that in the city of Tauris he is not held in such veneration as in the other places, for which reason it is said that he has left it and gone to stay at Casin,[1] seeing that he was not esteemed there as he wished. The city is divided into two factions, one called Nausitai, and the other Himicaivartu, which comprehend the nine municipal districts, five in one and four in the other, and all the citizens, about twelve thousand in number. These factions had always been at enmity, and slaughtered each other every day, nor could the king or any others put a stop to it, as the hatred between them had lasted more than thirty years.

<small>Factions at Tauris.</small>

Certainly, one may say that the chiefs of districts are more masters of the city than the king, since the origin of their discord was that the price of meat having risen a little higher than usual, the chiefs of the districts went to the palace of the sultans and killed all the servants, and the sultan himself, if there was anything against him; then they went to the houses of those servants who were not present, broke in the doors, killed them, and carried their heads to the palace. Nor did they do these things secretly, so that from that time no attempt has been made against their freedom; so much so, that in past times they have slain sultans only to preserve some one of their privileges.

<small>A curious and remarkable case.</small>

And since this city is the metropolis of the whole empire, it seems to me that I ought to say something about it.[2] This city, therefore, is situated in a large plain not far from some hills, and in the neighbourhood of a height where used to be an ancient castle, as may be seen from the ruins; its circumference, although it has no walls, is fifteen miles and more in a long shape. From a place called Nassa, as far as the gate of the city, towards Casbin, is almost a short day's journey in distance, with, however, numberless gardens and open places. The streets are forty-five in number, and in each there is a grove of trees, so that one may say

<small>Situation of the city of Tauris.</small>

---

[1] Kasween.   [2] See Angiolello.

that there is a garden for every street. The air is most salubrious in winter as well as summer. The fruits surpass those of every other country in goodness and quality. This city is commercial, as in it the goods and caravans of all parts of the kingdom come together, but its business has suffered much from war. As, for instance, in the past, two (loads) of silk, with which the country abounds, were worth more than four hundred sequins, and are now worth only two hundred. The merchandize which comes viâ Ormus, is taken care of by no one, as the route used to be through Aleppo, where there is now no traffic. They are still brought to Constantinople by land, and thence taken to Bogdania,[1] being dispersed through Poland, Denmark, Sweden, and other places, but the expenses are so great, that the profits are very small, in spite of the risk, as told me by some Armenians whom I met in Tauris, and afterwards in Tripoli. Commerce was still on the downhill road, until an English gentleman,[2] named Mr. Thomas, of London, arrived in this city with a great quantity of cloth through Muscovy, with the title of ambassador from the queen. Having died, the ruler of Siruan[3] took away all his things, so that his companions had to spend a great deal of money to get them back; so that, on this account, one cannot hope to negotiate or continue traffic with these countries.

In the kingdom of Carassam[4] they worked cloths of silk and especially velvets, which are equal in excellence to the Genoese; in other parts they work on smooth stuffs and damask, but not with the finish they have in Italy. In this country of Persia there are no mines of gold and silver or of copper, but only of iron; so that those who introduce silver from Turkey gain twenty per cent., gold fourteen and

Silken goods.

Mines.

---

[1] Moldavia.

[2] Alcocke, or Anthony Jenkinson, who came with a letter from Queen Elizabeth to Shah Tamasp in 1561.

[3] Shirvan.   [4] Khorassan.

fifteen per cent., and copper sometimes eighteen and sometimes twenty per cent.; it is true that there are great expenses, as the exportation of metals is forbidden.

<small>No duties in Persia.</small> This king, unlike other states, gets none of his revenues from duties, as they do not exist in this kingdom, but has a sixth part of the produce of the land, of corn and other plants; on vines and grass land, for one thousand archi of ground an annual payment of sixty-six pieces of gold, which is rather more than four sequins of gold. Archi are a measure, of which ten go to an ordinary field; so that one pays less than half a ducat for a field, and houses pay five per cent. on their rent. Christians in some regions pay five, in <small>Taxes on houses.</small> others seven and eight ducats, per house, according to the goodness and wealth of the country they inhabit. And of animals, for every herd of forty sheep he receives a tribute of fifteen bisti a year, which make three ducats of our <small>Male animals do not pay tribute in Persia.</small> money, but which male animals do not pay; for every cow they paid the sum of two ducats a-year of our money, and so on; these make up the income of the king, which is said <small>Income and expenditure of the King of Persia.</small> to amount to three millions of gold. The expenditure, which really comes from the treasury, is very small, as he is under obligation to pay only five thousand soldiers, called Curzi, who act as his body-guard, and are selected from the best and finest men in the realm; nor these even does he pay in money, but gives them uniforms and horses, putting on them whatever value he thinks fit in advance for their salaries.

He has eleven sons, and each of them has a sumptuous and separate court, but no one knows what he gives them. There are fifty sultans, by whom all the soldiery of the kingdom is made up, as it is divided into fifty parts, except that which he and his sons keep, which is not subject to governors. These same commanders have the charge of from five hundred to three thousand horsemen each, and from the regions assigned to them get as large an income as will support their retainers and cavalry, and enable them to muster them frequently; so that the king, in case of war, has nothing else to do but to send messengers to the sultans a month or two before, who, as they are always prepared, come without difficulty to the rendezvous. In all, they may amount to sixty thousand cavalry, notwithstanding that on paper the muster is much higher. They are generally men of fine aspect, robust, well-made, of great courage, and very warlike. They use for arms swords, lances, arquebuses, which all the soldiers can use; their arms also are superior and better tempered than those of any other nation. The barrels of the arquebuses are generally six spans long, and carry a ball a little less than three ounces in weight. They use them with such facility, that it does not hinder them drawing their bows nor handling their swords, keeping the latter hung at their saddle-bows till occasion requires them. The arquebus then is put away behind the back, so that one weapon does not impede the use of another.

Soldiery of the King of Persia easily brought together.

Persian arms.

The horses are so well trained and are so good and handsome that there is now no need to have them brought from other countries; this has happened since the arrival of Sultan Bayazeth,[1] who fled into Persia with some magnificent Caramanian and Arab horses, which were given away throughout the country, and afterwards when he was executed by order of the king, there were a thousand horses and mares in existence. On this account there has never

Persian horses and how they were introduced.

---

[1] Bayezid, the son of Suleyman, after his rebellion in 1556, fled for safety to the Court of Tahmas, who received him with favour at first; but, his mind becoming embittered against him, caused his followers to be dispersed and slain, and Bayezid himself to be cast into prison. Suleyman used all the means in his power to have Bayezid delivered into his hands, but Tamas would not consent; but afterwards, in consideration of a large sum of money, agreed to allow him to be made away with. Bayezid, accordingly, was strangled, with his four sons. (From Augerius Busbequius Legationis Turcicæ. epist. 4.)

been so fine a breed, and the Ottomans even have not got one like it. This Bayazeth also brought thirty pieces of artillery, which were taken to San Marco, towards the Caspian Sea; but not so the money and other spoils.

The strength of the king lies in his having caused them to lay waste the country on the frontiers of the Turk on every side for six days' journey in distance, and to pull down every castle in the district, in order to strengthen himself by the Turks having no inclination to seize and hold it. I shall now speak of the relations and understandings between him and the neighbouring princes.

This king has pretensions and claims to the countries taken from him by the Ottoman emperors, on one side from the river Euphrates to Babilonia, on the west to the countries of Benbech[1] and Lesser Armenia, in which are comprised Urfa,[2] Merdin,[3] Bira,[4] Adiligus Bitis,[5] Van, Vastan, Cassan,[6] Calasci, Haligan, Baiiburdt,[7] and other places. This king has the allegiance and dependence of a Christian named Lentul[8] Deghi, Prince of the Georgians, who is his tributary, and pays every year twenty thousand ducats; he has his state near the Caspian Sea. This prince, in case of war with the Ottomans, could assist with ten thousand Georgian horse, all robust and valiant men.

There are also some Turkish chiefs named Chindi inhabiting certain mountains in Lesser Armenia, towards the Mediterranean;[9] and these Chindi, when all united, may amount to seven or eight thousand cavalry, of great excellence, and always eager to fight against the Turk.

This is all, most Serene Prince and most Illustrious

[1] Diarbekr.   [2] Orfa.   [3] Mardin.   [4] Bir.
[5] Aradh el Jivaz and Bitlis.   [6] Kashan.   [7] Baiboort.
[8] Lentul Ogli, or Levent Ogli.

[9] These I suppose to be the Kizzilbashes of the Deyrsun and Kara Dagh, near Marash. They are still inveterate enemies of the Turks, though inhabiting their territory. Their religious tenets assimilate more with the Persians.

Noblemen, that in the space of one and twenty months passed since the day I left the feet of your Highnesses to go to Persia, till my return, I have diligently observed of the affairs of that realm.

FINIS.

ERRATA AND NOTES.

Page 5, Note, *for* "tancel", *read* "tawil", long. Uzun means long in Turkish, and Zeno is right in giving it the secondary sense of great; the Turks claim Artaxerxes Longimanus to have been of Turkish race, because with them long arms are esteemed a sign of power and greatness.

Page 8, *for* "Ikindjis", *read* "Akinjys".

Page 24, "ne dentider", probably "neh deria-dir", what a sea it is, Turkish, not Persian.

Page 70, "Occota Cau", probably "Oktai Khan".

Page 79, Note, *for* "Quzbvassi", *read* "Kas-ovahsy".

Page 81, "Arphaemiler", Arpa-eminy, master of the barley.

Page 136, "bosdocan", buzdugan, a mace, a word nearly obsolete in Constantinople; it is preserved in Wallachia.

Page 143. These columns are still standing, and have some inscriptions, apparently Phœnician, upon them.

Page 207. Sheibani Khan; for an account of his life and death, see M. Vambery's *History of Bokhara*.

INDEX.

Amasia, 37
Amida (Diarbekir), 6
Ardebil, 42
Astrabad, 113
Astrakhan, 114

Barbaro, 15, 21, 33, 93
Bitlis, 8, 157

Calo Johannes, 9, 178
Casimir, King of Poland, 33
Chalderan, battle of, 59-61, 120
Contarini Ambrosio, 33

Derbend, 44, 113, 185, 186
Despina, wife of Uzun Hassan, 9, 13, 14, 18, 41, 42, 71, 146, 178, 179

Erzingan, 7

Gaza, battle of, 128-130
Genealogy of Kara Yusuf, 1
——————— Shah Ismail, 5
——————— Shah Abbas, 48

Hassan Beg or Uzun Hassan, 1, 73, 183
Hyder Sheikh, 42, 43, 73, 100, 101, 184

Ismail, Shah, 46, 48, 103, 122, 137, 152, 187, 190, 191, 211

Jezirah, 150

Kafur el Ghouri, 126
Kharput, 148
Khoi, 165
Kurds, 157

Malatia, battle of, 25-29, 86-88, 181, 182
Mamelukes, 129, 133
Mardin, 148
Matthias Corvinus, 34
Mazenderan, 49
Morenigo, Pietro, 21
Murad Khan, 53, 55, 105, 192

Orfa, 98, 143, 144

Pancratio, 97
Persian army, 16, 17, 65
——————— games, 111

Selim Sultan, 58
Sert, 156
Shebban Kara Hissar, 23
Sheibani Khan, 55, 110, 115, 117, 158, 207
Sinan Pasha, 128, 132
Suleyman Sultan, 213

Tabriz, 166 178-224
Tahmasp Shah, 211
Tiflis, 97
Tomant Bey, 127, 131
Turkish army, 22, 62, 79, 83

Van, 159, 187
Vastan, 161
Violante, wife of C. Zeno, 9

Yakub, son of Hassan Beg, his death, 99, 183